DOGMAS IN LITERATURE AND LITERARY MISSIONARY

TEXT, READER AND CRITIQUE

Edited by

Önder Çakırtaş
Bingol University, Türkiye

Series in Literary Studies

VERNON PRESS

Copyright © 2024 by the Authors.

All rights reserved. No part of this publication may be reproduced, stored in a retrieval system, or transmitted in any form or by any means, electronic, mechanical, photocopying, recording, or otherwise, without the prior permission of Vernon Art and Science Inc.
www.vernonpress.com

In the Americas:
Vernon Press
1000 N West Street, Suite 1200,
Wilmington, Delaware 19801
United States

In the rest of the world:
Vernon Press
C/Sancti Espiritu 17,
Malaga, 29006
Spain

Series in Literary Studies

Library of Congress Control Number: 2023946268

ISBN: 978-1-64889-919-5

Also available: 978-1-64889-695-8 [Hardback]; 978-1-64889-793-1 [PDF, E-Book]

Product and company names mentioned in this work are the trademarks of their respective owners. While every care has been taken in preparing this work, neither the authors nor Vernon Art and Science Inc. may be held responsible for any loss or damage caused or alleged to be caused directly or indirectly by the information contained in it.

Every effort has been made to trace all copyright holders, but if any have been inadvertently overlooked the publisher will be pleased to include any necessary credits in any subsequent reprint or edition.

Cover design by Vernon Press. Cover image by JL G from Pixabay.

Contents

Acknowledgement — v

Preface — vii

Introduction: Literary Blindness and Conviction: The Dogmatics of Literature and the Politics of Literary Missionary — ix
Önder Çakırtaş
Bingöl University, Türkiye

PART I:
Toward Monopolized Literature: The Dogmatization of Fiction and Theory — 1

Chapter 1
The Amateur as De-Construction Worker: Demolishing Methodological Silos in Academic Literary Studies — 3
Kristen Schiedel
Dalhousie University, Canada

Chapter 2
Rethinking Some Literary Dogmatic Views of Virginia Woolf and Vladimir Nabokov — 25
Yeşim Sultan Akbay
Süleyman Demirel University, Türkiye
Betüre Memmedova
Süleyman Demirel University, Türkiye

PART II:
Literary Representation and Literary Missionary of Dogma — 51

Chapter 3
Undogmatic Perspective as an Antidote to the Imperial Hubris in J. M. Coetzee's *Waiting for the Barbarians* — 53
Seçil Erkoç Iqbal
İnönü University, Türkiye

Chapter 4
**Brecht's Epic Theatre: Demystifying the Dogmatic Tradition of
Aristotelian Drama in the Western Theatre** 77
Onur Ekler
Hatay Mustafa Kemal University, Türkiye

Chapter 5
**Multiply Fabulous: The Sacred in the Feminine Body in Jeanette
Winterson's *The Passion*** 103
Sezgi Öztop Haner
Dumlupınar University, Türkiye

Chapter 6
**Sermons on Joint: Bob Marley, Bokonon and the Religio-lyrical
Affair with State Apparatuses** 129
Ankit Raj
Government College Gharaunda, India
Nagendra Kumar
Indian Institute of Technology Roorkee, India

Contributors 147

Acknowledgement

I would like to thank Associate Professor Betüre Memmedova, who pioneered this book. Thanks to her guidance and assistance, I was able to call for the book, and the participants contributed. Huge thanks to all contributors to this book.

I am also grateful to my beloved wife and children, whose time and energy I have wasted.

Preface

The emergence of this text was inspired by the discussions that I had with my dear professor Betüre Memmedova, sometimes face-to-face, mostly by phone and e-mail. We both love literature, and I think this love occasionally drags us into the middle of heated debates on literature. Sometimes we have agreed, sometimes we have been quite at odds with each other. But we produce literature, which – I think – is the best ending to this adventure.

This book has gone through a rough route. The limitations of the subject necessitated me not to include many texts, especially after the peer review. For this reason, a book-length study with few chapters was formed on the way of choosing effective texts.

While I was writing the introduction to the book, a massive earthquake hit Southern Türkiye that partially affected the city I was in. We had many losses. Onur Ekler and Seçil Erkoç Iqbal, two of the contributors to this book, were also located in the earthquake zone, and Onur Ekler was directly affected and injured by the earthquake. In this difficult and necessary progression, we have nevertheless managed to finish this book. For this reason, I would like to attribute this book to those who struggle even in the worst of times.

In memory of my student Meliha Çam and all earthquake victims...

Bingöl, April 2023

Introduction:
Literary Blindness and Conviction: The Dogmatics of Literature and the Politics of Literary Missionary

Önder Çakırtaş

Bingöl University, Türkiye

In *Literature and Dogma*, Matthew Arnold discusses the inevitability of reading religious books, especially the Bible, with a scientific and literary interpretation rather than a dogmatic one and comments upon the "*precision* and *definiteness* of religious thought" (4) as described by the *Guardian* to refer to dogmatic theology. Arnold's curiosity for religious readings covers rhetoric about what kind of interpretation literature involves and perhaps deserves. So, one of the questions that plague one's critical mind in Arnold's discussion is, 'is literature *precise* and *definite*?' A likely answer to this question would probably lead to completely differing dilemmas and questions. Two of the most crucial inquiries that might arise are 'is literature dogmatic?' and 'are there dogmas in literature?'

It would be appropriate to turn to what and how literature commentators and readers have experienced to seek answers to these questions. Marxist scholar Terry Eagleton, to give an example on defining literature, argues that literature has a controversial mission when dealing with *factual* and *fictional*, and that for a very long time, some authors have argued that literature is a vehicle of two distinct carters that tell historical facts on the one side, and cover fiction on the other (1-2). What emerges here is not the role of literature as a truth-teller but rather a lasting impression it leaves on readers. How literature is interpreted is shaped by the narratives and intertextual accounts of the new literary and literature-based texts. The text, as an ultimate product of the perception formed in the mind of its creator, performs another possible mental transformation. It is here that literature seems to serve a mission of transmitters that become, regardless of their position, literary ambassadors and missionaries. However, the power of literature in perception might play a sharp *definite* role as soon as it goes beyond admiration. At this stage, the readers, in proportion to the power created in their own perception, turn into a missionary of literature and immerses themselves in literary dogmas. The resilience/transience of literature in perception may transform the interpreter, reader, and analyst into a hermit as well as a militant. The adventure of reading, which begins with the experience of taking pleasure, takes a course towards the construction of literary dogmas.

This comes to what Roland Barthes suggests as a kind of critical framework of pleasure in reading. As Mary H. Snyder puts forward, "In *The Pleasure of the Text*, Roland Barthes discusses the pleasure in reading a text, but he is careful not to encourage readers to become controlled by the texts they read" (110). Such a powerful practice of control can be explained by literature's ability to overwhelm and capture the reader. But the position in which the reader places themselves might exemplify that literature has evolved the mind towards a dogmatic mechanism.

The existence of dogmas in literature becomes visible depending on the readers' positioning themselves as regards the gradual standardization and hegemonic domination of dogmatised criticism. Quite frankly, in his defence of the New Criticism in *The Criticism and Truth*, Barthes mentions the subtle difference between the critic and the judge and discusses how the literary commentator's attitude in criticism puts forward an approach to making sense of language. So much so that the meaning of a new text written by reinterpretation might, as Barthes puts it, "open the way to unforeseeable relaying of meaning" as long as "the true 'criticism' of institutions and languages does not consist in 'judging' them, but in *perceiving, separating, dividing*" (3). The focal issue may arise from the fact that the literary readers and commentators might not realize whether they are a critic or a judge where they position themselves. It may also be due to the fact that literary readers and commentators have surrendered themselves to common fashion and have had to submit to the mainstream to a great extent. If, for instance, the idea or what is signified is shaped by a narrative of an idolized or cult author, literary tabooization and dogmatization take on more and more rapid precedence.

Frank Ritchie, in his revealing essay 'Literary Dogma' emphasizes, "A creed, so long as it is merely the expression of the genuine belief of an individual, is innocent enough," (535) and he continues, "but when it is put forth with the sanction of a well-known name, and when its promulgator is inspired with a missionary spirit, it is apt to exercise an unwholesome influence" (535). There are, of course, various instances of such kind of missionary in the literature. Virginia Woolf, for instance, wrote stupendous works that turned out to be well-known, and in 1928 she delivered a lecture at Cambridge University, where women were once not allowed, that formed the basis for the celebrated *A Room of One's Own* (1929). Her metaphorical wit, "a woman must have money and a room of her own if she is to write fiction," (4) which she ingeniously expressed in her work, has been recognized as a cult by various people, especially suffragette writers, and women, and practically everyone seems to be blindly attached to the idea that 'a woman without room and money cannot write'. But does this 'blindly' acceptance have to do with the fact that Woolf was already a famed writer when she proclaimed this history-defying motto? Probably, the

Introduction

answer is yes. Undoubtedly, Woolf is quite right when she claims that a woman writer, if she desires to be an authoress, should have a room of her own and a salary or money of her own. However, it does not mean that otherwise, female writers cannot write. There are a huge number of examples to claim the opposite. The Bronte sisters, Jane Austen, to mention but a few, never had a room of their own. Even Simone de Beauvoir herself confesses that "I didn't have a room of my own. In fact, I had nothing at all" (qtd. in Gobeil). Interestingly, even those who could afford a room of their own, preferred other ways of 'accommodation'. Maya Angelou, for instance, wrote mainly in a hotel room; Tony Morrison wrote with a paper on her lap. Fortunately, there are recently a number of notes against this statement. One of them is by Ida Rae Egli, titled *No Rooms of their Own* for which Raymond F. Wood wrote a review and added some more names who did not have their own room but survived to write.

> A case might be made out for Dame Shirley, writing from her log cabin at Indian Bar, where things might have been a bit tight, and a spare room was probably not available, and certainly for poor Lucy Young, an Indian girl who was captured and sold into "apprenticeship" (slavery) by renegade whites, but who lived to dictate her memories later on in life. (139)

However, the most poignant is Asja Bakic's 'Not All Writers Can Afford Rooms of Their Own'. She rents a flat, and that's what she says: "Had Virginia Woolf been forced to walk Mayor Bandic's gravelly paths in search of inspiration, her cult essay would've sounded quite different" (Bakic).

More remarkably, one of the rudiments that makes up the socio-cultural and every so often political aesthetics of dogmatic literature might be the ones that shape the literary theories. Doing a comprehensive study on this subject, Sára Tóth suggests some stimulating views on this. In her article specifically devoted to Northrop Frye's views on literary theory, Tóth presents the literary and dogmatic interpretations of religious texts on the basis of Christianity and underlines that "literary or poetic language, the language of story and image, takes precedence over the dogmatic or conceptual interpretations of texts" (185). At first glance, this view may seem counter-intuitive to the one we consider in this book. However, the author discusses the power of literary words on the reader, based on Frye's critical texts, and writes about the mystical power of literary elements uses theories to overcome even dogmatic thoughts in religious texts. As she emphasizes somewhere, "considering that it is literary or poetic language that can sustain such paradoxes (see Frye, *Words with Power* 109), it is not surprising that mystics, otherwise respectful of the creeds, repeatedly turned to literary devices to describe experiences often at odds with official dogma" (187). This enchanting and overpowering supremacy of words can, in a literary sense, feed people's dogmatic passion for literature. As such, literary theories can be part of this 'dogma' climate. Roland Barthes's 1967 essay on an introductory literary theory, for example, 'La mort de l'auteur' ('The Death of the Author'), can be reckoned as one of them to which some readers have developed a dogmatic commitment. It seems so unfair and unjust towards writers. In the same vein, some scholars vehemently protested against those who applied this conflicting theory to Shakespeare. "Does it matter who wrote his works" (Mena 14) exclaimed some critics considering the opposite view sceptically. And that is what is dangerous: to consider all the literary theories by prominent critics and philosophers unchallenging. Recently, even very reputable writers and critics do not consider the theory very reliable and state that "the time for the dead author is over. Now is the age of Living Dead authors" (Erikson). After all, one should not forget that theory does not mean 'it is', rather, it means 'it might be'. This theory is good for experimenting. Several academics used it at the exams giving students modernist or realist texts without mentioning the writer and having them determine the literary movement and genres, but to kill the author is not to kill everything? The meaning of the text goes through the words and it is the author himself who primarily gives meaning to the word.

Examples abound. Indisputably, one of the most vital hitches that arise is connected to the 'reader's intention'. In a way, it is the reader who undertakes the missionary role of the literary text. To put this in two exemplary questions, does every text in which Western writers treat Easterners have an Orientalist point of view? Or does the reader produce it? Does the work of every woman writer have feminist elements? How exactly do biases work in the interpretation of a text? How does the reader's intention affect the fate of the text? Or how accessible is the idea that a text, whether lyrical or prose, is shaped entirely or indirectly by the reader's emotions? Taking all this into account, an inevitable question arises: do literary readers/scholars become blind as they are trapped in the depths of literature? To an astonishing extent, in various literary texts, characters who have been enlightened as a result of their trials with books and wisdom have become physically and often metaphorically blinded. In *Oedipus the King*, while Oedipus allegorically pays for the 'blindness' concealed in his wisdom, Marlowe's book monster Dr. Faustus takes the stage with a different metaphor of blindness. Readers then become blinded to the extent that they immerse themselves in the magic words of literature. A woman reading Woolf suddenly thinks that 'a woman without a room cannot write', while a reader of Faustus may blindly wage war on words to find a way to be arguable with God. Thus, Barthes' critical warning resonates: the necessity of paying attention to not to be controlled by literature. What Kenneth Jernigan proposes as 'Is literature against us?', then sounds reasonable.

Introduction

> The literary record reveals no single theme or unitary view of the life of the blind. Instead, it displays a bewildering variety of images—often conflicting and contradictory, not only as between different ages or cultures, or among the works of various writers, but even within the pages of a single book. (Jernigan)

Literature, then, is mind-directed as much as it is directing the mind. Blindness occurs when this trick manipulates the mind. Thus, literature becomes a dogmatic cult. It is about how the author and/or reader-writer who undertake the task of a literary missionary can take ownership of the text to which they are blindly attached; that is, to borrow the term Edward Said has emphasized at one point, this is about "the curriculum and the ideology of study" (128).

The nature of the book consists of titles that meticulously address the possible answers to several questions proposed above. In this respect, not only reader-centered but also author-centered dogmatic elements have been examined by different academics with original ways of thinking and writing. The skeleton of the book is built around two main topics. Part one, titled 'Toward Monopolized Literature: The Dogmatization of Fiction and Theory', covers, in general, sub-chapters that examine the dogmatization of literature around the idea of monopolization of thought in literature and theories. Part two, 'Literary Representation and Literary Missionary of Dogma', covers studies that examine the 'missionary' role of various texts on the representation of dogma in literature and, thus, the authors of these literary texts. The style and analysis of each author allows readers to produce different meanings through the 'dogmatization of literature' and to witness how the mind is manipulated.

It will be a little exaggeration to state that the topic of literary dogma has so far received short shrift from literary critics as well as from academics. This being the case, the percentage of submitted critical chapters is encouraging. They demonstrate a great interest in the issue. In the first part, there are three chapters. In the first chapter of this part, Kristen Schiedel discusses post-criticism, or amateurism, as "a methodology that is well-positioned to challenge academic dogma as it may occur in literary studies" (8) Schiedel explains his point in the context of the relation of knowledge with experience, as, to him, knowledge evolves into power and thus leads to the formation of dogmatic academic theories. In the following subdivision, Yesim and Beture's essay provides a detailed discussion of some dogmatic views and attitudes by foremost modernist writers Virginia Woolf and Vladimir Nabokov. The authors refute their oft-quoted statements and claims, which have been considered axiomatic and unquestionable.

The second part of the book begins with a thought-provoking chapter by Seçil Erkoç Iqbal, who takes an undogmatic approach based on binary oppositions in J. M. Coetzee's *Waiting for the Barbarians*. The author, who almost *deconstructs* deconstructive criticism around elements that do not adopt dogmatic approaches, offers examples of the non-dogmatic nature of binary oppositions as represented in the aforementioned piece. In the second chapter, which reveals one of the most interesting parts of the book, Onur Ekler explains the genesis and evolutionary dogmas of the European theatre with the unshakable foundation of the Aristotelian tradition. The author claims that thanks to pioneering figures such as Bertolt Brecht, who revolutionized modern theatre, theatre meets an un-dogmatic tradition, and argues that with the introduction of modern subjectivities to European theatre, it began to be purged of Aristotelian representations and abandoned dogmas. In the next chapter, Sezgi Öztop Haner critiques dogma as a religious image and a metaphorical object. Discussing the dogmatism of Christianity around sexism in Jeanette Winterson's *The Passion*, the author makes interesting remarks on the dogmatization of general gender roles in the binary opposition of masculinity and femininity. In the last chapter, Raj and Kumar analyse Louis Althusser's Ideological State Apparatuses and Serawit Bekele Debele's modes of state control of religion to perform a comparative study of Rastafarianism in Jamaica and Bokononism (a fictitious religion) in San Lorenzo (a fictitious banana republic in Kurt Vonnegut's *Cat's Cradle*). In the chapter, the authors revisit the postcolonial state injustices in the two nations, compare the religious icons (Bob Marley and Bokonon) of the oppressed and their differing religious responses to the state, and go on to show how religion and religious dogma can be appropriated to act for or against the state.

Last but not least, it is hoped that the book will, to some extent, fill the gap and serve as a motivation for further research in this field.

Works Cited

Arnold, Mathew. *Literature and Dogma: An Essay Towards a Better Apprehension of the Bible*. London: Smith and Elder Co. 1963.

Bakić, Asja. 'Not All Writers Can Afford Rooms of Their Own: Rethinking the Romance of Writing When There Are Bills to Pay.' *Literary Hub*. March 21, 2019 https://lithub.com/not-all-writers-can-afford-rooms-of-their-own/ Accessed: 11 March 2021

Barthes, Roland. *The Criticism and Truth*. London: Bloomsbury. 2007.

Eagleton, Terry. *Literary Theory: An Introduction*. Oxford: Blackwell Publishing. 1996.

Erikson, Steve. 'The Author as the Living Dead.' *Steven Erikson's Blog*, 26 Oct. 2020, https://steven-erikson.org/the-author-as-the-livingdead/ Accessed: 11 March 2021.

Gobeil, Madeleine. 'Simone de Beauvoir, 'The Art of Fiction No. 35.' Translated by Bernard Frechtman. The Paris Review. ISSUE 34, SPRING-SUMMER. 1965, https://www.theparisreview.org/interviews/4444/the-art-of-fiction-no-35-simone-de-beauvoir

Jernigan, Kenneth. 'Blindness: Is Literature Against Us?' Banquet of the Annual Convention of National Federation of the Blind, July 3, 1974, Chicago. https://nfb.org/images/nfb/publications/convent/banque74.htm

Mena, Ricardo. *Ver, Begin*. CreateSpace Independent Publishing. 2015.

Ritchie, Frank .'Literary Dogma'. *Longman's Magazine, 1882-1905*; London Vol. 35, 1990, Iss. 210: 535-540.

Said, Edward W. *The World, The Text, and the Critic*. Cambridge: Harvard University Press. 1983.

Snyder, Mary H. 'Adaptation in Theory and Practice.' The Oxford Handbook of Adaptation Studies, edited by Thomas Leitch, Oxford University Press: New York, 2017, pp. 101-115.

Tóth, Sára. 'What Does Literature Say?: The Problem of Dogmatic Closure—from Romanticism to Northrop Frye.' ESC: English Studies in Canada, vol. 37 no. 2, 2011, p. 185-200. doi:10.1353/esc.2011.0023.

Wood, Raymund, F. Review of *No Rooms of Their Own: Women Writers of Early California, 1849-1869*, by Ida Rae Egli. Southern California Quarterly, 81(1), 1 April 1999, pp. 138–139. doi: https://doi.org/10.2307/41171935

Woolf, Virginia. *A Room of One's Own*. London: Hogarth Press. 1935.

PART I :
Toward Monopolized Literature:
The Dogmatization of Fiction and Theory

Chapter 1

The Amateur as De-Construction Worker: Demolishing Methodological Silos in Academic Literary Studies

Kristen Schiedel

Dalhousie University, Canada

Abstract

This chapter discusses the field of post-criticism, also called amateurism, and the potential this field has to bridge dichotomizations of academic methodologies and lived experience. This chapter references critical theory from scholars such as Saikat Majumdar, Aarthi Vadde, Elizabeth Anker, Rita Felski, Bruno Latour, Toril Moi, and Michael Polanyi. It also includes examples from two contemporary works of fiction, Claire Louise Bennett's *Pond* and Janette Winterson's *Stone Gods*, to demonstrate the benefit of both surface and depth readings and argues that we shouldn't hold one in higher esteem than the other when performing critical readings.

Keywords: post-criticism, amateurism, surface readings, depth readings

***

Amateurism, also called post-criticism, is, as defined by Saikat Majumdar and Aarthi Vadde, a method of scholarship that does not dichotomize academic and public writing or theory and lived experience. As such, I argue in this chapter that amateurism is a methodology that is well-positioned to challenge academic dogma as it may occur in literary studies. This methodology, well-established by scholars such as Elizabeth Anker, Rita Felski, Bruno Latour, Saikat Majumdar, Michael Polanyi, and Aarthi Vadde, does not by any means eschew the thorough and rigorous practice of critical thought; rather, it recognizes that knowledge, especially within the humanities, has historically been associated with "expertise," which, in turn, when it is "aligned with power" (Majumdar and Vadde, 4), can allow for and perpetuate dogmatic theoretical approaches within the academy. This dogma often, in turn, encourages "the hermeneutics of suspicion" (Paul Ricoeur), or "suspicious readings" (Eve Kosofsky Sedgwick), that approach a literary text as though it's hiding something that the expert must uncover and expose by imposing on it the "correct" reading. This understanding that there is or can be a "correct" reading encourages the academic silo-ing that can lead to the creation, execution, and perpetuation of academic dogmas. Amateurism responds to this insularity by encouraging a post-critical approach grounded in an ethos of loving attention and pleasure, and therefore traverses this dogmatic divide.

I want to say right from the beginning that I'm not trying to pick a fight: I have the utmost respect for all fields of literary criticism and my colleagues who are active in these fields. I'm also not positing an equation in which everything that is not amateurism/post-criticism = academic dogma. Rather, I'm trying to make space for amateurism in an ongoing conversation *about* academic dogmas. In other words, amateurism does not purport to be independent of or in competition with other critical fields. For example, similar to fields such as affect theory, amateurism encourages an approach that is embodied and affective: the "'post' of post-critique [amateurism] denotes a complex temporality: an attempt to explore fresh ways of interpreting literary and cultural texts that acknowledges, nonetheless, its inevitable dependency on the very practices it is questioning" (Anker and Felski, 1). The goal of amateurism, while acknowledging this dependency, is to "adopt new tools; to move from a spirit of debunking to one of assembling, or from critique to composition" (Latour qtd. in *Critique*, 15). Such readings of "assembling" and "composition" are referred to in the field of amateurism as "loving readings" (Felski, 57; Felski, 1-2; Attridge, 31), which are readings driven by passion, care, and intimacy, that take a post-critical approach which asks what kind of world the text is imagining, building, and offering to us (Felski, 1-2). The central questions posed in an amateur/post-critical approach, "what gets built and shaped" by a text and "what affordances and opportunities does literary form and experience open up" (Anker and Felski, 20), are also central to the potential of this field to question and respond to academic dogmas, especially in literary studies, if and when they occur. This chapter will first provide a survey of exigent and emergent post-critical theory; second, will provide a practical application of this potential by following Toril Moi's post-critical approach in asking "why this" of texts proposed for study so as to "open up a much wider range of affective as well as interpretative possibilities, allowing for forms of admiration as well as critique" (Anker and Felski, 20); and, third, will perform what Stephen Best and Sharon Marcus, among others, term a "surface reading" of a text so as to model the pleasure- and use-value of loving readings (I'll be using Jeanette Winterson's *Stone Gods* in this subsection).

Amateur and Professional

To distinguish between amateur and professional and to potentially also bridge that distinction, I will work closely with the research Derek Attridge puts forward in "Praise of Amateurism" so as to parse out the potential for, in the words of Saikat Majumdar and Aarthi Vadde in their introduction to the anthology in which Attridge's piece appears, and which is my favourite way to think about the potential for amateurism and professionalism not as opposites but rather as companions: "criticism in an expanded register" (23). I will then draw on the work of Trevor Ross to attend to a brief history of legislative changes that, in turn, invoked changes to the cultural and social implications of literature as a "vehicle of opinion" (2) or a "vehicle for articulating personal experience" (113). This brief history will lay the groundwork for a discussion on what defines *capital L* Literature so as to transition into a discussion of what kinds of literature we're talking about when we talk about literary studies, what happens when literature becomes knowledge and vice versa, and what makes a "good reader".

To begin, I need to clarify some of the terms I'll be using in this subsection because I think that we sometimes use some of them synonymously when really they're not. For example, the first difference I want to make clear is that I won't be using the words "scholar" and "critic" interchangeably. Although critics may produce scholarship, and scholars may perform criticism, these are still two distinct titles with distinct operations. Moreover, I want to clarify how and why we can consider critics as amateurs without denigrating the work that academics do. I find that Majumdar and Vadde offer the most comprehensive yet concise distinction between scholarship and criticism and that Attridge offers the same in his distinction between amateurism and professionalism, and I'll start with Attridge because that makes most sense from a logical, building-block formulation. Although "the figure designated by the term 'amateur' has been the object of both praise and blame for two centuries," it was first used in the late-eighteenth century as "a neutral term close to its French meaning, 'lover' or 'devotee'" (Attridge, 31). Here is the first building block: amateur means lover. This is how we get the idea of "loving readings" (see Felski), and also how we can equate amateurism to pleasure. It's also how we can talk about the amateur as a critic, or the critic as an amateur, because love and pleasure aren't constricted to either an inside or outside position in relationship to the academy: criticism can incorporate pleasure, and pleasure can incorporate criticism. In this understanding, what amateurism is not, to be clear, is a derogatory classification: it's not a pejorative distinction between professionals, those who do things "professionally" (read: are skilled and do things well), and amateurs, those who do things "amateurishly" (read: are unskilled and do things less well) (Attridge, 31). It's a mistake to think that post-criticism uses these terms in the same way that, say, sports uses the terms professional and amateur athlete, and it's critically important to note that "amateur," in the way it's invoked in post-criticism, is not a term that positions a lay person in contrast to a professional. In fact, when we mean "lay person," we say "lay person." It's also a mistake to generalize professionals as the antithesis of amateurs. Rather, to be amateur means to act from an impetus of loving care and devotion to the object of attention, and, in this way, professionals can be amateurs and vice versa. There is less of a divide here than a bridge, and this is the second building block: professionalism isn't invoked to discredit amateurism, and amateurism isn't invoked to undervalue professionalism (Attridge, 36). Next, the terms critic and scholar differ in the institutional adherence typically enacted by each. For example, Majumdar and Vadde argue that, although both the critic and the scholar "can be either amateur or professional... they can also find themselves shifting affiliations depending on the context at hand" by which they mean that a scholar is more likely to be bound by the conventions of the academy than a critic might be, since a scholar's scholarship is, in terms of "satisfying the requirements of university assessment and academic publishing," bound by an established standard (12). To this end, Majumdar and Vadde distinguish between critic and scholar by saying that "criticism is more likely to be amateur in ethos than scholarship, which necessarily becomes professional in ethos" due to its adherence to institutional academic conventions (12). To reiterate: what I've provided here is a legend or key for how to navigate the language of this chapter. The crucial takeaway, the third building block, should be that none of these terms, amateur, critic, professional, or scholar, are used to establish any sort of hierarchy, or are used in a derogatory way.

Now, let's take this legend and these building blocks into a brief history of legislative changes in the world of letters: prior to May 3rd, 1695, all manuscripts slotted for publication went through a censorship process before being printed; on this date, however, "a bill to renew [this] Licensing Act failed to emerge from committee" (Ross, 1). What this meant was that literature was no longer subject to the pre-publication stricture of governmental/committee approval. However, as Trevor Ross points out, this did not mean that literature was "emancipated" in any total sense: "for decades thereafter, governments regulated the press through a mixed battery of legal and economic measures" and "proceedings for seditious libel, stamp taxes, restrictions on parliamentary reporting, control of distribution through the post, and the reestablishment of trade monopolies under the Copyright Act all served to limit the extent and fervor of printed communication" (1). Even though literary emancipation was still tempered in these ways, Ross argues that "the end of licensing was [still] as consequential for English society as the revolutionary settlement of 1688-1689 was for its political order and the financial revolution of 1694 for its economic" (1). The end of this licensing act was so consequential because it meant that "the scope of licit free speech widened measurably over the next century, with a free press ever more loudly heralded as the 'bulwark of the English constitution'" (1). Moreover, the expansion of free press encouraged the enactment of Copyright Law, which "uncoupled anti-piracy from censorship" (1). It is this "uncoupling" which "transformed authorship into a profession and publishing into an industry" (1). Thus, we get to the vast and amorphous category of "literature," which means what, exactly?

One of the courses I took during my MA degree operated under the working definition of literature to mean "a piece of writing that could be approached and analyzed through a variety of theoretical lenses." Now, however, I'm a bit stuck on this definition because, while I do think that it's inclusive enough to incorporate amateurism when we think of amateurism/post-criticism as a theoretical lens, I also think that it may have the limitation of confining amateurism to an academically sanctioned lens which implies that the theory work associated with it must be performed by someone with the necessary skills (read: expert). It also begs the follow-up questions: must a text be analyzable to be considered literature, and does a text that has the potential to be analyzed without actually undergoing any analytical treatment still fit the bill? And, maybe more pressing, can we, professionals and amateurs and professionals as amateurs, ever really read without doing some kind of analytical work given our inability to escape our ideological subject positions?

These questions are not unique to my own wonderings but instead, show up with fair regularity in post-structural methodologies or lines of inquiry. In brief, post-structuralism is interested in the sign and the signifier and the disparity between the two. A Saussurean understanding of signs and signifiers tells us that the relationship between the sign and the signifier is arbitrary, in large part because language is a social phenomenon: for example, the word "tree" is a *sign* that is used to *signify* that which we recognize as a tree, even though there is nothing inherently "tree-ish" about a "tree"; rather, we've assigned that thing the sign of "tree" so that we have a common point of reference and can therefore communicate. Post-structuralism, with which we associate theorists like Paul de Man and Jacques Derrida, and the practice of deconstruction that follows, is intensely interested in the gap between sign and signifier, and what work might be done and undone in this gap: in other words, this practice looks for oppositions, binaries, and hierarchies in a text, and deconstructs them to reveal that the text isn't necessarily saying what it purports to because meaning is abundant and limitless rather than pre-ordained. This methodology looks for things in the text that are taken for granted as "natural," and demonstrates the ways in which they are indeed not natural but are rather a construction of knowledge: "whatever is natural, taken for granted, essentialized, or transparent becomes the critic's target: such qualities are seen as not only theoretically inadequate (in failing to acknowledge the linguistic and cultural construction of reality), but also politically troubling (in "naturalizing" social phenomena and thereby rendering them immune to criticism and change)" (Anker and Felski, 8). A common entry point for this kind of scrutiny is a suspicion of allegory: since allegory is something standing in for something else, a specific part gesturing toward a more general whole, for example, a character standing in for an ideology. Critics have long been suspicious of ways in which allegory might allow for the naturalization of constructed "truths." For instance, Anker and Felski argue that "the dissemination of deconstructive ideas in the 1970s and 1980s led to an intensifying skepticism about such modes of political interpretation, which were condemned for presuming, in a naive fashion, a clear parallel between a signifier inside and a signified outside the text" and that, in turn, "allegory became a cause for suspicion, accused of imposing false unities and hierarchical structures on to literature: the allegorically minded critic, it was argued, did not know how to read" (Anker and Felski, 7). "Knowing how to read" is a crucial point here, and I'll return to it in the subsection on "Knowledge and Education." For now, though, I want to focus on the ways in which the suspicion of readings that presume a contingent rather than the arbitrary relationship between "signifier inside" and "signified outside" the text offers us another working definition of literature: "what defines literature, in this line of thought, is its capacity to engage in self-conscious commentary on the indeterminacies and aporias of language, thereby eluding the overconfident reader" and, moreover, "by staging refusals of closure, resolution, or truth, literary works serve, in Paul de Man's words, as "allegories of the impossibility of reading" (7). What I really think is most crucially missing from both of these definitions, though, is 1) "a piece of writing that could be approached and analyzed through a variety of theoretical lenses," and 2) "what defines literature, in this line of thought, is its capacity to engage in self-conscious commentary on the indeterminacies and aporias of language, thereby eluding the overconfident reader," is a consideration of the reader, or the voice of the public in determining what is and isn't literature.

Here again, I'll turn to Ross for some history on when and how the authority of the individual reader/speaker, and the accumulation of readers/speakers into the more general "public," became somewhat troubled: "the more public speech was liberalized… the more literature's public role seemed less easy to define" because even though "literary writings had long been valued for both preserving traditions and transforming them… by the later eighteenth century, these functions were changing"; for example, "poetry fulfilled fewer instrumental uses" and, "most striking, perhaps, was how little authors by then subscribed to the old faith in the power of poetry to refine language, honor worthies, or inspire obedience to prevailing norms" (Ross, 5). However, it's widely accepted that, as Ross says, literary works, or I'd add the invocation or deployment of literary works by authoritative institutions, still had and have this power, especially the power to "inspire obedience to prevailing norms," particularly through "new mechanisms of cultural reproduction: canonical works were protected as national heritage, marketed for their prestige value by large publishing ventures, and studied in programs aimed at schooling the citizenry" (5). What I mean by the invocation or deployment of literary texts by authoritative institutions is rooted in Pascale Casanova's discussion of literary wealth and Rebecca Walkowitz's discussion of literary underdogs. Casanova, in *The World Republic of Letters*, defines having "literary wealth" as a country having a history of literary production so well-defined and well-established (read: old), that they get to set the standard of what is and isn't "literature," what styles are fitting for literature, and therefore what is accepted as "standard" around the world (23). This means that countries with literary wealth can trade their literary production history on the world economic stage in order to pay for the right to determine what gets read, what gets taught, what wins awards, what gets disseminated to the widest audience, and therefore, by extension, largely what gets produced. Literary underdogs writes Walkowitz, influenced by and expanding on Casanova's argument, are "those books produced outside of Western Europe and the United States" (29). Countries that are literary underdogs do not set the standard for what we consider classics or books that everyone should read: that standard is evaluated and defined by those countries that have literary wealth.

The question remains, though: does the public have a say in determining what is or isn't literature, or does public instruction by authoritative institutions have the only say in this determination? This question can be further complicated by considering who, amongst the public, has more of a say than others, which in turn raises an accessibility/disability consideration that is far beyond the scope of this chapter. So, while acknowledging that this is a much bigger issue than the subset of ideas upon which I'm specifically focusing, I'm going to reel it back in, for now, to my previous discussion of what we mean when we use the term "literature," and inject Ross's, not so much definition as guiding coordinates, that "the idea of 'literature' came about as a response to a deepening ambivalence over the role literary writings were to play in democratic society" (6). However, while we can perhaps quantify the level of ambivalence, we can't, in fact, qualify the nature of this ambivalence because "it is premised on an incoherent notion of public" (6). And we're now back to the question I posed at the outset of this paragraph which I then immediately said I couldn't answer in the scope of this paper: who and/or what is the public? That's okay, though, because there's still a way into this discussion without having to definitively answer that question (which is a relief) because, as Ross points out, "with popular sovereignty, the public acts with supreme authority, but in setting protocols of speech for itself, it paradoxically limits its authority in the very act of exercising it," which means that "the modern notion of the public as an agent of change is marked by *irresolvable* ambiguity" (6, emphasis mine). "Irresolvable" means it's most definitely not solvable in this chapter, so let's press on as we're able, which, in this case, is to move from a discussion of literature and collective instruction to a discussion of knowledge and education the distinctions and similarities between these two containers, and how they're implicated in our discussion of amateurs, professionals, amateurs as professionals, and potential pitfalls for academic dogmas.

Ways of Knowing

On the topic of education and, in particular, English Lit, we all know that you don't have to scroll very far down the first page of Google search results to see that a degree in English is often seen as more of a passion project than a viable start to a successful career path. Indeed, a Forbes article extolling the virtues of an English degree (Stoller-Lindsey, n.p.) links readers to updated stats on trade-schools.net that, as of March 2022, show a satisfaction rate of 45.7% for students in the U.S. who have majored in English. This is in comparison to students who majored in Accounting and Computer Science, which have satisfaction rates of 85.2% and 85%, respectively. This probably doesn't come as a shock since both Accounting and Comp Sci are highly regarded as having relevant and enduring "use-value." I'm not here to prove that English degrees also have high use-value because even in writing this chapter, I'm standing on the shoulders of giants who have already made eloquent and compelling cases to the affirmative.

However, when I'm inevitably called upon to defend my field, I sometimes get frustrated by "why now" follow-up questions that wonder why literary study matters *now*, when we have things like the climate crisis, the ongoing violence against Black and Indigenous People of Colour, the growing wealth gap, and the reversal of Roe v. Wade going on (to name only a few contemporary issues). But then I realize that the question I'm really being asked is, "so what?" And here we have the ultimate question, the question that we, as literary scholars/critics/professionals/amateurs, should always be keeping forefront in our minds: what about the current sociopolitical moment necessitates the consideration of why stories, epistemologies, and stories as epistemologies, are particularly important. While I wholeheartedly believe the answer to this question is "because it's always important, fullstop," I'm also extremely cognisant of the ways in which the zeitgeist informs academic research and scholarship, perhaps more so than the inverse. So, although I think the "why now" and the "why ever" questions are crucially considered together, I also think that the "why now" question invokes a particular spatiotemporal avenue into the discussion of "why ever" that can't and shouldn't be overlooked.

To parse out the importance of both the distinction and similarities between these questions, I will first draw on the work of Blythe McVicker Clinchy, who, in her seminal 1996 essay "Connected and Separate Knowing: Toward a Marriage of Two Minds", identifies and defines two distinct ways of knowing, which, as the title suggests, she calls "separate" and "connected". Separate knowing involves separating an idea from the context in which it arose and assessing it independently based on a set or series of rules that have been proven through some kind of accredited methodology, scientific or otherwise: Separate knowers will, according to Clinchy, "examine [my] arguments with a critical eye, insisting that I justify every point... looking for flaws in my reasoning, considering how I might be misinterpreting the evidence I present, what alternative interpretations could be made, and whether I might be omitting evidence that would contradict my position" (Clinchy qtd. in Nagoski and Nagoski, 144-5). Clinchy is also then quick to qualify her definition of separate knowing by adding that "the standards you apply in evaluating my arguments are objective and impersonal; they have been agreed upon and codified by logicians and scientists" (Clinchy qtd. in Nagoski and Nagoski, 145). This is to say that "separate knowing," like many "depth" readings, can and does serve an important and codified purpose. If the suspicion called for in separate knowing sounds like the suspicion invoked in Eve Kosofsky Sedgwick's definition of a suspicious reading or like Stephen Best and Sharon Marcus' definition of symptomatic readings, it's because it can also metamorphose into those. Here I will spend a bit of time getting into these definitions and the impetus behind them. To begin, the terms "surface" and "depth" readings will be crucial to many subsections of this chapter and thus warrant careful consideration. Stephen Best and Sharon Marcus, in "Surface Reading: An Introduction," begin to distinguish between surface and depth readings by tracing "interdisciplinarity" to "the acceptance of psychoanalysis and Marxism as metalanguages" in the 1970s and 80s: "it was not just any idea of interpretation that circulated among the disciplines, but a specific type that took meaning to be hidden, repressed, deep, and in need of detection and disclosure by an interpreter," a "way of reading" that "went by the name of 'symptomatic reading'" (1). Let's not forget Fredric Jameson's famous line in his 1981 publication *The Political Unconscious: Narrative as a Socially Symbolic Act* that "if everything were transparent, then no ideology would be possible, and no domination either" (61). Symptomatic reading is conflated with depth reading, or a reading in which you "plumb the depths" for hidden meaning in the text's "unconscious" (Best and Marcus 1-2). You can see, then, the similarities between Clinchy's definition of "separate knowing" and Marcus and Best's definition of "symptomatic" reading.

What Clinchy calls connected knowing, on the other hand, looks to context as an aid in explanation and understanding rather than as a distraction and "involves coming to understand an idea by exploring it within its context (Nagoski and Nagoski, 145). In a review of Clinchy's definitions, Emily Nagoski and Amelia Nagoski argue that "connected knowing" is aptly named as such "because it doesn't separate an idea from its context; it insists that we can only understand something if we also understand how it relates to the context it comes from" (Nagoski and Nagoski, 145). Nagoski and Nagoski further explain that, "if separate knowing separates wheat from chaff, connected knowing explores the relationship between the wheat and the chaff, seeking to understand where each comes from and why they accompany each other" (Nagoski and Nagoski, 145). Connected knowing, by this definition and explanation, is as much about the ways we go about knowing or the process of coming to know something as it is an evaluation of that which is to be known; connected knowing is a disposition of constant engagement with and awareness of historical, social and cultural context. Connected knowing, then, has similarities to what Best and Marcus mean by "surface readings": reading a text with the idea that it could be saying exactly what it seems to be saying in the context in which it is saying it, rather than covering up its true meaning through the application of literary devices. Best and Marcus, speaking from their own experience as scholars, say that, as "those who cut [their] intellectual teeth on deconstruction, ideology critique, and the hermeneutics of suspicion," they are the "heirs of Michel Foucault, skeptical about the very possibility of radical freedom and dubious that literature or its criticism can explain our oppression or provide the keys to our liberation" but that, "watching eight years of the Bush regime" (this article was published in 2009: no doubt Best and Marcus would have had lots to say about the Trump regime also) "may have hammered home the point that not all situations require the subtle ingenuity associated with symptomatic reading, and they may also have inspired us to imagine that alongside nascent fascism there might be better ways of thinking and being simply there for the taking, in both the past and the present" (2). I want to reiterate here, though, that while I agree with Best and Marcus, I don't take an either/or position when it comes to surface and depth readings (and I don't believe they do, either): the argument that there "might be better ways of thinking and being there for the taking" shouldn't relegate all deconstructive work to the realm of symptomatic reading.

Further to this point, deconstruction offers us much value through the way in the way it encourages us to question epistemology, ontology, and epistemology that is mistaken for ontology. I'll break this down. Epistemology is the study of knowledge and ontology is the study of being. So, what I mean when I talk about the danger of mistaking epistemology for ontology is that many "Absolute Truths," for example, that gender is a binary is the easy reference here, are actually constructions of knowledge rather than inherencies of being. Sticking with the gender binary example, arguments that position gender as biology assign gender to the realm of ontology, an inherency of being, rather than the realm of epistemology, a way of thinking that has been culturally constructed and culturally perpetuated through colonial education. I am of the belief that there are *very few* Absolute Truths, and so I appreciate methods of inquiry that seek out and challenge purported truths to the end of exposing the artifice of constructed knowledge. However, the practice of interrogating "absolutisms" must also extend past what's done in this practice also to include the practice itself: we need to consider a "meta-interrogation," or interrogation of interrogation, and consider that not *absolutely* everything is hiding something. I align myself here with Toril Moi, who argues that "we must learn to recognize situations in which suspicion is *not* called for" and that "critical readings existed well before professional literary critics began to believe that critique requires a particular version of language, meaning, and texts, or a particular method of reading" (32, emphasis in original). What this means is that there are innumerable "good readers" who haven't been "trained" to be suspicious and yet still read critically. By far, my favourite idea of what makes a reader a "good" one comes from Derek Attridge, who says that "good readers... readers, that is, who are sensitive to formal properties of works, [are] alert to their handling of meaning, cognizant of their relations to other works (contemporaneous, earlier, later), and... open to being surprised and changed by what they experience" (43). We can be alert without being suspicious and, moreover, we can be more open to being surprised and changed by what we experience if we don't approach a text with our minds already made up that what the text is saying on a surface level will/can never be what is actually being said.

Moreover, though, surface reading does not necessarily stand in direct opposition to symptomatic reading; rather, while surface reading can be used to critique symptomatic reading, it can also be used to compliment and/or expand on these types of readings: "we take the surface to mean what is evident, perceptible, apprehensible in texts; what is neither hidden nor hiding; what, in the geometrical sense, has length and breadth but no thickness, and therefore covers no depth" so, in other words, "surface is what insists on being looked at rather than what we must train ourselves to see through" (Marcus and Best, 9). Hopefully I've made clear here how I'm comparing "surface reading" to Clinchy's idea of "connected knowing." What I want to emphasise most here is that even though the surface doesn't need to be "seen through," it also doesn't prevent further exploration into the depths. This is one of the primary reasons we needn't be suspicious of the surface: because it's transparent rather than opaque and neither necessitates nor hinders further inquiry.

For a practical application of what I'm arguing here, let's take, as an example, Claire-Louise Bennett's *Pond*. Published in 2015 and set in an undisclosed location, but which we can assume based on the description is Ireland, this text accounts for episodes of an unnamed narrator who has recently left her position as a doctoral candidate and retreated to a small, remote, isolated coastal town to purposely and purposefully live a remote, isolated life. This book is formally quite unique since it presents what many have called a series of short stories, but that I instead am more inclined to think of it as a collection of free-verse narrative poems. The narration style, free indirect discourse told entirely in first-person except for the last entry (story, poem), which is told in third person, is quite poetic in both language and structure: for example, the shortest entry in this collection, "Stirfry," is only three lines long and uses white space to indicate line breaks:

> I just threw my dinner in the bin. I knew as I was
> making it I was going to do that,
>   so I put in it all the things I never want to see again (71)

However, the text also offers longer, more formally structured, and narratively driven sections in which we get most of our information about the narrator and her retreat: we learn in the entry titled "Morning, Noon & Night" that the narrator's dissent from academia follows a conference presentation at which she was criticized for grounding her argument in what we can infer is an amateur methodology (as I've discussed it previously in this paper, not in the sense of work done by a lay-person).

Describing her interest in her presentation topic as being "not necessarily in a meritorious way," the narrator says that "my interest was far too personal and not strictly academic and so my methodology came across as nostalgic and my perspective rather naïve since I ignored the usual critical frameworks which were anyhow quite incomprehensible to me" (11). Her argument, that "in the whole history of literature love is quite routinely depicted as an engulfing process of ecstatic suffering which, finally, mercifully, obliterates us and delivers us to oblivion," doesn't "go down very well" and is, in fact, "considered rather unsophisticated" (11) at a conference on the topic of the work of an unnamed playwright with the aim of "reputedly reassessing... by and large that violence [in this playwright's oeuvre] had hitherto been widely interpreted as nothing more than a dramatic strategy designed to shock" (12). Our unnamed narrator interjects in this formal conversation that she "could never quite accept" the premise about violence and shock value because "how on earth is there anything shocking about violence?" (12). In so doing, and in positing that "love is indeed a vicious and divine disintegration of selfhood and that artistic representations of it as such aren't at all uncommon or outlandish and have nothing whatsoever to do with endeavouring to shock an audience," she attempts to "establish a perennial language of love that testifie[s] to the abominable emancipation that is brought on by want of another," by referencing not only "Sappho, Seneca, Novalis, Roland Barthes, Denis de

Rougement and... Johan Huizinga," but also "lyrics by PJ Harvey and Nick Cave, with the somewhat misplaced intention of demonstrating that it just never stops" (12). There are two things in particular I want to take from this example. The first is that the criticism lodged against the narrator's conference presentation, that her approach is "naïve," rings true to other criticisms of amateur readings, surface readings, or readings of admiration rooted in connected knowing that this course of inquiry is "irrational, as if the only alternative to the scientific method and logical reasoning is nonsense" (Nagowski and Nagowski, 146), or questions of how "can surface reading be anything other than a tacit endorsement of the status quo, the academic version of resignation's latest mantra, 'It is what it is?'" (Marcus and Best, 13). Here, criticism lodged against the narrator, that her argument is "naïve," is made possible by academic dogma that gatekeeps knowledge by dismissing any kind of criticism that isn't governed by the strictures of established expertise of traditional academic methodology. In this case, the disparity between academic and public writing or theory and lived experience is something the narrator can't reconcile and therefore contends with by leaving the academy altogether.

The second thing is that this text works well as an example both for the merits of amateurism or, in the words of Majumdar and Vadde, the critic as an amateur, and also for a commentary on analogy and literality. In other words, this text makes a metacommentary on surface and depth readings. The title of this collection, *Pond*, seems to welcome an intertextual comparison to Thoreau's Walden Pond: we have a narrator who leaves behind public life to retreat to an intentional and deliberate way of living beyond the constraints of society or, as Bennett writes in an article for *The Irish Times* that she wrote about *Pond*, the constraints of what Calvino calls "anthropocentric parochialism" because "in solitude you don't need to make an impression on the world" and, as such, "the world has an opportunity to make an impression on you" ("On Writing *Pond*," n.p.). However similar this may seem to Thoreau's impulse for *Walden*, we learn in the entry titled "Something" that the title of the book refers to a sign that reads "Pond" beside the pond beside which the narrator lives:

> She [the narrator's landlady] went off to place a cautionary notice next to the pond – which, by the way, has absolutely no depth whatsoever. If it were up to me I wouldn't put a sign next to a pond saying pond, either I'd write something else, such as Pig Swill, or I wouldn't bother at all. I know what the purpose of it is, I know it's to prevent children from coming upon the pond too quickly and toppling in, but still I don't quite agree with it. (36)

This revelation reads a bit like a tongue-in-cheek metacommentary on the practice of "plumbing the depths for meaning," in the words of Best and Marcus, and the ways in which that kind of distrust of literality can lead us to miss the point: the point here being a sign announcing "Pond" when, really, any passerby should be able to easily identify the nature of the small body of water without requiring instruction.

Moreover, this is also a commentary on the ways in which the depths, after being plumbed for meaning, are signified by literalities that, in their attempt to "gotcha!" the hidden meaning of analogy, become themselves barriers to the admiration of the depths. In the same interview I mentioned above, Bennett says that, although "one sets off to investigate, you see, to develop the facility to really notice things so that, over time, and with enough practice, one becomes attuned to the earth's embedded logos and can experience the enriching joy of moving about in deep and direct accordance with things," nonetheless this "vital process" is "invariably… abruptly thwarted by an idiotic overlay of literal designations and inane alerts so that the whole terrain is obscured and inaccessible until eventually it is… as if the earth were a colossal and elaborate deathtrap" (Bennett, *Pond*, 36). In this way, "with enough time and practice becoming attuned to the earth's embedded logos," the practice of "becoming attuned" is a receptive act: with time and practice and the kind of practice that spans time, we can learn to orient our curiosity in a practiced way, with "practiced" here not meaning honed into any kind of particular expertise, but rather honed into curiosity, wherein curiosity honed into curiosity means becoming open to limitless potentiality that traverses the divide between surface and depth rather than being confined to either side of the binary. I want to draw a connection here between Ross's argument about the public exercising their popular sovereignty with supreme authority and depth readings that are also symptomatic readings doing the same, insofar as to say that each "paradoxically limit their authority in the very act of exercising it" (Ross 6): to plumb the depths without acknowledging the surface, to look for what the pond analogizes rather than to look at the pond as a pond, is to miss the meaning that is right there and self-evident. Moreover, Bennett explains this to her readers in the form of an analogy: the recollection of the narrator's landlady erecting the "Pond" sign to signify the water leads to the narrator considering the myriad "literal designations and inane alerts" that obscure any meaning that the world might be putting forth itself, just as the sign "Pond" limits any "pondness" the pond might perhaps convey independent of its given name.

Further to this line of thinking, to read *Pond* as simply an iteration of Thoreau's Walden Pond would be a mistake since Bennett's narrator is reaching far beyond the limitations of Thoreau, who, even in his isolation, was still bound by the conventions of sanity in the sense that cultural norms are considered "sane." Reviewing Bennett's *Pond* in *The New Yorker*, Jia Tolentino writes that it's important to note that, while "Thoreau might have siphoned insight from his surroundings[,] Bennett's narrator osmoses into hers completely"

("Pleasantly Insane," n.p,). The difference between "siphoning" and "osmosing" is the difference between "taking" and "receiving". When we think of siphoning or taking in terms of symptomatic readings, we can think about those kinds of readings "taking" authority from the meaning they reveal about the text; alternatively, when we think of osmosing or becoming in terms of receiving authority through loving attention and admiration, we can think about the devotion of the amateur as that word etymologically reaches back to the French meaning of "lover" or "devotee."

Although this kind of devotion might go against some standard academic norms and, like the narrator's conference presentation, be considered "naïve," Tolentino advises against reading the narrator and, by extension, her practice of osmosis, as insane: "the narrator of *Pond* is not insane, it's important to note"; rather, "she is sensitive to the point of being porous, but she is also lucid, practical, and excruciatingly cognizant of what is normal... It's in her house, in her garden – alone with herself, and unravelling – where she can return to her real business of magnifying a quality of exquisite attention to the point of irrationality, a mind deliberately astray ("Pleasantly Insane," n.p.). I think, here, that Nagoski and Nagoski's rebuttal to the criticism lodged against connected knowing, to which I'm paralleling amateur readings, is also useful: "connected knowing is careful, effortful, often slow, and *intensely rational*, meaning it follows predictable patterns and progression... that integrates emotion into the information needed to understand an idea" and that "it's also imaginative, requiring the listener to *suspend* their emotional reactions to differences and allow themselves to try on a viewpoint distinct from their own" (146, emphasis in original). Osmosis in this sense, or approaching a text as a connected knower or amateur, means *becoming* in the processual sense of the word. In other words, meaning isn't made; rather, it's made and remade, discovered and rediscovered, received and re-received, in perpetuity. Moreover, osmosis means movement toward equalization and, in this way, I think it's similar to Angela Leighton's metaphor of "fellow travellers" (qtd. in Wood, 61) referring to critique and admiration: whereas "siphoning" connotes taking particular information at will and through force, osmosis connotes a reciprocal transference and re-transference to keep the scales always and forever balanced, with information moving from side to side as needed to maintain equilibrium. We can also extend this metaphor to the critic as an amateur, with the subject then moving back and forth between professionalism and amateurism as needed to maintain equilibrium. All this to say: connected knowing does not necessarily pit surface readings against depth readings; rather, it has the potential to amalgamate both.

Knowledge and Education

I've focused so far in the first subsection on the ways in which we acquire/gain/make knowledge, and how these ways of making knowledge contribute to the distinction between amateur and professional and, in the second subsection, on the ways in which the public enacts, does not enact or, maybe more importantly, undoes its authority by paradoxically limiting it. I now want to turn to a consideration of how we define knowledge, both within and beyond the academy, and if/how we distinguish between knowledge and education.

First, I'd like to return to the idea of use-value. In the introduction to this chapter, and in the early lines of the first subsection, I briefly touch on the age-old debate about whether or not art can have use-value: is it art if it has a use? or is it then considered craft? or can use-value itself be considered art? or can we consider the provision of pleasure to have a kind of use-value? In any case, and since I've most definitely exceeded the limit of how many unanswerable questions I can introduce in one chapter, we need to acknowledge that literature is something to which we, socially, culturally, governmentally, have associated a use-value, and the use we've given it is collective instruction. However, the actual *value* of this use-value has been called into question dating back to the late eighteenth century, when people began expressing "skepticism over the value of [the] discourse[s]" of "literature and the arts" and therefore "began wondering whether literary writing lacked utility as a medium of knowledge, exhibited stylistic features too divergent from the mainstream of public debate, or purveyed beauty and affect that could be appreciated only at a remove from the distractions of public life" (Ross, 6). This debate is ongoing: humanities departments are underfunded, arts degrees are undervalued, and, let's not forget, English majors, as of 2022 in the U.S., only reported a satisfaction rate of 45.7 percent.

We know that particular kinds of knowledge-making and particular kinds of knowledge are privileged in Western society. We also know that, as Majumdar and Vadde claim, "as societies become more knowledge-dependent, the ability to claim expertise becomes more aligned with power, profit, and influence" (4). This is dangerous, and we've already seen this danger manifest in public reactions to "fake news," for example, the insurrection at the U.S. Capitol building on Jan. 6th, 2021. We also run the risk of knowledge being aligned with power within the academy if and when expertise is used as a guide for gatekeeping that knowledge. To complicate this idea further, Majumdar and Vadde ask whether or not literature "with a capital L" can even be considered "a domain of knowledge" at all (8). In considering literature as a domain of knowledge (and/or vice versa?), we must also consider to what extent the need for one might presuppose the other. In other words, as Majumdar and Vadde argue, "professional [literary] scholars certainly need literature to be institutionally recognized as knowledge for our livelihoods, but that need does not do justice to what literature, as a subset of imaginative and finely written works, actually is" (8-9). So, what is it, then? In his seminal book *Literature and the Taste of Knowledge*, Michael Wood writes that "literature characteristically offers something harder – in the sense of the 'hard' sciences – than understanding and something softer than what we often imagine knowledge to be" (54). Wood, notably, also acknowledges that we can't really define "knowledge" except by describing it as what it's not, as in it's not "opinion or belief... awareness or experience" (55); although I agree with Wood that opinion or belief seem somehow to be too intangible to be called knowledge (opinion doesn't belong in the category of either knowledge or wisdom, but I'm tempted to classify "belief" as perhaps a kind of "wisdom" rather than knowledge), I disagree that awareness and experience aren't in their own right types of embodied understanding which I, and I'm not alone (see Sonya Renee Taylor's *The Body Is Not an Apology*, Bessel van der Kolk's *The Body Keeps the Score*, and Elaine Scarrey's *The Body in Pain* as just a few of examples), would consider knowledge.

This disagreement aside, what Wood is getting at is that the conversation around the use-value of art and literature, and whether or not literature "lack[s] utility as a medium of knowledge" (Ross, 6), is the wrong conversation to be having because it paves the way for us to think of literature through the metaphor of a "holiday," the metaphor here being that reading a book is like taking a holiday (Wood, 60). This metaphor invariably breaks down because, as Wood argues, "literature does not simply refresh us so that we can return to nonliterary work, it helps us to do the work of deciding what we do and do not know... to repeat, [literature] renders all knowledge hypothetical, it pretends to affirm when it is not affirming," and yet "every pretend affirmation could also be the real thing, crying out for testing" (60). What I especially appreciate about Wood's consideration here is that he doesn't qualify the kind of testing that literature allows knowledge to undergo by equating that testing with any one literary methodology or even with the academic study of literature at all. Rather, he quotes Angela Leighton's claim that "if wanting poetry to be about something is criticism's shortsightedness, wanting it not to be about anything may be poetry's: conversations between the two, however ill-tempered and high-flown, are still those of fellow travellers" (Wood, 61). In making this reference to critique and admiration being "fellow travellers," and, I think it's fair to say we can extend this metaphor to the critic and the amateur, or in any case to the respective impulse of each, he posits that literature and knowledge operate in a symbiotic relationship that encourages critical thought through curiosity rather than demanding a particular kind of critical thought that stems from a particular academic methodology. In other words, he's taken the amateur/expert debate out of the equation because, by positing that "literature renders all knowledge hypothetical," he's located his position further than that debate could ever take us. If literature does, in fact, render all knowledge hypothetical, then there is simply no use for the kind of gatekeeping of literary knowledge that attempts to contain this knowledge to methodological silos of literary scholarship within the academy.

Surface and Depth Readings of/in Jeanette Winterson's *Stone Gods*

I'm going to conclude this chapter with my own close reading from Jeanette Winterson's *Stone Gods* as a culmination of what I've been discussing so far: amateurism and professionalism, ways of knowing, knowledge and education, surface and depth readings, and readings of admiration and critique. I've agreed throughout this chapter with Toril Moi's advocation that "surface reading" and "depth reading", or readings of "admiration" and "critique," should not be pitted against each other [because] any discussion of one always already invokes the other (33), and I argue that the treatment of poetry in Jeanette Winterson's *Stone Gods* is a useful and effective (and affective) case study of what Moi is saying, and more broadly what I'm saying in this chapter. I chose this book for a case study first and foremost because I love it. Although I was very tempted to write, "I love this book because," and then provide a justification of my enjoyment, I'm going to purposely not do that in an effort to have my own pleasure in reading it be enough justification for why I love it. For additional information about my choice, though, I've produced scholarship on this book and taught it in an academic setting to my first-year Global Lit class, so, in that sense, it's also well suited for my case study because I've considered it in my capacity as an amateur, scholar, and professional, and the overlap between these positions.

The Stone Gods, written in 2007, is, in very basic terms, premised on the need to find a new planet to support human life after Orbus, the planet upon which humans live at the outset of the novel, declines to the point of no longer being habitable. Winterson structures this novel in four parts: "Planet Blue," "Easter Island," "Post-3 War," and "Wreck City." Each section involves a love story between a human woman, Billie, and a female robot, or *robosapien*, Spike, with the exception of the section titled Easter Island, in which Billy and Spikkers are both human men. Much like the love story aspect, time itself in this novel doesn't follow a linear progression but rather reveals itself to be both cyclical and palimpsestic at the same time.

Now on to the plot points relevant to my argument: Captain Handsome, a space adventurer, is charged with exploring the universe to find another planet, which he does find and names Planet Blue, that can support human life. However, on one of his expeditions to find this planet, he flies through what he thinks is a field of space debris but actually turns out to be books and pages of remnants of the canon of human literary production (Winterson, 49). He gathers these materials and brings them into his ship and builds a library of sorts (49), but because some of these texts are full books, but more are loose pages or fragments, his library is incomplete in more ways than one: it neither accounts for all texts ever written, nor does it necessarily offer complete versions of the texts for which it can account. As such, one line of poetry becomes a repeating motif throughout the book: "She is all States, all Princes, I, nothing else is…" (7). Without context or history, Handsome understands this to be a line of love poetry that he quotes again and again throughout to his love, the robot named Spike, who was originally created to be a competent astronaut plus sex robot for space missions.

Handsome's reading of this line is a surface reading, or a reading of admiration, based on one line of what he does not and can not know to be John Donne's "The Sun Rising," but admires nonetheless for its essential qualities as the part becomes a whole into and of itself, rather than a part of the original:

> Busy old fool, unruly Sun,
>   Why dost thou thus,
> Through windows, and through curtains, call on us?
> Must to thy motions lovers' seasons run?
>   Saucy pedantic wretch, go chide
>   Late school-boys and sour prentices,
>   Go tell court-huntsmen that the king will ride,
>   Call country ants to harvest offices;
> Love, all alike, no season knows nor clime,
> Nor hours, days, months, which are the rags of time.
> Thy beams so reverend, and strong
>
>   Why shouldst thou think?
> I could eclipse and cloud them with a wink,
> But that I would not lose her sight so long.
>   If her eyes have not blinded thine,
>   Look, and to-morrow late tell me,
>   Whether both th' Indias of spice and mine
>   Be where thou left'st them, or lie here with me.
> Ask for those kings whom thou saw'st yesterday,
> And thou shalt hear, "All here in one bed lay."
>
> She's all states, and all princes I;
>   Nothing else is;
> Princes do but play us; compared to this,
> All honour's mimic, all wealth alchemy.

> Thou, Sun, art half as happy as we,
> In that the world's contracted thus;
> Thine age asks ease, and since thy duties be
> To warm the world, that's done in warming us.
> Shine here to us, and thou art everywhere;
> This bed thy center is, these walls thy sphere.

Handsome doesn't know that his line, "She is all States, all Princes, I, nothing else is…," is just a piece of a larger whole, and neither would a reader who does not catch nor understand the intertextual reference to Donne, since indeed only this one line is ever mentioned and it's not at any point contextualized, which results in the reader potentially having the same isolated experience with it as does Handsome.

I suggest that there is a way to read this scene as admiration for a beautiful line of poetry that is otherwise unknown or unrecognized; in other words, there is a way to read these words as beautiful in their own right and that there is also a way to read this scene critically by following the intertextual reference to Donne's "The Sun Rising" and the way in which the speaker of that poem addresses the sun to tell it that, in its duty and obligation to warm the whole world, it needs to go no further than the window of the room the speaker shares with their lover, since the world has been reduced to them and them alone: "She is all states, all Princes I, nothing else is".

Whether you admire the surface, the words as words, or you dig into the depths, the words as an intertextual reference, I argue that the same world-building action is occurring. Here I mean world-building in the standard understanding, as in *The Stone Gods* is a work of non-realist science fiction, and therefore, Winterson needs to build the world in which it occurs, but I also mean world-building in the sense of what Rita Felski means when she describes "loving readings" as those that are "driven by passion, care, and intimacy" and endeavour "to understand what kind of world the text is imagining, building, and offering to us" (1-2). On the surface, Handsome's singular scrap of poetry, "She is all States, all Princes I, Nothing else is," is in itself building a world: it's the framework and infrastructure upon which Handsome is attempting to build the "new world" for which he's exploring the galaxy: he's building this new world with and for his love. In the depths, this scrap of poetry is also referencing a physical world made completely redundant by the love of two people. Either way, we arrive at the same reading, which I think is best represented in Spike's dialogue as she gives Billie the first tour of the spaceship commissioned to find Planet Blue:

> Spike turned to me, smiling… 'Look over here. I want to show you something and to explain something.' She stood up and went over to the

pages pasted on the wall. She pointed at one of the yellowing texts… She said, 'On the official space mission, when we hung in our ship over Planet Blue, Handsome came aboard for the celebrations. While the crew were making the film record, the first shots to be replayed back to Orbus, Handsome got out his book of poetry. Everyone laughed at him, but he insisted that only a poet could frame a language that could frame a world. Underneath the digital images of Planet Blue, he wrote, *She is all States, all Princes I, Nothing else is.* (66)

Later, when this second mission to Planet Blue fails, and all of the crew members face inevitable death because, in scientifically engineering the extinction of the dinosaurs that inhabited the planet by re-routing an asteroid to make an impact and cause a dust cloud to block the sun, they've also ensured their own death by hypothermia, Handsome, in defeat, says to Spike "poetry didn't save us, did it?" and Spike replies "Not once, but many times" (78). Whether you read Handsome's scrap of poetry as just that, the one line *as* the poem, or you follow the implication all the way through to Donne's "The Sun Rising" and infer into *The Stone Gods* the references to a world that both shrinks and at the same time expands to contain and bolster the love of two people, poetry itself is the world-building project being undertaken; it is the material with which Handsome and Spike build their world, the world in which they ground themselves for support, protection, and purpose. Likewise, whether I, as the reader, ground myself in the surface of the depths matters not when doing either gets me to a place I want to be, a place that is justified in my desire to want to be there and also by my devotion to it.

Works Cited

Attridge, Derek. "In Praise of Amateurism." The Critic as Amateur, edited by Saikat Majumdar and Aarthi Vadde. Bloomsbury Publishing, 2019, pp. 31-48.

Bennett, Claire-Louise. *Pond*. Riverhead Books, 2015.

—. "On Writing Pond." The Irish Times, 26 May 2015. https://www.irishtimes.com/culture/books/claire-louise-bennett-on-writing-pond-1.2226535

Best, Stephen and Sharon Marcus. "Surface Reading: An Introduction." *Representations*, vol. 108, no. 1, 2009, pp. 1-21.

Casanova, Pascale. *The World Republic of Letters*, translated by Malcolm DeBevoise. Harvard UP, 2007.

Critique and Postcritique, edited by Elizabeth S. Anker and Rita Felski. Duke UP, 2017.

Donne, John. "The Sun Rising." *Poems, Poets, Poetry*, second edition. Helen Vendler, editor. Bedford, 2002.

Felski, Rita. "Context Stinks." *New Literary History*, vol. 42, no. 4, 2011, pp. 573-579.

Jameson, Fredric. *The Political Unconscious: Narrative as a Socially Symbolic Act*. Cornell UP, 1982.

Majumdar, Saikat and Aarthi Vadde, editors. *The Critic as Amateur*. Bloomsbury Publishing, 2019.

Moi, Toril. "'Nothing is Hidden': From Confusion to Clarity; or, Wittgenstein on Critique." Critique and Postcritique, edited by Elizabeth S. Anker and Rita Felski, Duke UP, 2017, pp. 31-49.

Nagoski, Emily and Amelia Nagoski. *Burnout: The Secret to Unlocking the Stress Cycle*. Ballantine Books, 2020.

Ross, Trevor. *Writing in Public: Literature and the Liberty of the Press in Eighteenth-Century Britain*. JHU Press, 2018.

Stoller-Lindsey, Nina. "Here's Why We're Underestimating the Value of English Majors." *Forbes*, 26 July 2017. https://www.forbes.com/sites/learnvest/2017/07/26/heres-why-were-underestimating-the-value-of-english-majors/?sh=1443027730d4

Tolentino, Jia. "A Work of Fiction that Will Make You Feel Pleasantly Insane." *The New Yorker*. 11 July 2016. https://www.newyorker.com/books/page-turner/fiction-that-will-make-you-feel-pleasantly-insane.

Walkowitz, Rebecca. *Born Translated: The Contemporary Novel in an Age of World Literature*. Columbia UP, 2017.

Winterson, Jeanette. *The Stone Gods*. Penguin Books, 2007.

Wood, Michael. *Literature and the Taste of Knowledge*. Cambridge UP, 2005.

Chapter 2
Rethinking Some Literary Dogmatic Views of Virginia Woolf and Vladimir Nabokov

Yeşim Sultan Akbay
Süleyman Demirel University, Türkiye

Betüre Memmedova
Süleyman Demirel University, Türkiye

Abstract

The present chapter was encouraged by the lack of study in the field of literary dogmas. Dogmas are generally thought to be related to religion, but they exist in every field, literature being no exception. The chapter proves that in light of new developments and changes in literature, some statements and ideas by distinguished authors have undergone major re-evaluations and revisions. Among these renowned names, the British modernist and feminist writer, critic, and essayist Virginia Woolf and the Russian-born American novelist, poet, and prominent entomologist Vladimir Nabokov hold a special place. For a long time, few critics dared to question their dictums. However, recently, a number of writers and critics have raised their voices against their pronouncements. Virginia Woolf's famous assertion that to become a writer, a woman needs a room and money of her own have been under scrutiny by such writers and critics as Emily Hodgson Anderson, Carol Goodman, Lawrence Durrell, and many others. The chapter presents a detailed account of their views gained from their own experience. The research focuses not only on Vladimir Nabokov's contradictory opinions on the novel genre expressed in *Lectures on Literature* but also on his literary snobbery as regards such established authors as Jane Austen, Thomas Mann, Henry James, Rainer Maria Rilke, Nikolai Gogol, Fyodor Dostoevsky, and even Leo Tolstoy. He undermines and underestimates them by degrading and insulting words like 'a pale porpoise', 'dwarfs or plaster saints'. To him, *their names are engraved on empty graves, their books are dummies, they are complete nonentities.* Nabokov's dogmatic assertions that we learn nothing even from the most reliable historical novels, that all the novels are fairy tales, and that all the writers are great deceivers are challenged and refuted in the study. Our objections to these unacceptable ideas are supported by prominent critics such as Azar Nafisi, Priscilla Meyer, Emily Temple, Sally Vickers, Kate Bernheimer, and J. K. Rowling. Literature is not something static: it is constantly changing and getting enriched and varied with new movements, genres, literary theories, and concepts. Diversity has always characterised literature. Immanuel Kant's statement, *The death of the dogma is the birth of morality*, related to religion, is well valid for literature as well. In literature, the death of literary dogmas is the birth of critical thinking, revision, and rethinking of the ideas, maxims, and quotations of eminent writers that have been accepted without questioning. Literary critics and academicians need an open mind coupled with a critical eye to refute dogmas. Only in this case is it possible to reveal the dogmatic implications in literature.

Keywords: Literary Dogmas, Dogmatic Assertions, Re-evaluations, Virginia Woolf, Vladimir Nabokov

***

Art is neither complete rejection nor complete acceptance of what is. It is simultaneously rejection and acceptance, and this is why it must be a perpetually renewed wrenching apart. The artist constantly lives in such a state of ambiguity, incapable of negating the real and yet eternally bound to question it in its eternally unfinished aspects.

—Albert Camus, "Create Dangerously"

By way of preface, let us say that on none of the matters to be discussed do we affirm that things certainly are just as we say they are: rather, we report descriptively on each item according to how it appears to us at the time.

—Sextus Empiricus, "Outlines of Scepticism"

Introduction

The issue of literary dogmas has been, so far, the neglected area in literature. The present chapter deals with some dogmatic attitudes expressed by Virginia Woolf in her insightful book *A Room of One's Own* (1929) and contradictory assertions about the novel genre by the Russian-born American writer Vladimir Nabokov in the famous book *Lectures on Literature* edited by Fredson Bowers in 1982. With Virginia Woolf as a leading representative of women's literature and female voice and Nabokov as one of the greatest modern male writers in the world, the chapter will try to refute the dogmatic implications in their works. The statements that were considered unchallenging are now being reassessed by a number of writers and critics who put forward fresh interpretations.

The word of Greek origin, *dogma*, means *opinion*. To be more exact, it means "that which one thinks is true" and comes ultimately from the Greek "dokein," which means "to seem good" or "think" (*Merriam-Webster*). Unfortunately, however, the word has narrowed its meaning to "a belief or set of beliefs that is accepted by the members of a group without being questioned or doubted" (*Britannica*). Usually, the word refers to the field of religion (see Arnold), but there are dogmas in every field, literature being no exception.

The idea to analyse literary dogmas came to us with Roland Barthes' "The Death of the Author" theory which was blindly accepted for decades in academia. No one considered his theory unfair and unjust towards writers (see Akbay; ch. IV). It is not only literary theories by prominent writers and critics that are accepted without questioning but also some claims by distinguished authors on various issues concerning literature. Those who accept all the literary theories without a critical eye and consider them to be unchallengeable and axiomatic seem to ignore the fact that literary theory does not mean *it is*; rather, it stands for the probability of analysing and interpreting a literary work from a wide range of perspectives.

However, what causes more concern is that the line of demarcation between art and literature is getting increasingly blurred. This fact has become prominent during the postmodernist period when some literary works are far from exciting strong feelings in the reader, something art and literature are meant to do. In the opening lines of her essay "Modern Fiction," Virginia Woolf wishes that the newly written literary works were better than the old ones. She expresses her disappointment about the quality of some literary pieces: "We do not come to write better; all that we can be said to do is to keep moving, now a little in this direction, now in that" (*Selected Essays* 6). It remains to wonder how this unparalleled modernist writer would judge today's literature and art, the two fields that have always been inseparable. On the one hand, she would be pleasantly or unpleasantly surprised at the great variety of new genres such as hysterical realism, dirty realism, prison literature, neuro novel, Twitter novels, lucid fiction, cli-fi, graphic novel, manga (Japanese graphic novels), doodle fiction, bizarro (using absurd and grotesque elements), mythopoeia, bit punk (referring to the technology of the 80s) and mystery genre (which is not only about murder any more), xenofiction (stories about extra-terrestrials) and many others. On the other hand, she would hardly find a good number of postmodernist or feminist novels appropriate as a literary piece. She might be shocked by the lack of moral themes and ethics as well as by the loss of "elegance and virtue" (see Tuttleton) in them, the qualities that unfortunately belong to the past only.

Most critics accept Virginia Woolf's contradictoriness without questioning. For Nasrullah Mambrol, *A Room of One's Own* can be confusing because it puts forward contradictory arguments ("Analysis of Virginia Woolf"). The Twenty-First Annual International Conference on Virginia Woolf, titled "Contradictory Woolf" [1], is another confirmation of the writer's ambiguities. Before addressing these ambiguities, Woolf should be given credit for being modest and self-critical in chapter one of *A Room of One's Own*, where she wants her readers to tell the truth from lies and "decide whether any part of it is worth keeping" (4). As the passage of time shows, every word in this immortal essay is "worth keeping" (*A Room* 4). However, despite all the merits and virtues of the book, some assertions by Virginia Woolf have been under close scrutiny in literary essays and articles. One of the dogmatic cases is considered Virginia Woolf's universally accepted statement that "a woman must have money and a room of her own if she is to write fiction" (*A Room* 4). Metaphorically, no one can deny the wisdom of the quote in Woolf's seminal work *A Room of One's Own*. Virginia Woolf's dictums must have been relevant when she wrote them in 1929, looking back at the previous centuries when female writers had no access to the literary world when even the prominent nineteenth-century laureate poet Robert Southey was convinced that "literature cannot be the business of a woman's life" (329). However, recently a number of writers and critics have raised their voices against this cliché phrase. They present a large number of examples refuting this thought.

Female Writers Looking for a Personal Space

Victoria Chang, an American poet and children's writer, for instance, wrote "in a windowless room. Not in a room at all" (14). Professor Emily Hodgson Anderson does her writing on her multi-functional kitchen table. Pointing out the positive developments in the position and stature of women since 1929, the writer nevertheless has no room of her own: "I spend much of my intellectual life at our table [dinner table], in a room that is not a room, in a space with no doors to close" (Anderson).

The writer also questions Woolf's assertion about interruption and concludes that "Interruptions, the very structure of Woolf's essay suggests, are not always occasions to be mourned" (Anderson). She names a large number of writers and poets who sought interruption rather than privacy in the rooms of their own. It turns out that it was not only Maria Edgeworth who greeted interruption but a great many writers and poets such as Samuel Taylor Coleridge, David Hume, W. Wordsworth, and Wittgenstein, to mention but a few. As she states, it

---

[1] University of Glasgow, Scotland, 2011.

was with interruptions that "In my life, I've finished many a memo, reader's report, work email, lesson plan, and book review... at the dining room table, tilting my computer screen away from my boys" (Anderson). She quotes Maria Edgeworth's confession to her woman writer friend, who at times welcomed interruption:

> I remember once... I was just in the solitary melancholy state you describe, and I used to feel relieved and glad when the tea-urn came into the silent room, to give me a sensation by the sound of its boiling. (Anderson)

Carol Goodman, on the other hand, wrote wherever she could write as a writer: "in cafés and restrooms, on trains and planes, sometimes using improvised materials such as the backs of envelopes" ("Home of Her Own"). When Robert Phillips went to interview Simone de Beauvoir in her place, he noticed that "The apartment had no separate den or study; her writing was done in the corner of the dining room, the typewriter being put away every evening" ("Elizabeth Spencer"). Simone de Beauvoir herself confessed that "I didn't have a room of my own. In fact nothing at all" (qtd. in Gobeil). According to Ian S. MacNiven, the biographer of the British novelist and dramatist Lawrence Durrell (1912-1990), the latter, too, embraced interruptions. To MacNiven, Durrell had "no quiet place and no time to write" (717), his second novel fifteen years after the publication of his first novel. But, when he set pen to paper, he had "never felt in better writing form," although "under more difficult circumstances" (718). Andrea Bajani (1975—), the contemporary Italian writer, can write everywhere: "In bars, on trains, on benches" but never at home though he can afford a convenient space for writing ("Love is Space"). Though Sidney Offit believes that focus and concentration are of utmost importance to writers in the process of creating, they still welcome interruption (see Offit).

The late British writer Penelope Fitzgerald's (1916-2000) writing career is compelling in itself. Interestingly, she is also one of those welcoming interruptions.

> Women adapt in a peculiar way to the battle against Time and Nature. I started writing during my free periods as a teacher in a small, noisy staff room, full of undercurrents of exhaustion, worry, and reproach, and for a long time after I gave up my day job I missed the staff room, and, sitting in peace and quiet, could scarcely get anything written. I had thought of both of them—peace and quiet—as the absence of certain things. That's not so, they are positive, but to my dismay I found they worked against each other. In the tranquillity of my own room, overlooking a garden with a large pear tree, I found I was waiting obsessively for an interruption and even ready to welcome it. (*House of Air* 510)

Jane Austen (1775-1817) did not have a room of her own and was often the target of interruptions, yet she was able to write six masterpieces on a small round table. Moreover, in her 2017 *The New York Times* review, Professor Devoney Looser considers the fact of Jane Austen's writing in secret[2] a fiction and myth ("Jane Austen Wasn't Shy"). Austen was not writing secretly; actually, it was Jane Austen's father, an avid reader himself, who asked Fanny Burney's publisher to read his daughter's manuscript of *First Impressions*, the would-be *Pride and Prejudice*. However, the publisher Cadell refused the request even without reading it. Mary Oliver (1935-2019), the famous American poet and writer, the winner of *The National Book Award* and the *Pulitzer Prize*, kept writing "walking with her notebook around the woods" ("I Got Saved"). It is quite clear that most female writers were exposed to interruptions but kept writing under all kinds of circumstances.

Throughout *A Room of One's Own*, Virginia Woolf expresses her concern about women who could not write for lack of money. However, it is surprising that she does not mention Margaret Oliphant, the most prolific (more than 120 works—over 100 novels—in about fifty years) and professional author of Victorian England. It should be noted that neither Sandra Gilbert nor Susan Gubar included her in the *Norton Anthology of Literature by Women* (1979). Margaret Oliphant (1828-1897), described as "a penniless, undaunted little Scottish 'scribbling woman'" (*House of Air* 40) by Penelope Fitzgerald, was one of the many female writers who grappled with financial issues throughout her writing career. She, who would generally write under the name Mrs. Oliphant, wrote without a room of her own, writing "in the intervals of housekeeping and sick-nursing" (*House of Air* 42). Though she never welcomed interruption, Margaret Oliphant hardly "had two hours undisturbed (except at night, when everybody is in bed) during my whole literary life" (qtd. in Mundhenk 391). After marrying her glass-painter cousin, it was she who became the breadwinner of the household throughout her marriage. After her husband's death, she was left pregnant with two children to take care of and nearly a debt of £1,000 (*House of Air* 43). She triumphed over all the difficulties a Victorian woman could have faced in Victorian England. Though highly acclaimed by her contemporary critics, writers, and even Queen Victoria, she undeservedly slipped into oblivion after her death. Relying on Emily Blair (see *Virginia Woolf and the Nineteenth-Century Domestic Novel*), Ana Clara Birrento, in the introduction to her book *The Autobiography of Margaret Oliphant: The Story of a Woman - A Landscape of the Self*, states, "the damaging influential voices of Leslie Stephen and his

---

[2] See "Jane Austen hid her manuscripts or covered them with a piece of blotting-paper" (*A Room* 66).

daughter" (13). For the reliability of the case, the following quotation is given at length:

> Like her father, Virginia Woolf found Oliphant guilty as a writer and as a woman (Blair 2007). Relegating her to a second-rate position, as a mere scribbler, Woolf set the tone of criticism until the 70s, writing in Three Guineas one of the fiercest attacks on the novelist, accusing her of selling her brain and of prostituting culture, of enslaving her intellectual freedom in order to survive and to bring up her children. Woolf suggested that reading Margaret Oliphant's fiction left the reader's mind and imagination dirty as the continuous writing of marketable fiction had made the novelist complicit with the political evils of a patriarchal system. Virginia Woolf would therefore disavow the novelist's struggle with the material conditions that the middle-class woman writer faced. According to Blair (2007), Woolf's appreciation of Oliphant revealed a literary hierarchy that created aesthetic value by distancing it from economic necessity. But if, according to Woolf, the exhaustion of Oliphant's creativity hindered her to write a few good works, Elizabeth Jay, on the other hand, considers that all the reviewing fuelled her talent; being an avid reader of the work of other writers, English or foreign, was an enriching experience and gave her a cosmopolitan vision of the English affairs. (Birrento 14)

As if echoing Ana Clara Birrento, Jessica Gildersleeve blames Woolf for a lack of empathy with less privileged women:

> But Woolf seems to lack an awareness of her own privilege and how much harder it is for most women to fund their own artistic freedom. It is easy for her to advise against "doing work that one did not wish to do, to do it like a slave, flattering and fawning." ("Guide to Classics")

The fact that Mrs. Oliphant was neglected until the 1970s and was considered "a novelist who wrote too much and too quickly, with an eye to the market" (Birrento 7) is a sad example of a dogmatic attitude towards the Victorian female writer. Mrs. Oliphant speaks from experience when in her novel *Sheridan* (1883), she claims that "the middle of life is the testing-ground of character and strength" (144). She is one of those women who truly justified her life, which was a life of bravery and a life of great difference. After Merryn Williams' *Margaret Oliphant: A Critical Biography* (1986) and Elizabeth Jay's *Mrs Oliphant, "A Fiction to Herself": A Literary Life* (1995), Margaret Oliphant's fame has been revived to a great extent. No doubt that Mrs. Oliphant, like Aphra Behn, also deserves flowers on her grave.[3]

The Victorian English poet and fiction writer Charlotte Mew (1969-1928) also went through a life of torment, working "against the obstacle of poverty, severe bouts of depression, and taxing familial responsibilities that included caring for her demanding, widowed mother as well as her beloved and delicate younger sister" (Merrin 201). Much remains unknown in her life, except the fact "that it was a long struggle not only with poverty but with adversity and private sorrows that finally overcame her" (Untermeyer 167). After her father's death, she felt obliged to "make a living" and "decided to earn money by writing" (*Charlotte Mew* viii). Although her artistic powers failed to heal her depressive moods, eventually leading her to suicide with a bottle of Lysol, her artistic merits were highly appreciated and admired by the great writers of her time. The great Thomas Hardy considered Mew the best female poet of her time, "who will be read when others are forgotten" (qtd. in Orel 59). Moreover, along with Ezra Pound and Siegfried Sassoon, she was admired by Virginia Woolf, who called her the "greatest living poetess" (qtd. in Parini 15). In a male-dominated society with financial insecurities,

> Charlotte Mew triumphed. She achieved the writing of poetry of beauty, originality and intensity. In a culture that regarded poetry as a supremely male vocation (niches were granted to poetesses writing ladylike verses) she made her voice heard. (*Charlotte Mew* xi)

The late-blooming British novelist, short-story writer, poet, biographer, essayist, and Booker Prize winner Penelope Fitzgerald started writing her novels when she was going through the most challenging times of her life; poverty, homelessness, unhappy marriage (though never mentioned and complained by her) were only but few of them. The treatment of such difficult phases of life was a value inherited from her immediate family and has never become an obstacle withdrawing her from hope and will to write. Her neighbours would recall that the Fitzgeralds never had proper food; either pasta or cold fried eggs (Lee 101). She would cut down her clothes to make clothes for her children when they were babies (Lee 122), would dye her hair with tea bags (*So I Have Thought* 145), mend her shoes (*So I Have Thought* 49), and watch her barge home *Grace* sink. Despite the difficulties she endured and often welcomed, she wrote nine novels, three biographies, a collection of essays and reviews, as well as a collection of short stories after sixty in twenty years. She became the focus

---

[3] "All women together ought to let flowers fall upon the tomb of Aphra Behn which is, most scandalously but rather appropriately, in Westminster Abbey, for it was she who earned them the right to speak their minds" (*A Room* 65).

of notable critics who kept asking, "How did she do it?" (see Barnes). Katherine A. Powers felt admiration for her writing talent:

> Fitzgerald knew exactly who she was, and never allowed the circumstances of her life —the blighted prospects, descent into poverty and homelessness, marital trials, crumby jobs, condescension from literary insiders—to blind her to her own gift of greatness. ("Penelope Fitzgerald")

Like "Balzac and 19th-century writers, black and white" (qtd. in Young), Maya Angelou (1928-2014), the African American female writer, poet, essayist, autobiographer, and female activist, does not see something improper in writing for money. In her chronology of seven autobiographical books,[4] she vividly depicts her long years of squalor and abuse. She worked as a cook, singer, waitress, dancer, and even a prostitute to make ends meet. For Angelou, writing was a means of survival until she became an acclaimed writer and poet. The titles of her obituaries reveal the positive effects of poverty on a black woman writer fighting against not only privation but also racial discrimination with a childhood trauma of sexual abuse.[5] Maya Angelou was the author of 36 books—thirty of which became best-sellers. Her legacy no doubt will endure.

Octavia Estelle Butler (1947-2006) was another African American writer who had to battle against chronic poverty. Butler decided to be a writer at the age of nine, in a household where they could hardly fill their stomachs. While fighting with dyslexia, she took on numerous odd jobs to survive as a writer. It is to her credit that she excelled in a male-dominated genre, science fiction. Despite the harsh conditions she had to write in, Octavia Butler

> published 15 novels and short story collections in her lifetime, received a MacArthur genius grant, and earned two Nebula and two Hugo awards, both esteemed recognitions in publishing. And despite dying unexpectedly of a stroke at age 58 in 2006, her legacy still lives on; "In 2019, the Los Angeles Public Library named its studio space the Octavia Lab in her honor" (Jean-Philippe).

---

[4] See *I Know Why the Caged Bird Sings* (1969), *Gather Together in My Name* (1974), *Singin' and Swingin' and Gettin' Merry Like Christmas* (1976), *The Heart of a Woman* (1981), *All God's Children Need Traveling Shoes* (1986), *A Song Flung Up to Heaven* (2002), *Mom &Me & Mom* (2013).

[5] See "The Life of Poet Maya Angelou, From Poverty to Presidential Prizes" by Karen Grimsby Bates in *NPR*; "Maya Angelou Whose Chronicle of her Dirt-Poor Upbringing Became a Literary Sensation" by *The Telegraph*; "Writer Angelou's Optimism Overcame Poverty, Hardship" by Anne Ferrer in *The Press Reader*; "Maya Angelou's Arkansas: Dignity and Poverty in the Depression" by Ben Cosgrove in *Time*.

The worldwide recognised author J. K. Rowling (1965–), who wrote the seven-volume *Harry Potter* series (1997-2007), is one of the female writers who rose "From Poverty to Billionaire Status" (Hamre). Rowling was a poor single mother who went through severe depression having suicidal thoughts. In a 2008 Harvard University commencement speech, she described her state as being "poor as it is possible to be in modern Britain, without being homeless... By every usual standard, I was the biggest failure I knew" (qtd. in Newman xi). She would write some parts of the volume at coffee shops with her daughter sleeping next to her; she would go without a meal when there was only enough food to feed her daughter. However, she regarded the overcoming process as something necessary for life and growth:

> I cannot criticise my parents for hoping that I would never experience poverty. They had been poor themselves, and I have since been poor. And I quite agree with them. It is not an ennobling experience. Poverty entails fear, stress, and sometimes depression. It means a thousand humiliations and hardships. Climbing out of poverty on your own efforts, that is something to pride yourself on. But poverty itself is romanticised only by fools. (qtd. in Howe 105)

The *Harry Potter* collection was rejected twelve times, but Rowling never gave up. The writer is now the world's first billionaire author, with the *Harry Potter* series selling more than five hundred million copies.

A critical survey of roomless female writers proves that what they needed was not a room but rather a personal and spiritual space, a word not synonymous with 'room' and 'place'. The writers who managed to create their own spaces resisted patriarchal theories of space according to which the feminine implies body, private and opaque. They succeeded in transcending all three barriers, blessing readers with books of enduring impact (see Denis). The space these female writers created and internalised allowed them to keep and promote their autonomous selves. Sometimes, it was a voyage into the inner space of "elsewhere" (see Quawas); another time, it was "unlearning to not speak" (Gilbert and Gubar 83); more often, it was a "departure from the unsatisfactory reality of life in an alienated and alienating society" (Quawas 107). But most importantly, it was a space where they cherished a belief that writing "is spreading out its roots in the deepest places of (their) heart" and that without writing, they would die (Rilke 16). It must be for all this supernatural strength of the *weak* and their enormous power of "storytelling and the art of tenderness" (Popova) that had Olga Tokarczuk (the 2018 Polish Nobel laureate in literature) "bow low" ("Banquet Speech") to all these women authors of the past. Like Tokarczuk, every reader, no doubt, feels them "standing behind" ("Banquet Speech") and hears their voices, the voices of the voiceless.[6]

"Talent Is Its Own Excuse"[7]

The Russian-American (post)modern novelist, poet, critic, and prominent entomologist Vladimir Nabokov (1899-1977) is no less idiosyncratic as a critic than a writer. Like many famous writers, he is not without literary snobbery. His antagonistic attitude towards female writers is well-known. In his letter to Mark Aldanov, the Russian émigré writer, Nabokov undermines famous women writers by saying, "You have so many writing women! Be careful—it's a sign of a provincial literature" (qtd. in Meyer and Trousdale 480). Also, he wrote to the American writer and literary critic Edmund Wilson about his negative opinion as regards women writers as a whole: "I dislike Jane, and am prejudiced, in fact, against all women writers. They are in another class" (qtd. in Meyer and Trousdale 490). Despite this statement, in his *Lectures on Literature*, along with the works of such world-renowned writers as Charles Dickens, Gustave Flaubert, Robert Louis Stevenson, Marcel Proust, Franz Kafka, and James Joyce, Nabokov scrupulously analyses Jane Austen's famous novel *Mansfield Park*, though not considering it a masterpiece, but "the work of a lady and the game of a child" (10). Also, in his foreword to *Strong Opinions* (1973), the author refers to Jane Austen as *great*. It is worth mentioning here that the late Sterling Professor and literary critic Harold Bloom refutes the ideas like those of Nabokov and compares Austen with Shakespeare (see Bloom 51). Richard Whately, too, draws parallels between Austen and the Great Bard of Stratford of Avon for her outstanding skills in characterisation (qtd. in Tuite and Johnson 333). Ruth Wilson, in her book *The Jane Austen Remedy*, enthusiastically declares how rereading Jane Austen's novels transformed her life and made her happy as never before (see Wilson). Her observation once again does prove that each rereading of prominent writers rewards us with new revelations and epiphanies.

---

[6] Excerpt from Olga Tokarczuk's speech: "Today it is exactly one hundred ten years since the first woman won the Nobel Prize in Literature – Selma Lagerlöf. I *bow low* [emphasis is mine] to her across time, and to all the other women, all the female creators who boldly exceeded the limiting roles society imposed on them, and had the courage to tell their story to the world loud and clear. I can feel them *standing behind* [emphasis is mine] me" (Tokarczuk).

[7] Anton Pavlovich Chekhov's letter to his brother Nikolai Chekhov; Moscow, March, 1881: "This talent places you above millions of people, for there is only one artist for every two million people on earth. It places you in a very special position: you could be a toad or a tarantula and you would still be respected, because *talent is its own excuse* [emphasis is mine]" (Chekhov 49).

Nabokov's attitude to Virginia Woolf deserves special attention in that it shows how inconsistent he is in some of his assumptions. Priscilla Meyer accounts Nabokov's dismissal of Woolf to his jealousy of her innovative literary experiments he was interested in and perhaps for his resentment at Woolf's negative criticism of male writers in her *A Room of One's Own*. The critic blames him for *cryptomnesia*[8] ("Cryptomnesia")—unconscious plagiarism—and supports her belief by quoting Nina Berberova, the Russian writer: "I gradually got used to his manner of . . . taking something from a great author and then saying he'd never read him" (qtd. in Meyer and Trousdale 490). In fact, Nabokov read all of Woolf's oeuvre and was inspired by her literary experiments though he never alluded to her works. Priscilla Meyer convincingly shows the parallels between Nabokov's novel *Pale Fire* and Woolf's *Orlando*, which Nabokov deemed vulgar. Also, the article points out the affinities between Nabokov's *The Real Life of Sebastian Knight* and Woolf's *Jacob's Room*. In her conclusion, Priscilla Meyer emphasises Nabokov's contradictory perspective towards Woolf:

> Despite Nabokov's dislike of women writers in general and Woolf in particular, he seems to have systematically adapted both plot and thematic elements from her work in order to consider the identity and techniques of the artist, the relationship between authorial self and history, and the possibility of a mystical communion among the living and the dead. His choice to disguise his relationship to her important contribution to the prose fiction of his era perhaps reflects his strenuous effort to transcend his personal anguish in his art. Like Pnin crying in spite of himself at the Soviet propaganda film, Nabokov resisted the sentiment Woolf evoked, including the model of madness and suicide associated with her biography. (qtd. in Meyer and Trousdale 518-19)

Even in his novel *Bend Sinister* (1947), Nabokov's snobbery reveals itself in the statement of one of his characters:

> He remembered other imbeciles he and she had studied, a study conducted with a kind of gloating enthusiastic disgust. Men who got drunk on beers in sloppy bars, the process of thought satisfactorily replaced by swine-toned radio music. Murderers. The respect a business magnate evokes in his home town. Literary critics praising the books of their friends and partisans. Flaubertian farceurs. (11)

His contradictory reflections on great writers hardly hold water. It must be noted that his dislike of some great writers is not limited to female writers only. He considers Rainer Maria Rilke and Thomas Mann as "dwarfs or plaster saints"

---

[8] The term was first used in 1901 by the psychiatrist Theodore Flournoy.

compared to Kafka (*Lectures* 255). Also, he was far from appreciating such irreplaceable writers of all time as Fyodor Dostoyevsky and Leo Tolstoy. Sadly, for him, Henry James was "a pale porpoise" (Hardwick). Emily Temple, the author and the managing editor at *Literary Hub*, whose writings are always inspiring and illuminating, holds a different view on Nabokov's literary scepticism in terms of great writers. Though being reserved about many of his "ecstatically transgressive opinions" (Temple), she nevertheless takes delight in his sincerity, which she takes as an act of courage. She quotes his essay in which he attacks Edmund Wilson, who used to be his closest friend:

> Mr. Wilson must accept my instinct ... to take digs at great reputations. ... I refuse to be guided and controlled by a communion of established views and academic traditions, as he wants me to be. What right has he to prevent me from finding mediocre and overrated people like Balzac, Dostoevski, Sainte-Beuve, or Stendhal, the pet of all those who like their French plain? (qtd. in Temple)

In his interviews, he goes even further, adamantly announcing his condescending attitude toward such eminent writers and poets as Ezra Pound, the writer, philosopher, and critic Albert Camus, and the American writer and Nobel Prize winner William Faulkner. His remark, "Their names are engraved on empty graves, their books are dummies, they are complete nonentities insofar as my taste in reading is concerned. Brecht, Faulkner, Camus, many others, mean absolutely nothing to me" (qtd. in Temple) is hardly justified. To him, Boris Pasternak's *Doctor Zhivago* is "melodramatic," William Faulkner's novels "an absurd delusion," the great Russian writer Nikolai Gogol is "a worthless writer," Ernest Hemingway is a writer of "bells, balls and bulls," a writer he loathes, Joseph Conrad is a writer having "a souvenir-shop style" (qtd. in Temple).

Apart from his antipathy to some outstanding female and male writers, his contradictory opinions on the novel genre also pose a number of questions. It is unbelievable that such a great and meticulous writer with a keen eye on the details in the novel, who was over-sensitive about every aspect of literature, who demanded "of his students the passion of science and the patience of poetry" (*Strong Opinions* 15), could be so opinionated about the novel genre. Nabokov's contentions that "great novels are great fairy tales" (*Lectures* 2), and "Fiction is fiction. To call a story a true story is an insult to both art and truth. Every great writer is a great deceiver, but so is that arch-cheat Nature" (*Lectures* 5) can hardly be justified and need to be questioned.

Some writers and critics consider it quite natural for the novels to contain elements of fairytale and myth. Sally Vickers is firmly convinced that in all the literary genres, we "find unapologetic representations of fairy stories" and wonders why "anything to do with witches, wizards, ghosts, spirits, and fairies is considered at best whimsy, at worst tosh" ("Why we need fairies"). For this, she blames "the undeniable increase of the reign of those grim twin *isms*, reductionism, and materialism" ("Why we need fairies"). A contemporary fabulist and fairy tale review founder Kate Bernheimer refutes Nabokov's claim in an editor's note, "Form is Fairy Tale, Fairy Tale is Form," and believes that "all great literary works owe everything to fairy tales" (13). In one of her interviews, J. K. Rowling observes the fantasy elements in the novel:

> I think… there will always, always, always be books about magic, discovering secret powers, stuff that you're not allowed to do. It exists in adults, too. There's a small part of you that wishes you could alter external things to be the way they ought to be. (qtd. in Steffens 24)

This claim of the author reminds one of Samuel Taylor Coleridge's phrase "willing suspension of disbelief" (497) mentioned in the fourteenth chapter of his 1815 *Biographia Literaria*. The phrase means that it is natural for the reader and the viewer not to think critically and logically while getting involved in the work of art and take it as something natural. It was perhaps for this reason that *Harry Potter* became a bonafide phenomenon.

A book definitely has much more to say than its form, structure, style, and imagery, the literary elements Nabokov focused on most in his *Lectures on Literature*. It teaches us almost everything about human nature, behaviour, and condition. It is this life knowledge gained from books that are compelling for readers. It is not only the common reader who gleans insights from literature but writers as well. Leo Tolstoy

> was a believer in the novel not as a source of entertainment but as a tool for psychological education and reform. It was, in his eyes, the supreme medium by which we can get to know others, especially those who might from the outside seem unappealing and thereby expand our humanity and tolerance. ("Leo Tolstoy")

Azar Nafisi emphasises the positive role of literature in politics and social life. For her, it is beyond any doubt that "democracy and human rights are sustained, in part, by literature itself" and that "literary fiction is a crucial force within democracy itself" (qtd. in Fassler). Wendy Lesser, in the prologue of her *Why I Read*, states that she owes her knowledge of nineteenth-century England, France, and Russia to the novels she has read. She is very persuasive in her account: "Those fictional images and experiences are now so much a part of my own mind that superimposed reality pales by comparison" (Lesser 3). Moreover, "The Paris of Balzak, Zola, or Proust" is more real to her than "the actual Paris" (Lesser 10). Another writer's confession also deserves attention: "I've experienced the delight of melding with fictional characters whose life experiences had nothing to do with mine countless times" (Melynczuk). All these experiences Azar Nafisi calls "heartbreaking power" and considers it "beautiful" (qtd. in Fassler). Joseph Dobrian asserts that

> the truly great, truly timeless novels are those that contain wisdom that will always be wisdom, that leave you with an epiphany. Those that make you tell yourself, at the end, "I never thought of life that way," or, "That's just what I've felt all along but never could systematise in my mind." But they mustn't leave you completely happy, completely sad, or completely anything, if they are to be great and timeless. Style is valuable, but substance is all. The true immortals are the novels that leave you almost stunned, awed beyond words, by what a great story you've just read. ("What makes fiction timeless?")

Ursula K. Le Guin, in a *Paris Review* interview, emphasises how books enriched her: "A very good book tells me news, tells me things I didn't know, or didn't know I knew, yet I recognise them—yes, I see, yes, this is how the world is" (qtd. in Als). Also, she adds: "Fiction —and poetry and drama—cleanse the doors of perception" (qtd. in Als). To the question to whom she was measuring her works, the writer gives the names of "Charles Dickens, Jane Austen. And then, when [she] finally learned to read her, Virginia Woolf" (qtd. in Als). The American technical writer, literary historic and novelist Jon Michael Varese goes even further as regards Charles Dickens, claiming that we read Dickens's novels because they inform us "in the grandest way possible, why we are what we are" ("Why are we still reading Dickens").

Without mentioning Vladimir Nabokov, James Edwin Mahon, in his persuasive article "Novels Never Lie," argues against those who consider the novel to be nothing but a product of imagination: "If something is a lie then it is not a literary work of any kind, and if something is a literary work, and being a lie, are mutually exclusive categories" (323). The critic cites Jean-Paul Sartre and C. A. Higgins, who also consider the novel genre to be completely the author's imagination. However, James Edwin is of the opinion that "even if all of the statements in a novel are untruthful, however, the novel is still not a lie" (qtd. in Mahon 326). Considering a lie an assertion and misrepresentation, the critic excludes the possibility of the novel being a lie. To him, even such genres as *pseudo-gossip-lit* novels as well as *non-historical* novels are not lies. According to the critic, the same goes for *roman à clef* novels as well. The term *roman à clef* means a novel with a key, which is always justified by the plot though the authors of such novels always deny that they created their protagonists on the base of a real-life figure. The twentieth-century British writer Somerset Maugham's novel *The Moon and Sixpence* (1919) took the famous French Post-Impressionist artist Paul Gaugin's life as the basis for his protagonist Charles Strickland (see Maugham). In this novel, there are so many *keys* about Gaugin's life that during its publication, the majority of the reading audience considered the novel to be the great painter's biography. His other novel, *Cakes and Ale: or The Skeleton in the Cupboard*, is a camouflaged story of the British writer Thomas Hardy, his first wife Emma Lavinia Gifford's oddities in particular. There are also many clues behind the plot of such novels as *The Bell Jar* by Sylvia Plath; *The Sun Also Rises* by Ernest Hemingway, *Tender is the Night*, *The Last Tycoon* by F. Scott Fitzgerald, and *Human Bondage* by Somerset Maugham, which leave no doubt that the novels mentioned above actually describe the tumultuous lives of their authors. It is noteworthy that, in this case, the demarcation line between *roman à clef* novels and *biofiction* is very blurred.

Vladimir Nabokov holds a contradictory opinion about historical novels as well, which cannot be accepted either: "Can anybody be so naive as to think he or she can learn anything about the past from those buxom best-sellers that are hawked around by book clubs under the heading of historical novels?" (*Lectures* 1). Avrom Fleishman (1971) differentiates the novel from a historical novel as follows: "When life is seen in the context of history, we have a novel; when the novels' characters live in the same world with historical persons, we have a historical novel" (3-4). In her article "Historical Fiction: Towards a Definition," Bryony D. Stocker (see Stocker 65-80), and Sarah Johnson in her article "Defining the Genre: What are the Rules for Historical Fiction?" (see Johnson) try to elucidate the definition of the historical novel without undermining its significance.

The genre has been on the literary agenda since the first half of the nineteenth century when the father of the historical novel Walter Scott came forward with his historical novel series *Waverley*. Fusing fact and fiction, the genre adds a new dimension to literature. It is undoubtedly a gateway to the enormous information about a great variety of issues, such as the horrors of the wars, the disturbing realities of genocide, colonisation, racism, immigration, and forced migration. Most importantly, it takes the reader to distant pasts allowing him to compare the past and present and the lessons learned and unlearned.

What the eighteenth-century German philosopher and poet Novalis (Fritz von Hardenberg) said about the novel genre goes more for the historical novel: "Novels arise out of the shortcomings of history" (qtd. in Clark and Sears 114). In other words, novels compensate for things untold by history. In his article "What Can You Learn from A Historical Novel?", Daniel Aaron expresses the same thought differently: "Good writers write the kind of history good historians can't or don't write" (62). In one of his interviews, the famed Mexican novelist Carlos Fuentes Macias uses the term *ideal history*, which aims to "vitalise all aspects of the past that have not yet been expressed" (qtd. in Anadón 5). The writer also wonders if literature is "what history conceals, forgets, or mutilates" (qtd. in Aaron 62). Jerome De Groot devotes his book *The*

Historical Novel to the genre from a variety of aspects. In his introduction, De Groot states that "at present the historical novel is in robust health, critically and economically" (1). Himself a writer of historical novels, Crystal King, is convinced that "historical fiction is more important than ever" and claims that "reading historical fiction has colored my decisions and changed my actions— I truly believe it has made me a better person" ("Historical Fiction is More Important Than Ever"). If Vladimir Nabokov lived today, he would be surprised by the vast number of historical novels written in the twenty-first century. Crystal King presents ten authors of historical novels, among whom he names Jenna Blum, Anjali Mitter Duva, Jenni L. Walsh, Stephanie Dray, Marjan Kamali, Caroline Wood and Tim Weed (See King).

The next dogmatic view by Nabokov is related to the identification of the reader with his fictional characters. To him, to identify oneself with a character in the book "is the worst thing a reader can do" (*Lectures* 4). The review of literature on the readers' identification with narrative characters reveals literary critics' great interest in the issue. Marcus Cheetham et al., in their article "Identifying with fictive characters: structural brain correlates of the personality trait 'fantasy'", quote about thirty critics, among them philosophers and psychologists, who evaluated this issue (see 1836-44). The issue of identification has been taken so seriously by critics and psychologists that it has become a literary theory with its own ideas, principles and terms. Jonathan Cohen emphasises the importance of a theory of identification not only as regards novels and films but also media, communication and television programs: "identifying with a fictional character lies at the core of many media experiences, be it reading a novel, watching a movie, or playing a video game" (qtd. in Felnhofer et al.).

Moreover, David Morley's statement refutes Nabokov's erroneous idea about identification: "One can hardly imagine any television text having any effect whatever without that identification" (209). He observes that the reader goes through cognitive and emotional empathy during the reading process. Kobie van Krieken et al. present a study on identification as "a dynamic process" realised through six dimensions: "a spatiotemporal, a perceptual, a cognitive, a moral, an emotional, and an embodied dimension" (1190). Hermione Lee, in her biography *Virginia Woolf,* eloquently describes the emotional bond between the reader and the book. For Lee, reading Virginia Woolf's books creates "a free union"; it is "like a very intimate conversation or an act of love. That longing for loss of self, entry into an other" (*Virginia Woolf* 404), are inevitable outcomes of the reading process.

Rita Felski, in her article "Identifying with Characters", wishes critics were more scrupulous about the theory of identification and would not come to hasty conclusions "before it is fully seen" (77). For the critic, the issue of identification is not determined by empathy alone but depends on the identity and self of the reader or viewer:

> Identifying involves ideas and values as well as persons; may confound or remake a sense of self rather than confirming it; and is practiced by skeptical scholars as well as wide-eyed enthusiasts. (qtd. in van Krieken et al. 1190)

A good example of how strongly a reader can build empathy with the characters is given by Camden Hotten et al.: "The Irish politician Daniel O'Connel is reported to have thrown Charles Dickens' *The Old Curiosity Shop* out of the window of a riding train after reading the part in which the heroine, little Nell, dies" (qtd. in van Krieken et al. 1190). The politician's erratic behaviour is hardly surprising given that the universal and timeless theme of death is likely to evoke powerful emotions in the reader. In most famous novels, death is *functional*,[9] that is, it changes the course of the action in the novel and significantly affects the reader. Another puzzling example of exaggerated identification is when actors playing negative roles become objects of scorn. When encountered by viewers, they are even exposed to insults and accusations.

Not only the readers but also some great writers too identified themselves with the cherished characters of their creations. The nineteenth-century renowned French writer Gustav Flaubert's statement '*I am Madame Bovary*' (Madame Bovary, c'est moi) is well known. The author must have meant what was later called "The Madame Bovary syndrome" by French philosopher Jules De Gaultier by which he meant "chronic affective dissatisfaction with one's life" (Giesler 6). Though destructive and dangerous, Emma's romanticism appealed to Flaubert since his tendency for romantic ideas gave him away in his early works and letters. It is not accidental that to Nabokov, the novel is stylistically "prose doing what poetry is supposed to do" (*Lectures* 125).

Pride and Prejudice was Jane Austen's "own darling child," and Elizabeth Bennett, as she writes in a letter to her sister Cassandra, "as delightful a creature as ever appeared in print," and "how I shall be able to tolerate those who do not like her at least, I do not know" (Austen 137). To Jane Austen, Elizabeth Bennett's high spirit, a strong sense of self-worth, and her unconventional ideas of marriage, honesty, and morality were of great significance in a woman. Virginia Woolf, who was far from being sentimental while evaluating a novel critically, felt so absorbed and overwhelmed while reading Charlotte Brontë's *Jane Eyre* that "if someone moves in the room the movement seems to take place not there but up in Yorkshire" (*Women and Writing* 127).

---

[9] The term *functional death* belongs to Vladimir Nabokov (see *Lectures* 19).

A survey conducted at Durham University under the supervision of the writer and psychologist Charles Fernyhough yielded incredible results. It turned out that many of the 1500 respondents not only empathised with their favourite characters but also heard their voices and strongly felt their impact on their thoughts and actions. This unusual experience was called "experiential crossing" by Alderson-Day et al. (Alderson-Day 102). The novelist Edward Docx's observation definitely strikes a chord with the majority of readers. He gives precedence to fiction among other forms of art:

> The greatest film can't do that, and neither can a computer game. Only the novel can give you an intimate portrait of the complex cross-currents of human psychology, to the extent where you know another person's soul. And that's the most intimate thing in the world. (Loria)

Another research at the same university surveyed 181 authors "to find out just how common it is for writers to see, hear, or feel the presence of their characters" (Hawthorn).

The degree of identifying with characters in the novel changes from reader to reader depending on the readers' literary knowledge, reading experience, emotionality, and even as Kobie van Krieken et al. suppose, literary knowledge. The degree of identification is higher when the reader's vocabulary and semantics are good enough to comprehend the text. The readers usually identify with powerful and inspiring fictional characters whose experiences, sorrows, and joys resemble their own. It is these novels that haunt them long after they finish them. It must be for this reason that there are prequels and sequels to a number of masterpieces of English literature. Jean Rhys' prequel *Wide Sargasso Sea* to Charlotte Brontë's *Jane Eyre*, which gives the reasons for Bertha's insanity; Lin Haire-Sargeant's sequel *Heathcliff: The Return to Wuthering Heights*, in which Heathcliff is the narrator who gives a different story of his love for Catherine Earnshaw; and again Lin Haire-Sargeant's *Who is Jo March?: A Return to the World of "Little Women,"* the book giving a different fate of Josephine March, one of the characters in Louisa M. Alcott's *Little Women*, are but few of them.

The novel genre, with its multitudes of types, definitely teaches us a myriad of things. Vladimir Nabokov contradicts himself when, on the one hand, he calls the writer a "great deceiver" (*Lectures* 5); on the other, he sees in major writers a blend of a storyteller, a teacher, and an enchanter (*Lectures* 5). He claims that "we may go to the teacher not only for moral education but also for direct *knowledge*, for simple facts" (*Lectures* 5). There is further evidence of his polarity when in his interviews, he states that while writing his novels, including *Lolita*, neither having a social purpose nor conveying a moral message was his concern (*Strong Opinions* 16).

Conclusion

Immanuel Kant's statement related to religion, "the death of the dogma is the birth of morality" (qtd. in Cherry 34), is well valid for literature as well. In literature, the death of literary dogmas is the birth of critical thinking, revision, and rethinking of the ideas, maxims, and quotations of eminent writers that have been accepted without questioning. It is well known that literature is not static: it is constantly changing and getting enriched and varied with new movements, genres, literary theories, and terms. Diversity has always characterised literature. Good literature needs a keen eye of critics and readers to rise to all possible challenges of what we call real art, the art that teaches, haunts, and transforms us. As for the assertions mentioned above of outstanding writers, it should be noted that the passage of time makes its corrections.

If Nabokov applied his highly contradictory observations to novels of no worth and devoid of any aesthetic and literary value, his negative attitude perhaps could be accepted, but regrettably, he blacklists even masterpieces and historical novels. The masterpieces V. Nabokov undermines contain memorable characters, indelible ideas, but most importantly, universal truths acknowledged by generations of critics and readers.

Though she complained that *words failed her* (see *Selected Essays* 85-91; Macdonald), Virginia Woolf was the master of the word-making art of everything, even of *illness*[10] (see *Selected Essays* 101-110). On the other hand, she was the writer who used the conjunction *but*[11] most frequently, by which she admitted the ambiguity of things. Woolf's statements need revising and reassessing owing to the passage of time and the changing circumstances, whereas Nabokov's assertions about the novel genre and identification with characters are still entirely unjustifiable.

Nabokov's scorn of his fellow writers recalls to mind the science of *memetics*, the term coined by biologist Richard Dawkins in 1976, which is "the study of memes" (*Merriam-Webster*) and

> sees ideas as a kind of virus, sometimes propagating in spite of truth and logic. Its maxim is: Beliefs that survive aren't necessarily true, rules that survive aren't necessarily fair and rituals that survive aren't necessarily necessary. Things that survive do so because they are good at surviving. ("A New Key to Behavior")

---

[10] "On Being Ill" (1926).

[11] See Allen, Judith. ""But...I had said 'but' too often." Why "but"?" in *Contradictory Woolf: Selected Papers from the Twenty-first Annual International Conference on Virginia Woolf*, edited by Derek Ryan and Stella Bolaki, Oxford UP, 2012, pp. 1-10.

One can hardly deny the wisdom of the assertions in the above definition. Some contradictory ideas and thoughts by writers whose genius is never questioned could be put in doubt. Dogmatic views are detrimental to the quality of literature; in other words, literature should not deviate from the definition of art.

Works Cited

"A New Key to Behavior." *Los Angeles Times*, 20 Mar. 1999, https://www.latimes.com/archives/la-xpm-1999-mar-20-me-19202-story.html. Accessed 18 Feb. 2022.

Aaron, Daniel. "What Can You Learn from a Historical Novel?" *American Heritage*, vol. 43, no. 6, 1992, pp. 55–62.

Akbay, Yeşim Sultan. *Actualisation of Self in Penelope Fitzgerald's Non-Fictional World*. 2021. Süleyman Demirel University, PhD dissertation. *YÖK Tez Merkezi*, https://tez.yok.gov.tr/UlusalTezMerkezi/tezSorguSonucYeni.jsp.

Alderson-Day, Ben, et al. "Uncharted Features and Dynamics of Reading: Voices, Characters, and Crossing of Experiences." *Consciousness and Cognition*, vol. 49, 2017, pp. 98-109. *Science Direct*, doi:10.1016/j.concog.2017.01.003.

Allen, Judith. "'But…I Had Said 'But' Too Often." Why "But"?" *Contradictory Woolf: Selected Papers from the Twenty-first Annual International Conference on Virginia Woolf*, edited by Derek Ryan and Stella Bolaki, Oxford UP, 2012, pp. 1–10.

Als, Hilton. "Edward P. Jones, The Art of Fiction No. 222." *The Paris Review*, 2013, https://www.theparisreview.org/interviews/6283/the-art-of-fiction-no-222-edward-p-jones. Accessed 18 Apr. 2022.

Anadón, Jose. "Carlos Fuentes on Politics, Language, and Literature." *Worldview*, vol. 23, no. 9, 1980, pp. 5–7., doi:10.1017/S008425590004078X.

Anderson, Emily Hodgson. "No Room of One's Own." *Air/Light Magazine*, Issue 1, 2020, https://airlightmagazine.org/airlight/fall2020/no-room-of-ones-own/. Accessed 14 Nov. 2021.

Arnold, Matthew. *Literature & Dogma: An Essay Towards a Better Apprehension of the Bible*. Smith, Elder, 1873.

Austen, Jane. *Selected Letters*. edited by Vivian Jones, Oxford UP, 2004.

Bajani, Andrea. "Love is Space: Notes on Marriage and Creativity." *LitHub*, 2 May 2022, https://lithub.com/love-is-space-notes-on-marriage-and-creativity/. Accessed 10 May 2022.

Barnes, Julian. "How did she do it?" *The Guardian*, 26 July 2008, https://www.theguardian.com/books/2008/jul/26/fiction. Accessed 6 June 2022.

Bernheimer, Kate. "Form is Fairytale, Fairytale is Form." *Fairy Tale Review*, The White Issue, no. 4, Wayne State UP. 2015. p. 13.

Birrento, Ana Clara. *The Autobiography of Margaret Oliphant: The Story of a Woman — A Landscape of the Self*. Universidade de Évora, Centro de Estudos em Letras, 2011.

Blair, Emily. *Virginia Woolf and the Nineteenth-Century Domestic Novel*. State University of New York Press, 2007.

Bloom, Harold. *Novelists and Novels: A Collection of Critical Essays*. Infobase Publishing, 2007.

Camus, Albert. *Resistance, Rebellion, and Death: Essays*. Translated by Justin O'Brien, Vintage International, 2012.

Chang, Victoria. *Dear Memory: Letters on Silence, Writing and Grief.* Milkweed Editions, 2021.

Cheetham, Marcus, et al. "Identifying with Fictive Characters: Structural Brain Correlates of the Personality Trait 'Fantasy'." *Social Cognitive and Affective Neuroscience*, vol. 9, no. 11, 2014, pp. 1836-44. *Oxford Academic*, doi:10.1093/scan/nst179.

Chekhov, Anton Pavlovich. *Anton Chekhov's Life and Thought: Selected Letters and Commentary*. Translated by Michael Henry Heim and Simon Karlinsky. Northwestern University Press, 1997.

Cherry, Eric. *You Need Not Think Alike to Love Alike*. Unisoul, 2008.

Clark, Penney, and Sears, Alan. *The Arts and the Teaching of History: Historical F(r)ictions*. Springer Nature, 2020.

Coleridge, Samuel Taylor. "Biographia Literaria." *The Norton Anthology of English Literature*, edited by Stephen Greenblatt, 10th ed., vol. D, W. W. Norton, 2018.

"Cryptomnesia." *APA Dictionary of Psychology*. https://dictionary.apa.org/cryptomnesia. Accessed 16 May 2022.

De Groot, Jerome. *The Historical Novel*. Taylor & Francis, 2010.

Denis, Laura. "Annie Ernaux and the Space of Old Age." *Dalhousie French Studies*, vol. 106, 2015, pp. 69–78. *JSTOR*.

Dobrian, Joseph. "What makes fiction timeless?" *Press Citizen*, 8 Aug. 2017, https://www.press-citizen.com/story/opinion/contributors/writers-group/2017/08/08/what-makes-fiction-timeless/550646001/. Accessed 13 Apr. 2022.

"Dogma." *Britannica*. https://www.britannica.com/dictionary/dogma. Accessed 13 Jan. 2022.

"Dogma." *Merriam-Webster*. https://www.merriam-webster.com/dictionary/dogma. Accessed 13 Jan. 2022.

Empiricus, Sextus. *Sextus Empiricus: Outlines of Scepticism*. edited by Julia Annas and Jonathan Barnes, Cambridge UP, 2000.

Fassler, Joe. "Write to Transcend Space and Time." *The Atlantic*, 4 Nov. 2014. https://www.theatlantic.com/entertainment/archive/2014/11/why-america-needs-literature/382332/. Accessed 22 May 2022.

Felnhofer, Anna, et al. "Character identification is predicted by narrative transportation, immersive tendencies, and interactivity." *Current Psychology*, 2022. *Springer Link*, doi:10.1007/s12144-022-03048-4.

Felski, Rita. "Identifying with characters." *Character: Three Inquiries in Literary Studies*, edited by Amanda Anderson, Rita Felski, and Toril Moi, University of Chicago Press, 2020, pp. 77–126.

Fitzgerald, Penelope. *A House of Air: Selected Writings*. Harper Perennial, 2005.

—. *Charlotte Mew and Her Friends: With a Selection of Her Poems*. Fourth Estate, 1984.

—. *So I Have Thought of You: The Letters of Penelope Fitzgerald*. Fourth Estate, 2009.

Fleishman, Avrom. *The English Historical Novel: Walter Scott to Virginia Woolf.* John Hopkins Press, 1971.

Giesler, Audrey C. *Madame Bovary Syndrome: The Female Protagonist's Plight.* 2020. Eastern Kentucky University, Honors Theses. *Encompass*, https://encompass.eku.edu/honors_theses/780/.

Gilbert, Sandra M., and Gubar, Susan. *The Madwoman in the Attic.* Yale Nota Bene, 2000.

Gildersleeve, Jessica. "Guide to the classics: A Room of One's Own, Virginia Woolf's feminist call to arms." *The Conversation*, 23 Sept. 2020, https://theconversation.com/guide-to-the-classics-a-room-of-ones-own-virginia-woolfs-feminist-call-to-arms-145398. Accessed 23 Nov. 2021.

Gobeil, Madeleine. "Simone de Beauvoir, The Art of Fiction No. 35." *The Paris Review*, Spring-Summer 1965, https://www.theparisreview.org/interviews/4444/the-art-of-fiction-no-35-simone-de-beauvoir. Accessed 7 Oct. 2021.

Goodman, Carol. "A Home of Her Own – How Jane Austen Found the Space to Write." *Women Writers, Women[s] Books*, 26 Mar. 2019, https://booksbywomen.org/a-house-of-her-own-finding-the-space-to-write-jane-austen-by-carol-goodman/. Accessed 10 Feb. 2022.

Hamre, Eric. "From Poverty to Billionaire Status." *Medium*, 15 Sept. 2020, https://medium.com/skilluped/j-k-rowling-from-poverty-to-billionaire-status-4f083c7cc413. Accessed 20 June 2022.

Hardwick, Elizabeth. "Master Class." *The New York Times*, 19 Oct. 1980, https://archive.nytimes.com/www.nytimes.com/books/98/07/26/specials/hardwick-nabokov.html. Accessed 2 Feb. 2022.

Hawthorn, Ainsley. "Most Authors Can Hear Their Characters Speaking to Them." *Psychology Today*, 30 Sept. 2020, https://www.psychologytoday.com/us/blog/the-sensory-revolution/202009/most-authors-can-hear-their-characters-speaking-them. Accessed 6 July 2022.

Howe, Randy. *Here We Stand: 600 Inspiring Messages from the World's Best Commencement Addresses.* Rowman & Littlefield, 2009.

Jean-Philippe, McKenzie. "7 Octavia Butler Books That'll Transport You to a New World." *Oprah Daily*, 31 July 2020, https://www.oprahdaily.com/entertainment/books/g33459612/octavia-butler-books/. Accessed 12 June 2022.

Johnson, Sarah. "What are the rules for historical fiction?" *Historical Novel Society*, https://historicalnovelsociety.org/defining-the-genre-what-are-the-rules-for-historical-fiction/. Accessed 15 Dec. 2021.

King, Crystal. "Historical Fiction is More Important Than Ever: 10 Writers Weigh In." *LitHub*, 24 Apr. 2017, https://lithub.com/historical-fiction-is-more-important-than-ever-10-writers-weigh-in/. Accessed 16 June 2022.

Lee, Hermione. *Penelope Fitzgerald: A Life.* Vintage Books, 2014.

—. *Virginia Woolf.* Vintage Books. 1999.

"Leo Tolstoy." *The School of Life*, https://www.theschooloflife.com/article/leo-tolstoy/. Accessed 23 May 2022.

Lesser, Wendy. *Why I Read: The Serious Pleasure of Books.* Farrar, Straus and Giroux, 2014.

Looser, Devoney. "Jane Austen Wasn't Shy." *New York Times*, 15 July 2017, https://www.nytimes.com/2017/07/15/opinion/sunday/jane-austen-wasnt-shy.html. Accessed 10 Dec. 2021.

Loria, Kevin. "A Surprising Percentage of People Report Hearing Voices of Characters in Stories Even When They Aren't Reading." *Insider*, 4 Mar. 2017, https://www.businessinsider.com/readers-hear-the-voices-of-characters-from-books-2017-3. Accessed 24 June 2022.

Macdonald, Fiona. "The Only Surviving Recording of Virginia Woolf." *BBC*, 28 Mar. 2016, https://www.bbc.com/culture/article/20160324-the-only-surviving-recording-of-virginia-woolf. Accessed 13 Apr. 2022.

MacNiven, Ian S. *Lawrence Durrell: A Biography*. Open Road Integrated Media, 1998.

Mahon, James Edwin. "Novels Never Lie." *British Journal of Aesthetics*, vol. 59, no. 3, 2019, pp. 323–38. *Oxford Academic*, doi: 10.1093/aesthj/ayz034.

Mambrol, Nasrullah. "Analysis of Virginia Woolf's A Room of One's Own." *Literary Theory and Criticism*, 11 Oct. 2020, literariness.org/2020/10/11/analysis-of-virginia-woolfs-a-room-of-ones-own/. Accessed 15 Oct. 2022.

Maugham, William Somerset. *The Moon and Sixpence*. Penguin Books, 1993.

Melynczuk, Ascold. "Why My Favorite Characters to Write Are Often Unsympathetic and Unforgivable." *LitHub*, 27 Sept. 2021, https://lithub.com/why-my-favorite-characters-to-write-are-often-unsympathetic-and-unforgivable/. Accessed 11 Apr. 2022.

"Memetics." *Merriam-Webster*, https://www.merriam-webster.com/dictionary/memetics. Accessed 10 July 2022.

Merrin, Jeredith. "The Ballad of Charlotte Mew." *Modern Philology*, vol. 95, no. 2, 1997, pp. 200-17. *JSTOR*.

Meyer, Priscilla, and Trousdale, Rachel. "Vladimir Nabokov and Virginia Woolf." *Comparative Literature Studies*, vol. 50, no. 3, 2013, pp. 490–522. *JSTOR*, doi:10.5325/complitstudies.50.3.0490.

Morley, David. *Television, Audiences and Cultural Studies*. Routledge. 1992.

Mundhenk, Rosemary J., and Fletcher, LuAnn McCracken. *Victorian Prose: An Anthology*. Columbia UP, 1999.

Newman, Rick. *Rebounders: How Winners Pivot from Setback to Success*. Random House Publishing Group, 2012.

Nabokov, Vladimir. *Bend Sinister*. Penguin Modern Classics, 2012.

—. *Lectures on Literature*. Harcourt Brace Jovanovich, 1982.

—. *Strong Opinions*. Penguin UK, 2012.

Offit, Sidney. *Friends, Writers, and Other Countrymen: A Memoir*. St. Martin's Press, 2008.

Oliphant, Margaret. *Sheridan*. Harper & Brothers, 1883.

Oliver, Mary. "I Got Saved by the Beauty of the World." *On Being*, 5 Feb. 2015, https://onbeing.org/programs/mary-oliver-i-got-saved-by-the-beauty-of-the-world/. Accessed 4 Apr. 2022.

Orel, Harold. *The Final Years of Thomas Hardy: 1912-1928*. The Macmillan Press Ltd., 1976.

Parini, Jay. "Companionship was Everything." *The New York Times*, sect. 7, col. 1, 1988, p.15.

Philips, Robert. "Elizabeth Spencer, The Art of Fiction No. 110." *The Paris Review*, Summer 1989, https://www.theparisreview.org/interviews/2417/the-art-of-fiction-no-110-elizabeth-spencer. Accessed 7 Oct. 2021.

Popova, Maria. "Storytelling and the Art of Tenderness: Olga Tokarczuk's Magnificent Nobel Prize Acceptance Speech." *The Marginalian*, 21 Nov. 2022, https://www.themarginalian.org/2022/11/21/tenderness-olga-tokarczuk-nobel-prize/. Accessed 15 Dec. 2022.

Powers, Katherine A. "Penelope Fitzgerald: A Life, a Reading Life." *Barnes and Noble*, 2 Dec. 2014, https://www.barnesandnoble.com/review/penelope-fitzgerald-a-life. Accessed 8 June 2022.

Quawas, Rula. "Lessing's 'To Room Nineteen': Susan's Voyage into the Inner Space of 'Elsewhere.'" *Atlantis*, vol. 29, no. 1, 2007, pp. 107–22.

Rilke, Rainer Maria. *Letters to a Young Poet*. W. W. Norton & Company, 1993.

Southey, Robert. *The Life & Correspondence of the Late Robert Southey*. Longman, Brown, Green and Longmans, 1850.

Steffens, Bradley. *J. K. Rowling: People in the News*. Lucent Books, 2002.

Stocker, Bryony D. "Historical Fiction: Towards a Definition." *Journal of Historical Fictions*, vol. 1, no. 2, 2017, pp. 65–80. *ResearchGate*.

Temple, Emily. "The Meanest Things Vladimir Nabokov Said About Other Writers." *Literary Hub*, 20 Apr. 2018, https://lithub.com/the-meanest-things-vladimir-nabokov-said-about-other-writers/. Accessed 27 Feb. 2022.

Tokarczuk, Olga. "Banquet Speech." *The Nobel Prize*, 10 Dec. 2019, https://www.nobelprize.org/prizes/literature/2018/tokarczuk/speech/. Accessed 20 Dec. 2022.

Tuite, Clara and Johnson, Claudia L. *A Companion to Jane Austen*. Wiley, 2011.

Tuttleton, James W. "Louis Auchincloss: The Image of Lost Elegance and Virtue." *American Literature*, vol. 43, no. 4, 1972, pp. 616–32. *JSTOR*, doi: 10.2307/2924658.

Untermeyer, Louis. *Modern American and British Poetry*. Harcourt, Brace and Company, 1944.

Van Krieken, Kobie, et al. "Evoking and Measuring Identification with Narrative Characters - a Linguistic Cues Framework." *Frontiers in Psychology*, vol. 8, 2017, p. 1190. *National Library of Medicine*, doi: 10.3389/fpsyg.2017.01190.

Varese, Jon Michael. "Why are We Still Reading Dickens?" *The Guardian*, 4 Sept. 2009, https://www.theguardian.com/books/booksblog/2009/sep/04/why-reading-dickens. Accessed 15 Oct. 2021.

Vickers, Sally. "Why We Need Fairies." *UnHerd*, 21 June 2022, https://unherd.com/2022/06/why-we-need-fairies/. Accessed 23 June 2022.

Wilson, Ruth. *The Jane Austen Remedy: It Is a Truth Universally Acknowledged that a Book Can Change a Life*. Allen & Unwin, 2022.

Woolf, Virginia. *A Room of One's Own*. Harcourt Inc., 2005.

—. *Selected Essays*, edited by David Bradshaw, Oxford World's Classics, 2009.

—. *Women and Writing*, edited by Michèle Barrett, Harcourt Brace Jovanovich, 1980.

Young, Gary. "No Surrender." *The Guardian*, 25 May 2002, https://www.theguardian.com/books/2002/may/25/biography.mayaangelou. Accessed 20 May 2022.

PART II:
Literary Representation and Literary Missionary of Dogma

Chapter 3

Undogmatic Perspective as an Antidote to the Imperial Hubris in J. M. Coetzee's *Waiting for the Barbarians*[1]

Seçil Erkoç Iqbal[2]
İnönü University, Türkiye

Abstract

J. M. Coetzee's *Waiting for the Barbarians* (1980) is an allegorical work narrated by an anonymous Magistrate who oversees a border town located between the Empire and the native lands of the so-called 'barbarians.' Based on the tension between the imperial power holders and the 'barbarians,' the novel raises questions concerning the ambivalence pertaining to the discursive dichotomies set up between the self/other, civilized/barbarian, culture/nature, and victor/victim, among others. In such a sharply dissected atmosphere, the Empire considers everyone who does not relate to them as a threat to be exterminated. Therefore, the imperial self, blinded by its own intellectual short-sightedness, finds escape in creating 'shadow images' reflecting the darkest hues of its psyche. Still, it is the darkness of the 'civilized' that is eventually brought to light through the broken body of a barbarian girl, who is left crippled and half-blind at the hands of the Third Bureau's officials. Witnessing the extent of the brutality and inhumanity encoded in the dogmatic truisms of the Empire, the Magistrate can no longer remain silent about the horrendous tortures inflicted on the bodies and souls of the innocent natives who are systematically labelled as traitors suspected of sharing secret agendas with the 'barbarians.' As he starts seeing the darkness lurking behind the imperial mask(s), the Magistrate

---

[1] This study is a revised and extended version of the author's unpublished paper entitled "Ambivalence Unbound: Waiting for the Key or the Barbarians?" which was presented at the 10th International IDEA Conference: Studies in English. Boğaziçi University, İstanbul/Türkiye. 14-16 April 2016.

[2] Assist. Prof. Dr., Department of Western Languages and Literatures, İnönü University (Malatya/Türkiye) secil.erkoc@inonu.edu.tr, secilerkoc@hotmail.com.

himself turns out to be a scapegoat who ends up getting labelled as the betrayer inside and is exposed to physical and psychological violence. Through the undeniable presence of his bodily pain, the Magistrate manages to strip himself off the self-blinding bondages of the Empire and lets himself be penetrated by the 'truth' – that the distinction between the 'barbarian' and the 'civilized' is easily blurred. Within this perspective, it is argued that Coetzee's work does not simply problematize the permeability of the dichotomies within a linguistic system where meaning is constantly deferred. Emphasizing the corporeal presence of the barbarian girl and the magistrate through the physical suffering that they have undergone, the novel shows that the bodily and spiritual *pain* can be too deep to be put into words, but that does not mean that *it* does not exist. In this manner, without negating the seminal capacity of deconstructive criticism, this study attempts to portray how poststructuralism can also evolve into a dogmatic asset validating its own 'alter metanarratives.' That is why it is significant to develop a more welcoming and undogmatic attitude that is not stuck in the critique of either/or dichotomies but celebrates the multifarious nature of unmediated 'truth' and 'meaning' without crossing them out.

Keywords: J. M. Coetzee, *Waiting for the Barbarians*, Imperialism, Pain, Body

***

"Where civilization entailed the corruption of barbarian virtues and the creation of a dependent people, I decided, I was opposed to civilization; and upon this resolution I based the conduct of my administration."

—J. M. Coetzee, *Waiting for the Barbarians*

Dogma, as an expression, is associated with a prescribed set of beliefs and doctrines validated by a logocentric stance. What may be termed as a dogmatic outlook or perspective is imbued with a sense of fixity, sterility, and inertia feeding on an outdated methodology that can no longer be in tune with the fluid dynamics of the twenty-first century. Given the binary bending impetus of postmodernism, it would be a naive attempt to continue embracing the tenets of an authoritative standpoint which compartmentalizes meaning into sharply defined categorizations. However, it should also be noted that poststructuralist approaches can be tainted by a dogmatic attitude when they are merely seen as conceptual items to dismantle the hierarchical set of divisions between the artificially regulated binary oppositions. In other words, deconstructive criticism underscores the existence of an unsolidified momentum that is always deferred, hereby paving the way for the articulation of uprooted 'unrealities' in an ongoing interplay of signifiers. So conceived, this study intends to introduce an 'undogmatic' approach which acknowledges the arbitrariness of binary oppositions, yet it is not stuck in a totally negating principle that disavows the existence of a root cause which is always re-shaping itself in a process of becoming.

Within this perspective, the purpose of this chapter is to analyse J. M. Coetzee's (b. 1940) *Waiting for the Barbarians* (1980), which renders various interpretations possible since the novel is set on a critical ground problematizing the dichotomies between the civilized/barbarian, colonizer/colonized, sight/blindness, light/dark, nature/culture, and self/other among many others. As a South African writer, it is inevitable that Coetzee uses his pen as a medium to share his reflections on the historical legacy of his country in particular; as well as addressing the universal themes, including the relationship between the colonizer/oppressor and the colonized/oppressed, the implementation of injustice by the power holders, and the dynamics of the otherization process in general. Based on an allegorical groundwork – in that it is set in an unspecified time and place – *Waiting for the Barbarians* is narrated by an anonymous figure known as the Magistrate, who is the chief administrator of a frontier town located between the Empire and the lands inhabited by the so-called barbarians. Due to the rumours concerning the possible barbarian attack on the Empire, another authority figure, Colonel Joll, arrives to investigate the matter at hand, and he starts torturing the nomadic barbarians whom he keeps as prisoners. Not being able to do anything other than feeling sad for the victims, the Magistrate decides to help a young barbarian girl who is left crippled and partly blinded by the officials of the Empire. Soon he feels attracted to the girl and tries to heal her wounds by welcoming her to his room and then to his bed. When he is not able to have an ultimate grasp of her traumatic past, the Magistrate decides to take the girl back to her own people living in the heart of the desert. Upon his return to the town, he gets labelled as the collaborator with the barbarian enemy and turns out to be the next victim who is imprisoned, tortured, and humiliated by the 'civilized' guardians of the State. Despite suffering badly, the Magistrate goes through an illuminating experience that teaches him about the haphazard nature of the binaries, and in this metaphoric journey that is implemented via various levels, the barbarian girl acts as a guiding principle and/or root cause showing him the way out of the *labyrinth* – which stands for the dogmatic and the authoritative discourse(s) of the Empire.

Since its first publication in 1980, *Waiting for the Barbarians* has been studied extensively by various scholars. Considering its allegorical foundation, as the setting defies the regulatory tenets of time and space, it may be noted that *Waiting for the Barbarians* has a timeless quality that re-fashions itself in the process of contemplative flux; therefore, it continues paving the way for fertile analyses. The ongoing (in)action is also emphasized in the title, which accentuates the act of *waiting*, yet it is not explicitly revealed when and how *it* first started. Relatedly, in Constantine P. Cavafy's (1863-1933) poem, *Waiting for the Barbarians* (1904), from which Coetzee borrows the title of his novel, the Alexandrian-Greek poet introduces two anonymous speakers talking to each other and wondering about when the barbarians will arrive. Though the historical context is not clear, considering the references to the Senate, the Senators, and the Emperor in the poem, it is possible to assert that Cavafy's work connotes the ancient Roman Empire, and it conjectures the barbarian 'other' as a threat to the imperial 'self.' Obviously, in its construction of the dichotomy pertaining to the self and the other, Western civilization projects itself as the ultimate paragon of reason, moral superiority, culture, progress, and authority both on the practical and the discursive level. In this dogmatic scheme, barbarians are bound to be the direct opposite of all these fabricated projections of the Empire so that the imperial self can guarantee its 'unshakeable' status. Ironically enough, such a fixed status can also ruin itself from within because to sustain the role that is created on a discursive level, the 'self' needs the presence of the 'other' whose imaginary repercussions must be re-produced and re-constructed upon a linguistic, historical, and mythical spectrum that is rooted in a speculative basis. Therefore, as stated above, the act of *waiting* assumes a manipulative character that constantly postpones a sense of conclusion. In a similar fashion, elaborating on the dialogue between Cavafy and Coetzee's work, Maria Boletsi draws attention to "the progressive form of the verb in the title" (76) and argues that

> [it] points to the lack of closure in the process of waiting. It is a process without a definite beginning or end, as the advent of the object of waiting is eternally deferred. The use of the same title in Coetzee evokes the practice of sequels and raises the expectations that a sequel usually does: [...] the reader may expect the novel to take the scenario further and propose a solution by actually bringing the barbarians onto the stage. But the barbarians fail to appear again. The repetition of the title thus makes the act of waiting even more tantalizing and underlines the *omnipresence* and, yet *absence* of the barbarians. (76, emphasis added)

The absent-present quality of the barbarians has parallels to Jacques Derrida's interpretation of the "transcendental signified" which always remains outside of the text (Derrida 20). As one of the pioneers of the post-structuralist agenda, Derrida challenges the monopoly of meaning, for it is not possible to follow a direct route between a signifier and a signified in a textual space. Rather, there is an ongoing and unpredictable set of interactions within a signification process, and it can never lead to a systematic closure. As Gayatri C. Spivak also explains in his "Translator's Preface" to Derrida's *Of Grammatology*, "[s]ign will always lead to sign, one substituting the other (playfully, since 'sign' is 'under erasure') as signifier and signified in return. Indeed, the notion of play is important here. Knowledge is not a systematic tracking down of a truth that is hidden but may be found" (xix). In other words, 'knowledge' cannot be restricted to a dogmatic enclosure that is manifested methodically. On the contrary, it belongs to a space of becoming which upgrades itself in a constant flux of endless permutations. Therefore, the idea of the 'play' comes to the foreground and functions as a latitudinarian tool that challenges the autocracy of a single standpoint. "In this play of representation" as Derrida posits further, "the point of origin becomes ungraspable" (36). Within this scheme, it becomes difficult to ascertain the presence of a simple origin because it always defers itself. Paradoxically enough, the operation of the whole system does also depend on the inaccessibility of such an origin i.e., the transcendental signified, because its absence-presence can also lead the way out of a maze of dogmatic stances and regulations. In this framework – via Derrida's illuminating methodology – deconstruction disentangles the long-woven fabric of the logocentric dogmata and leaves the prototype of the egocentric 'subject' amidst loose ends which cannot be tied to any firm foundation. If the imperial self, as postulated by the ideologies of the Empire, continues following its own prejudices and embraces a myopic stance, then it becomes impossible to find a way out of the labyrinth.

The Magistrate, in his encounter with the barbarian girl, realizes that he has long been restrained by the impasses of this restrictive system which affects not only the mind but also the body of its subject-objects. On a discursive platform, the shiny and self-negating principles of the Western civilization, which have been used as sugar-coated measures to strengthen the prominence of the imperial 'self' over the barbarian 'other,' promise a golden cage to its inhabitants. To exemplify, blinded by his sense of duty to the *Empire*, the Magistrate cannot challenge *its* misconducts in the beginning. He does not want to leave his comfort zone, either: "I did not want to get embroiled in this. I am a country magistrate, a responsible official in the service of the Empire, serving out my days on this lazy frontier, *waiting* to retire" (Coetzee 8, emphasis added). Only after the Magistrate experiences the atrocities of the 'civilized' Empire by first hand and feels the pain of the body himself does he realize that not only his body but also his mind has been regulated by the dictums of the Empire. Thus, he leaves his position as a spectator to the shadow play of the 'civilization' and takes his first step into the byzantine rooms of the labyrinth, only to find out that he is to be guided by the invisible thread of the barbarian girl – who, just like a transcendental signified, escapes his attempts to lay claim over her. In this vision, the Magistrate – parallel to the figure of Theseus in Greek mythology – is able to come up against the Minotaur with the help of the barbarian girl/Ariadne and understands that he has long been feeding the 'monster' in himself. Thus, the sharp lines between inside and outside, human and monster, master and victim, civilized and barbarian, once again blur and become blunt.

In this manner, Terry Eagleton's (b. 1943) comments about the interchangeable status of the binary oppositions show that, similar to the way the Magistrate is not able to 'decipher' the traumatic story of the barbarian girl completely, the constructed version of the imperial 'reality' is nullified by an interplay of ambiguities, gaps, inconsistencies, and a sense of fluidity/becoming that cannot be encapsulated by the logocentric bias:

> Perhaps what is outside is also somehow inside, what is alien also intimate – so that man needs to police the absolute frontier between the two realms as vigilantly as he does just because it may always be transgressed, has always been transgressed already, and is much less absolute than it appears. [...] Such metaphysical thinking, as I have said, cannot be simply eluded: we cannot catapult ourselves beyond this binary habit of thought into an ultra-metaphysical realm. But by a certain way of operating upon texts whether 'literary' or 'philosophical' – we may begin to unravel these oppositions a little, demonstrate how one term of an antithesis secretly inheres within the other. (115)

Eagleton's reflections on the 'impractical' aspect of poststructuralism are quite telling because, as he has expressed above, we cannot simply return to a prelapsarian world that is marked by total harmony and coherence. It is true that, deconstruction is quite functional when it comes to uncovering the artificially constructed status of the discourses that try to legitimize the so-called superiority of the one side over the other. However, it also runs the risk of reducing everything to the status of a textual entity that cannot meet the practical demands of the material realm. Without taking strict sides with any of them – that is, the 'linguistic' and the 'material' turn – it is significant to find a middle course in between.[3] The Magistrate, in this respect, can be interpreted as epitomizing the passage from the linguistic to the material turn – first via his attempts to decode the inscriptions on the wooden slips that he has unearthed and then via his perverted fascination with the traumatized body of the barbarian girl. Not able to have complete dominance over any of them, he undergoes an *anagnorisis* which makes him realize the fact that neither the linguistic nor the material turn can be functional when they are totally disconnected from each other. Instead, as will be analysed in further detail

---

[3] In their co-authored article, "Material Ecocriticism: Materiality, Agency, and Models of Narrativity" (2012) Serenella Iovino and Serpil Oppermann state that the linguistic turn has revitalized the superiority of the discourse over the matter; therefore, the material world is projected as a phenomenon that is constructed by language. Material turn, on the other hand, "is a pronounced reaction against same radical trends of postmodern and post-structuralist thinking that allegedly 'dematerialized' the world into linguistic and social constructions" (75-76).

below, the Magistrate is to develop a material-discursive stance that takes note of both ends. Otherwise, the myopic/dogmatic vision of the Empire continues inscribing its own interpretations on the body and the psyche of its victims – only to erase and re-formulate them again.

Regarding the earliest stages of the systematic oppression of the 'other' on a linguistic/discursive level, the etymological background of the word *barbarian* should also be taken into consideration. First used by the Ancient Greeks, the successive repetition of the first syllable (*bar-bar*) refers to the unintelligible speech of a 'foreign' person who does not speak Greek. According to Boletsi, such an attitude has consequences on two levels: "on a first level, it signifies a lack of understanding on the part of the other, since the language of the other is perceived as meaningless sounds. At the same time, it suggests an unwillingness to understand the other's language and thus to make the encounter with the other a communicative occasion" (68). Totally enclosed on itself and restricted to a passive stance such as *waiting*, the civilized subject finds itself in a precarious position where its onto-political existence is both threatened and guarded by the absence-presence of the barbarians. If they do not appear, then the Empire is to start decaying – both materially and psychologically:

> Because night has fallen and the barbarians have not come.
> And some people have arrived from the frontiers,
> and said that there are no barbarians anymore.
>
> And now, what will become of us without barbarians?
> Those people were some sort of a solution. (Cavafy, lines 31-36)

As the closing lines of Cavafy's poem testify, no matter how systematic and comprehensive the domain of the civilization appears to be, it desperately needs the barbarians as a counter force from whom it continues deriving its ominous force and energy. While waiting for the so-called barbarians to emerge and attack the frontiers, the Empire not only generates and implements its own interpretation of what barbarism means but also re-writes a counter-image of itself repeatedly. In this re-writing process, the most effective medium of the civilization is the language which entails a documented version of the Empire's authority and control over the 'illiterate other' who is denied an unmediated history of its own. In this way, history, too, turns into an ideological tool distorting the lines between truth and fantasy, and what appears, in the end, is nothing more than a romanticized parable of the Empire. Similarly, in *The Colonizer and the Colonized* (1957), Tunisian novelist and thinker Albert Memmi (1920-2020) describes how the colonized is mythologized and represented by the colonizer. By drawing a mythical portrait of the 'other' as inferior, wicked, lazy, and backward, the colonizer "justifies his police and legitimate severity" because, as Memmi further explains in an ironic tone, "he must defend himself against the foolish acts of the irresponsible, and at the same time—what meritorious concern!—protect him against himself!" (126). However, all these ideological mechanisms are turned upside down and rendered ineffective when there are no barbarians visible on the horizon. Then, as Cavafy had aptly expressed at the dawn of the twentieth century – when the ideals of civilization and progress were soon to be demolished by the impending world wars – in the absence of the barbarians, the oppressive gadgets of the civilization including language, history, and parables can no longer operate thoroughly, and the 'civilized' subject ends up encountering its own isolation and moral barrenness. In other words, the 'cultivated' self understands the futile attempt to sharpen the distinction between the civilized and the barbarian, for the strict lines between them have long been blurred.

The ambivalent nature inherent in the interchangeable quality of the opposing poles, such as the colonizer and the colonized, the lover and the torturer, the comrade and the enemy, and in the broader perspective, the civilized and the barbarian enables *Waiting for the Barbarians* to be read through the lenses of deconstructive criticism. By calling into question the 'otherness' of the 'other' and showing the areas where the commanding voice of Colonel Joll and the Empire crumbles into pieces – in the face of multiple and flexible interpretations – Coetzee dismantles the dogmatic and ideological projections of a fixed meaning. Nevertheless, it should be kept in mind that Coetzee does not embrace a nihilistic stance that negates the guiding principles of ethical responsibility and conscience. As a postmodern writer, he is aware of the playful and unpredictable quality of the language, as well as the unsolidified relationship between the signifier and the signified – which are bound by a myriad of variations that always evade the reader/writer. In a similar vein, Susan V. Gallagher explains that "Coetzee's affirmation of the tentative qualities of language, his recognition of multiple interpretations, multiple voices, multiple languages, is an embrace of Others and a rejection of rigid authoritarianism" (*A Story* 124). Hence, Coetzee does not simply point at a textual space that is severely alienated from the realities of the physical world. Postmodern as he is, it is true that Coetzee problematizes the clear-cut distinctions between the binary oppositions, and he never assumes the position of a totalitarian voice in *Waiting for the Barbarians*. However, it does not mean that he strips himself off the ethical and political responsibilities of the author completely. On the contrary, he "refuses an authoritarian determination of the role of the writer" and challenges the idea that "there is a particular function that all writers must fulfill" (Gallagher, *A Story* 16). Then, it is possible to claim that Coetzee's application of the deconstructive method in his novel is not infertile and dogmatic because it is not stuck in a self-negating principle that takes shelter in a somewhat escapist understanding – that in an infinite "interplay of implications" there is no meaning (Derrida 246).

According to Coetzee, however, there is always more than what meets the eye on the surface, and the transcendental signified is too powerful to be reduced to the discursive projections of a logocentric approach. The impossibility of articulating the ultimate *truth*, which goes beyond the system of dichotomies, does not mean that *it* does not exist; rather, *its* absence-presence can only be discerned by amalgamating the linguistic and the material, the mind and the body, the physical and the metaphysical into each other. Within this context, the body of the barbarian girl becomes a material-discursive *tabula rasa* upon which the tyranny of the Empire is engraved. In her refusal to historicize/ romanticize what happened to her in the torture room, the barbarian girl disallows "her tortured body to be translated into language, [and] she prevents the othering that the magistrate's categorizations would impose in transforming her story into his own" (Wenzel 66). It is the pain of the suppressed 'other' that defies the attempts of linguistic articulation because no meaning-making practices of the imperial self can truly convey the agony of the body and the anxiety of the mind. Colonel Joll and the Magistrate's comments about the process of distilling the truth off the 'barbarian' prisoners exemplify how the Empire assigns itself the right to impose its own constructed version of reality on the 'other.' When the Magistrate asks the Colonel how he is able to understand whether the interrogated tells him the truth, the Colonel replies that it is thanks to the speaker's tone, which can only be recognized by training and experience (Coetzee 5). Upon being asked whether the tone of truth can be discerned in everyday speech, Colonel Joll goes on as follows:

> "No, you misunderstand me. I am speaking only of a special situation now, I am speaking of a situation in which I am probing for the truth, in which I have to exert pressure to find it. First I get lies, you see—this is what happens—first lies, then pressure, then more lies, then more pressure, then the break, then more pressure, then truth. That is how you get the truth." (Coetzee 5)

The Magistrate's subsequent observation of the Colonel's myopic standpoint, quite ironically, shows that it is the Empire that continues constructing lies and prioritizes them over the authentic and the unmediated version of the truth – which is rooted in the bodily pain: "Pain is truth; all else is subject to doubt. That is what I bear away from my conversation with Colonel Joll [...]" (Coetzee 5). Though the Magistrate does not share the Colonel's point of view, he is not powerful enough to stand up against him at this point. Not having yet endured the pain of the body himself, the hypocritical stance of the Magistrate gets validated when he tries to extricate the painful truth from the barbarian girl. The only difference between him and the Colonel is that the Magistrate's methods are much softer and appealing, but it cannot conceal the fact that they both serve the Empire: "It has not escaped me that an interrogator can wear masks, speak with two voices, one harsh, one seductive" (Coetzee 8). As Hania A. M. Nashef elucidates, "the magistrate and Colonel Joll can be seen as two sides of the same coin, the cruel and benevolent colonizer" (25). Belonging to the same ideological discourse, the Colonel and the Magistrate can follow different paths; however, it does not change the fact that they both head towards the same destination – for they are the products of the same Empire, which is constructed upon the aggrandisement of the imperial self. Then, no matter how hard they try to cover it or not, beneath their masks, they are both colonizers. In a similar vein, French philosopher Jean-Paul Sartre (1905-1980), explains that

> there are neither good, nor bad colonists: there are colonialists. Among these, some reject their objective reality. Borne along by the colonialist apparatus, they do every day in reality what they condemn in fantasy, for all their actions contribute to the maintenance of oppression. They will change nothing and will serve no one, but will succeed only in finding moral comfort in malaise. (21-22)

Read within the context of post-structuralist thinking, Sartre's juxtaposition of fantasy and reality is quite functional since it shows how the Empire blurs the distinction between the two for its own advantage. Moreover, it also shows the incompatibility of words/discourse and deeds/actions in a hypocritical spectrum shaped by the colonialist agenda. The erasure of the distinction between the good and the bad further underlines the deep-seated corruption of ethics and morals, which are emptied inside and turned into ideological apparatuses broadening the gap between the barbarian 'other' and the imperial 'self.' Indeed, the Empire and its subjects are both the playmakers and the referees of this 'infinite interplay of signifiers', which, quite paradoxically, creates its own constructed 'realities.' Then, it is possible to assert that deconstructive criticism or postmodernism as a more enveloping term cannot challenge its own shortcomings. Having relied on the prevalence of representations over the material reality for so long, the postmodern selves – who are embodied through the Colonel and the Magistrate in the novel – are bedazzled by their own radical and moral inertia to such an extent that they cannot see through the material realities. Perhaps, this is the reason why *Waiting for the Barbarians* commences with a direct description of Colonel Joll's sunglasses:

> I have never seen anything like it: two little discs of glass suspended in front of his eyes in loops of wire. Is he blind? I could understand it if he wanted to hide blind eyes. But he is not blind. The discs are dark, they look opaque from the outside, but he can see through them. He tells me

they are a new invention. 'They protect one's eyes against the glare of the sun,' he says. [...] 'At home everyone wears them.' (Coetzee 1)

Here, the home stands for the capital of the Empire. On a figurative level, everyone's wearing of dark glasses at home indicates how blind they are to the material/historical realities of their own time. It seems the imperial selves have been taking comfort in an inverted and illusionary version of the 'truth' – which is easily compensated by the ready-to-wear projections of the Empire. The frontier town, where the Magistrate is holding office, is geographically away from the capital. Hence, people living in the town are not as short-sighted as their fellow citizens living at home. Located between the capital and the desert where the barbarians are living, the frontier town is a liminal space where the 'civility' of the Empire and the 'brutality' of the barbarians intermingle. Out of this amalgamation, there appears a hybridized version of both parts, and it shows that there is a certain degree of light and dark present in each of them. The Magistrate's self-confrontation with the darkness lurking deep in himself, therefore, lights up the dark and initiates the early stages of his recovery from the imperial hubris:

> For I was not, as I liked to think, the indulgent pleasure-loving opposite of the cold rigid Colonel. I was the lie that Empire tells itself when times are easy, he the truth that Empire tells when harsh winds blow. Two sides of Imperial rule, no more, no less. [...] I said to myself, "Be patient, one of these days he will go away, one of these days quiet will return: then our siestas will grow longer and our swords rustier, [...] and the line that marks the frontier on the maps of Empire will grow hazy and obscure till we are blessedly forgotten." Thus I seduced myself, taking one of the many wrong turnings I have taken on a road that looks true but has delivered me into the heart of a *labyrinth*. (Coetzee 148-149, emphasis added)

The structure of the labyrinth, with its blind alleys, can be compared to an endless interplay of routes and passages that seem to lead nowhere. However, the entrance of the labyrinth does also function as its exodus. In this paradoxical construction, then, entrance and departure, salvation and destruction, freedom and captivity, and solution and problem overlap and indicate the dissolution of the binaries. According to Sue Kossew, in Coetzee's novel, "the entire concept of the possibility of access to knowledge and truth is challenged" (91), and she goes on to state that in this labyrinthine structure of the text, both the reader and the Magistrate encounter "three central 'keys'" which seem to illuminate their path (91). The keys are the barbarian girl, who functions as a 'decoder' for the Magistrate in his search for truth; the poplar slips which he has found while excavating the barbarian ruins – that also wait to be deciphered; and finally, the recurring dreams which the Magistrate tries to analyse, and which seem to come to a resolution towards the end of the novel (91). In his interaction with all of these, the Magistrate learns to move beyond the surface and to look deep within. Only then does he realize the discrepancy between the pain articulated and the pain experienced. Accordingly, as a follow-up to Kossew's ideas, it can be said that Coetzee does not necessarily disavow the existence of truth. Overall, it is the pain of the tortured body that defies the immaterial and ideological projections of the Empire. Coetzee, therefore, criticizes the mediated and the inorganic representation(s) of the real, which is hidden behind the silenced voice(s) of the oppressed bodies and souls. His concern is about the role of the author because it is possible that in his/her attempts to represent the pain of the 'other,' the author can also fall into the trap of representations and be further removed from the truth of pain. Then, his main challenge as an author, as Coetzee himself describes, is "how not to play the game by the rules of the state, how to establish one's authority, how to imagine torture and death on one's own terms" ("Into the Dark Chamber" 364). In other words, it is about embracing an undogmatic perspective that takes a clear note of the contradictions inherent in deconstructive criticism.

It is true that postmodernism is a practical tool – especially when it comes to problematizing the supremacy of authoritative discourse. However, in its total ignorance of the material realm, postmodernism itself becomes a meta-narrative that invalidates its own essence and dictum. In such a discursive realm marked by an endless play of signifiers, all human and nonhuman matter is reduced to the position of "a fretful midge," spinning endlessly without a certain aim and direction (Rossetti, line 36). The Magistrate, in this perspective, epitomizes the misplaced and disoriented self who "seems to be wandering in the wilderness of deconstructive criticism" (Gallagher, *A Story* 122). Nevertheless, in his struggle to find a way out of this wilderness – which becomes visible through the recurring dreams rooted in his subconscious – the barbarian girl turns out to be the unique guiding principle that promises the presence of ultimate meaning and salvation: "There is no hope of reaching *the other side*, but I plod on, carrying the girl, the only key I have to the labyrinth, her head nodding against my shoulder, her dead feet drooping on *the other side*" (Coetzee 95, emphasis added). Though the Magistrate terms it as a hopeless act in his dream, he manages to carry the girl back to her own people and crosses over to the other side – both literally and figuratively. In this manner, Coetzee insinuates that there is always a way out of the deconstructive wilderness; hence, he does not confine himself to the dogmatic and restrictive prescriptions of deconstructive criticism:

> Coetzee thus identifies the absence of moral authority that results in torture with the absence at the heart of contemporary literature since

the advent of deconstructive criticism. In a world without a moral center, in a world where barbarity hides behind all the faces of society, the author can only struggle to provide authority and meaning. Coetzee's fiction is full of gaps and absences, yet he nonetheless suggests that temporary presences, especially the presence of the storyteller, can at least approximate a moral and linguistic center. (Gallagher, "Torture and the Novel" 285)

Rather than enclosing ourselves in a textual space and reducing everything to the status of discursive representations, we need to pay more serious attention to the multi-dimensional dynamics of our own spatiotemporal existence. Underlining the need to develop more comprehensive approaches to be able to understand the present moment, Zekiye Antakyalıoḷu proposes an insightful inquiry regarding the function of literature and art in contemporary time and space:

Postmodern fiction with all its feathers made of self-reflexivity, metafictional voices, parodic/ironic intellectual language games, intertextuality and lack of essentialism can function no better than ostriches in representing our condition today. The best thing, or maybe the only thing, postmodernist fiction ever represented was representation itself. The kind of fiction which is only concerned with fictionality *per se* might not be the voice we need today. It is therefore not surprising nowadays to see novels, films and TV series with essential social, ethical and political concerns and warnings. (260)

As stated above, the allegorical repercussions of *Waiting for the Barbarians* earn the novel a timeless quality that addresses way beyond/before its time. The clash between the barbarian and the civilized has always been on the history scene; however, starting from the end of the twentieth century onwards it is no longer practical to elaborate on the intellectual and philosophical trajectories of this artificial division. Instead, it is necessary to bring the literal and the metaphorical together. The authors and the philosophers of the twenty-first century, therefore, are supposed to bear witness to the suffering(s) of the body, which belongs to the realm of the matter.[4] Given the intellectual and academic

---

[4] In *Meeting the Universe Halfway* (2007), Karen Barad criticizes the post-structuralist tendency to reduce everything to the position of linguistic articulations as follows: "Language has been granted too much power. The linguistic turn, the semiotic turn, the interpretative turn, the cultural turn: it seems at every turn lately every "thing"—even materiality—is turned into a matter of language or some other form of cultural representation. […] Language matters. Discourse matters. Culture matters. There is an

shift towards new materialisms,[5] posthumanism,[6] agential realism,[7] ecocriticism,[8] and ecological postmodernism [9] – among many other disciplines grouped under the umbrella term Environmental Humanities, the creative mediums of the new millennium, including art and literature can no longer ignore the significance of the corporality and the corporeal ontology. Moreover, the corporeal pain also indicates the passage to the semiotic dimension of language, which is not dominated by an authoritative meaning-making practice tool.[10] Unlike Colonel Joll, who is stuck in the symbolic order, the Magistrate has access to the semiotic dimension through bodily pain, humiliation, torture, and suffering. In this way, he not only bears witness to the

---

important sense in which the only thing that does not seem to matter anymore is matter (132).

[5] See Rachel Tillman, "Toward a New Materialism: Matter as Dynamic." *Minding Nature*, vol. 8, no. 1, 2015, pp. 30-35.

[6] See Başak Ağın Dönmez, "Recent Approaches in the Posthuman Turn: Braidotti, Herbrechter, and Nayar." *Relations*, vol. 4, no. 1, June 2016, pp. 105-115.

[7] "In agential realism's reconceptualization of materiality, matter is agentive and intra-active. Matter is a dynamic intra-active becoming that never sits still—an ongoing reconfiguring that exceeds any linear conception of dynamics in which effect follows cause end-on-end, and in which the global is a straightforward emanation of the local" (Barad 170).

[8] See Greg Garrard, "Ecocriticism." *Keywords for Environmental Studies*. Edited by Joni Adamson, William A. Gleason, and David N. Pellow, New York UP, 2016, pp. 61-64.

[9] "This account of postmodernism which regards language and reality, nature and culture, and discursive practices and the material world as completely intertwined, is known as 'ecological postmodernism.'" (Iovino and Oppermann 78)

[10] French feminist critic Julia Kristeva (b. 1941) argues that the patriarchal undertones of the symbolic aspect of the language cannot be challenged by mimicking its premises. On the contrary, a totally fresh synthesis should be introduced without necessarily essentializing the female as a stereotypical input. Every (wo)man has their own unique persona, so they cannot be described from a reductionist perspective. In this framework, Kristeva argues that the semiotic dimension of the language introduces an alternative path which is not stuck in Lacan's theory of the symbolic order. Semiotic realm is not discursive and immaterial; instead, it is associated with the nonverbal mediums of communication that are linked back to the body of the mother, and it underlines the pre-verbal existence of the self which cannot be controlled by the meaning-making practices of language. However, we cannot stay within the borders of this pre-verbal existence forever. Then, as Kristeva posits, we can have access to the semiotic realm through art and literature since they enable us to develop original ways of communication that challenge the formulated superiority of the patriarchal discourse. See Julia Kristeva, *Revolution in Poetic Language*. Translated by Margaret Waller (Colombia UP, 1984); Judith Butler, "The Body Politics of Julia Kristeva." *Hypatia*, vol. 3., no. 3, Winter 1989, pp. 104-118.

traumatic past of the barbarian girl but also becomes the 'other.' It is the bodily torture that erases all the differences between the 'civilized' and the 'barvarian.' Pain surpasses all the hierarchical demarcations and reminds us, once again, that we are all biological entities who are vulnerable before the unpredictable social, economic, political, and nature-cultural dynamics of our own times. Hence, as stated above, as opposed to the outdated paradigms of post-structuralism, which ends up transforming itself into a grand text and continues negating the presence of 'meaning,' a more welcoming and undogmatic perspective needs to be developed. Within this context, it is difficult to deny the capacity of fiction, for it is one of the most effective mediums for knocking down the barriers between the self/reader and the other/imaginary characters, and thereby enabling us to train and polish the rusted virtues of the twenty-first century, i.e., empathy and altruism.

To better understand how such an undogmatic vision can function as an antidote curing the egocentric hubris of the imperial self, it is beneficial to look at the interaction between the Magistrate and the barbarian girl closely – the former assuming the active and the latter the passive role(s). Since there is a sinister dialogue between all variations of constructed discourses validating the 'supremacy' of the powerful over the weak, it is not difficult to see how the Empire projects itself as an all-powerful actor penetrating the bodies and the souls of the barbarian 'other' through physical and psychological torture. As a result, the Empire functions as a 'super-power' mechanism trying to leave its mark on the suppressed body of the 'other.' In this respect, the Magistrate's frequent inclination to sleep with women stems from his unconscious desire to prove that he belongs to the Empire. Thus, he is supposed to perform well, just as the way the Empire is supposed to have dominance over the colonized land. However, there is also a kind of perverted relationship between the counter sides here: comparing the barbarian girl to a lady figure or to a beloved, it is possible to observe the way in which the Magistrate likes seducing her and takes pleasure out of her making him wait due to unspecified and enigmatic reasons. For the Magistrate, who takes on the role of an imaginary lover, it is fine to wait for a reasonable amount of time, as this allows him to refine himself so that he can come up with more effective tactics to seduce his target next time. What happens then if the beloved discloses herself, just as the way the barbarian girl exposes the most hidden secrets of her body, including her deepest wounds to the Magistrate? There she stands as a body, a mere surface that is ready to welcome any type of infiltration as she has already experienced the worst kind in the torture chamber. As an outsider, she does not belong to the Empire, so she is supposed to be explored and interrogated – not in the torture room this time, but in the bedroom of the Magistrate. The answer to the question above is that her being such open to accepting anything on the physical level causes the Magistrate to lose his potential. The barbarian girl's openness and indifference are contrasted with her not letting the Magistrate look closer into her soul and mind. She does not allow her true 'self' to be brought to the light, or perhaps the Magistrate is too blind to see through her at that time. On this account, rather than sleeping with her, he either prefers to fall asleep on his bed or visits the maid at the inn to consummate his desire. Obviously, he is drawn to the barbarian girl; however, by constantly delaying the action or refraining from having sexual intercourse with her, he tries to create the 'waiting' process by himself: "I see myself clutched to this stolid girl, unable to remember what I ever desired in her, angry with myself for wanting and not wanting her" (Coetzee 35). In this respect, he indirectly meets on the same ground with Colonel Joll and Warrant Officer Mandel as they all 'wait' for the barbarians to put on the symbolic dress that the Empire has woven for them. This is the reason why the Magistrate cannot situate himself in a stable position before the barbarian girl. His impotency to do so stems from the ultimate confusion in his mind:

> So I continue to swoop and circle around the irreducible figure of the girl, casting one net of meaning after another over her. She leans on her two sticks looking dimly upward. What does she see? The protecting wings of a guardian *albatros* or the black shape of a coward *crow* afraid to strike while its prey yet breathes? (Coetzee 89, emphasis added)

This is the moment when the Magistrate loses his command of the clear-cut distinctions between the binary oppositions in his life. From now on, all concepts intermingle into one another; sharp edges get rid of their protruding ends and leave their places to the prominence of circles. As a result, freedom turns out to be a confinement for him. Therefore, the Magistrate finds himself in a symbolic labyrinth that opens and closes on the barbarian girl. In such a platform, the Magistrate cannot discern the discrepancy between the barbarian and the civilized. In a similar vein, Gallagher argues that

> [t]hroughout the course of the narrative, the differences between barbarian and the settler are deconstructed. [...] in many ways it is the people of the Empire who are idle, slovenly, and dissolute. [...] Although the magistrate accuses the barbarians of tolerating disease and death, it is his soldier whose foot becomes infected during the journey into the desert because he has not followed the sanitary precautions established by the magistrate. (*A Story* 129)

Hence, the barbarians can be interpreted as the shadow images of the Empire. The civilization projects all the negative concepts inherent in its body/soul onto an outsider figure and thereby constructs a scapegoat for itself. As the Magistrate himself also declares in the novel: "But of what use is it to blame the crowd? A scapegoat is named, a festival is declared, the laws are suspended:

who would not flock to see the entertainment?" (Coetzee 131). However, the moment the victimized 'other' summons up his/her courage to redirect the mirror to the face of the victimizer – so that the imperial self can stand face to face with its own 'darkness' and 'barbarity' inside – the illusionary reflections get shattered to the ground. Colonel Joll's wearing of the sunglasses and Mandel's being depicted as a person who "will look behind that immobile handsome face and through those clear eyes as an actor looks from behind a mask" stems from the Empire's inclination to turn a blind eye to its own faults (Coetzee 84). The officials of the Empire are not courageous enough to confront their 'true' selves. In a similar vein, Hannah Arendt (1906-1975) states that "[truth] is hated by tyrants, who rightly fear the competition of a coercive force they cannot monopolize, and it enjoys a rather precarious status in the eyes of governments that rest on consent and abhor coercion" (236). Obviously, the Empire dictates its own conception of 'truth' on the 'barbarians' and aspires to create an indirect monopoly over the very object that it cannot control in any other way.

Then, is it possible to assert that the Magistrate is not a tyrant just because he does not hate the truth, but is attracted to it? To exemplify, he works on the ruins of the past and collects the wooden slips to be able to decipher them. He also examines the body of the barbarian girl, oiling and comforting her wounds, just as the way he puts oil on the artefacts so that they will not disintegrate. All these may be seen as testimonies that show how the Magistrate traces after truth. Nevertheless, it is important to decide whether he tries to dominate the victim or lets himself be dominated in return. It is not easy to come up with any concrete answer to this paradoxical impasse because the Magistrate stands at the crossroads where 'barbarity' and 'civilization' touch each other. In this respect, his being situated in a frontier town has fundamental implications because it illustrates how the Magistrate is torn between the polar sides, both psychologically and geographically. In other words, it can be said that he is the so-called embodiment of the amalgamation of the white and the black – a grey figure: "When she [the barbarian girl] doesn't look at me I'm a grey form moving about unpredictably on the periphery of her vision" (Coetzee 31). At one point, by turning into a passive onlooker to the tortures of Colonel Joll, the Magistrate gets associated with him; nevertheless, by being exposed to the attacks of the Empire, he 'becomes' the barbarian girl. In this intermediary position, the Magistrate cannot help feeling himself tainted by the sins of the Empire and tries to purify his soul through washing the feet of the girl. Still, complete purification comes only after he quits seeing the girl as an instrument and himself becomes an object of torture. As a result, he can no longer consider himself a saviour figure for the barbarian girl; on the contrary, he turns out to be the convict who is redeemed:

> If we consider this act [washing of the barbarian girl's disfigured feet] with the washing of feet in John 13, it suggests that the Magistrate tries to act as the girl's saviour, that he tries to purify her after she has been defiled, first at the hands of Joll and then by living as a prostitute. [...] However, if we associate it with the sinning woman's compulsion to wash Jesus's feet and anoint them with oil in Luke 7, the ritual suggests that it is the Magistrate who has become a prostitute, buying a life of leisure from the Empire by selling himself through silent complicity with a system of torture and oppression, and that he believes at some level that the girl will be his salvation. (Urquhart 12)

Here it is possible to see how Coetzee foregrounds the reversal of the roles between the colonizer and the colonized: The barbarian girl is no longer a figure to be exploited, and the Magistrate symbolically emasculates himself, for he cannot sleep with the girl in his chamber. All these changing conditions add to the bewilderment of the Magistrate, and he finds the ultimate solution in taking the barbarian girl back to her family. It may be interpreted as his struggle to get rid of his self-vision that is reflected in the eyes of the barbarian girl since he sees nothing in them other than his own emptiness, and it reduces him to a silent, passive position:

> I am disquieted. 'What do I have to do to move you?': these are the words I hear in my head in the subterranean murmur that has begun to take the place of conversation. 'Does no one move you?'; and with a shift of horror I behold the answer that has been waiting all the time to offer itself to me in the image of a face masked by two black glassy insect eyes from which comes no reciprocal gaze but only my doubled image cast back at me. (Coetzee 47)

In the absence of the barbarian(s) or the passive image, the Empire is paralyzed, for the 'waiting' process can no longer bear any fruit in the long run. The love game is transformed into a self-seduction activity; thus, the penetration process assumes a distinct character in that it begins to infiltrate itself from within: "I shake my head in a fury of disbelief. *No! No! No!* I cry to myself. It is I who am seducing myself, out of vanity, into these meanings and correspondences" (Coetzee 47, emphasis in original). The cry of the Magistrate is a moment of self-realization, which shows him that he has been living in a dream: "'You are living in a dream!' I say to myself: I pronounce these words aloud, stare at them, try to grasp their significance: 'You must wake up!'" (Coetzee 103).

As to elaborate more on the reversal of artificially constructed roles ascribed to the 'masculine' Empire and the 'feminine' barbarian(s), as well as the Magistrate's attempts at 'unsexing' himself, it is significant to understand why the Magistrate and the barbarian girl become intimate outside the walls of the border town – that is in Nature. It is generally evaluated as the Magistrate's pastoral escape into a romantic atmosphere. However, it would be a too optimistic interpretation considering the overall effect of the novel on the reader. Here, it is the barbarian girl who seduces the Magistrate, and while doing that, she restores the phallus of the Empire just to be able to prove its doomed incapacity in the end. The fact that she starts having her period after her union with the magistrate illustrates his incapacity to impregnate her – which is made apparent both to himself and to the others in the camp: "The girl is bleeding, that time of the month has come for her. She cannot conceal it, she has no privacy, there is not the merest bush to hide behind" (Coetzee 75). Therefore, the passivity of the Empire is brought to the light through the body of the female figure. In other words, the power mechanism renders itself ineffective by its own hand. The barbarian girl may not have the power of the discourse and the language – which are the iconic markers of the Empire; however, with her corporeal existence, she is able to defy the post-structuralist premises that have been celebrating the perseverance of the linguistic turn blindly. Having access to the semiotic dimension of the language, she deconstructs all the regulated prescriptions pertaining to the artificial division between the powerful and the weak, the active and the passive, the illuminated and the ignorant. Now that the barbarian girl is closer to her physical roots and away from the darkness of the Empire, she gradually gets rid of the heavy burden of being labelled as the 'other.' She is re-united with her own people who have been pushed into the mountains by the imperialist agenda of the 'civilized.' For the Magistrate, it is a surprising and unique experience because it is the first time, he has met a barbarian on equal terms – which, in a broader context, illustrates the earliest stages of his recovery from the imperial hubris that has been shaping/dictating his perspective:

> I have never before met northerners on their own ground on equal terms: the barbarians I am familiar with are those who visit the oasis to barter, and the few who make their camp along the river, and Joll's miserable captives. What an occasion and what a shame too to be here today! [...] And here I am patching up relations between the men of future and the men of the past, returning with apologies, a body we have sucked dry – a go-between, a jackal of Empire in sheep's clothing! (Coetzee 79)

The unequivocal tone in his reflections shows that, although the Magistrate is unable to impregnate the barbarian girl, paradoxically enough, he himself gets metaphorically pregnant to the unmediated truth, i.e., it is the 'barbarity' of the Empire to colonize the lands of peaceful people, to push them to the geographical/ideological margins, to usurp the body of an innocent woman, and to leave her half blind and half crippled. Passive as she is, the barbarian girl assumes the active role when she is away from the Empire, and she blurs the opposition between the active 'self' and the passive 'other.' Since the *truth* is accompanied by pain and suffering, the Magistrate cannot give birth to *it* without experiencing torture and humiliation himself. In other words, he is bound to be stripped of all the traces and the symptoms of the masked brutality inherent in the imperial self. The first stage of this symbolic purification starts with the Magistrate's being labelled as a collaborator with the 'barbarian' enemy and then his subsequent confinement by the Third Bureau of the Civil Guard. Upon learning about the accusation directed at him – that he has been "treasonously consorting with the enemy" (Coetzee 85) the Magistrate reacts as follows: "'We are at peace here,' I say, 'we have no enemies.' There is silence. 'Unless I make a mistake,' I say. 'Unless we are the enemy.'" (Coetzee 85). The Magistrate has already been questioning and criticizing the violence of Colonel Joll and the Empire. However, his visit to the depth of the desert and his peaceful encounter with the barbarians have transformed his vision totally, so now he is bold enough to announce that perhaps the barbarians they have been waiting for are not too far away, but they are just at their doorstep – they are the barbarians themselves.

Not able to face up to such an accusation, the Empire dismisses the Magistrate and sentences him to confinement. It causes him to feel liberated because the punishment marks the breaking of the enslaving bonds between the Magistrate and the guardians of the Empire. Nevertheless, the Magistrate is cautious enough not to project himself as a heroic figure, for he knows that if it was not for the charge against him, he would continue living as before: "It should not be so easy to attain salvation. And is there any principle behind my opposition? Have I not simply been provoked into a reaction by the sight of one of the *new barbarians* usurping my desk and pawing my papers?" (Coetzee 85, emphasis added). Addressing the guardians of the Empire as the new barbarians, the Magistrate unearths the darkness lurking behind the masks of the civilized. Still, his purification process is getting even more difficult because the change in his discourse and language can only be validated once his body/material also going through the pain of truth.

The Magistrate has been using the body of the barbarian girl through "the ritual of washing," where he explores her private parts in detail and takes a corrupt kind of pleasure out of her compliance (Coetzee 32). This time, however, it is the Empire that luxuriates in the sensation of torture because the fear of bodily pain gives the guardians of the Empire a watertight domination not only over the 'barbarians' but over anybody who has been announced as the 'other.' Suffering in the hands of the Warrant Officer, the Magistrate realizes how his bodily needs, including eating, sleeping, and evacuating, are gradually turning him into a beast: "Truly man was not made to live alone! I build my day unreasonably around the hours when I am fed. I guzzle my food like a dog. A bestial life is turning me into a beast" (Coetzee 87). After two months of confinement in the cell, he starts questioning the thin line between bestiality and civilization, delirium and sanity:

> I walked into that cell a sane man sure of the rightness of my cause, however incompetent I continue to find myself to describe what that cause may be; but after two months among the cockroaches with nothing to see but four walls and an enigmatic soot-mark, nothing to smell but the stench of my own body, no one to talk to but a ghost in a dream whose lips seem to be sealed, I am much less sure of myself. (Coetzee 104-105)

Confusion, puzzlement, uncertainty, ambiguity, and corporeal pain are, in fact, the symptoms that will be leading the way towards an undogmatic perspective. The Magistrate feels confused because he is to brush himself off the conceptual dust that has been blurring his vision for so long, and he is bound to suffer terribly. The last blow to his imperial 'self' comes during the mock-execution scene where the Magistrate is hung upside down in a woman's clothes – to entertain the 'civilized' residents of the town and to show how far the Empire can go when it comes to punishing its own subjects. Not able to express his suffering and agony in words, the Magistrate drifts away into the semiotic realm and starts speaking/feeling the same language of pain with the 'barbarians': "I bellow again and again, there is nothing I can do to stop it, the noise comes out of a body that knows itself damaged perhaps beyond repair and roars its fright. [...] 'He is calling his barbarian friends,' someone observes. 'That is the barbarian language you hear.' There is laughter" (Coetzee 132-133). From now on, the girl is nothing but the 'key' to the labyrinth because, just like her, the Magistrate has exceeded beyond the linguistic articulation of the *pain* and experienced *it* physically. Similar to the way in which the passive resistance of the 'barbarians' causes the Empire to retreat, the inactive condition of the barbarian girl also enables her to win over the Magistrate – the albatross and the crow fall victim to their own desires, the interrogator finds himself questioned, the illusion leaves its place to reality: "But alas, I didn't ride away [...] then in the light took a lantern and went to see for myself," and he finds the key (Coetzee 9-10).

In *Waiting for the Barbarians,* Coetzee illustrates how the imperial 'self' 'projects its shadow/cruelty onto the barbarian 'other' and develops a powerful discourse to validate its so-called 'civility.' The same idea is also exemplified in Cavafy's poem, where the Emperor and the Senate are described to be waiting in their best clothes for the arrival of the barbarians at the city gates, but the barbarians never appear. Thus, they return home accompanied by the realization that "Empire has no meaning without a subject to oppress, a subject by which to define itself" (Newman 127). In the novel, too, the barbarians never appear as a direct military threat to the Empire. On the contrary, "they provide a solution, a legitimate scapegoat on which to cast one's own brutality" (Gallagher, *A Story* 132). Then, one may wonder whether there will be an end to the act of 'waiting' in Coetzee's allegorical work, or is it destined to go on in a vicious circle, terminating only to be able to restart again? The novel starts with many questions to be answered, foreshadowing the constant question-answer traffic of the Empire's search for 'truth' – first in the torture room and then in the Magistrate's chamber. However, what if 'truth' is not hidden in the answer but in the question itself? Therefore, it would be helpful to concentrate not only on the interrogated but also on the interrogator, as the action promises to bear the 'truth' in the end, or the reflection of the 'truth' at least. Indeed, for the Magistrate, 'truth' lies in the ambivalence present in the false dichotomy pertaining to the artificial and dogmatic distinctions between the self and the other, for he himself witnesses how inhumane the 'civilized' Empire can be by firsthand. Within this framework, it has been attempted to introduce an undogmatic approach that does not embrace the binary bending impetus of deconstructive criticism blindly because such an act runs the risk of problematizing the manifestations of the 'material/corporeal' ontology. The corporeal existence of the barbarian girl is a grave marker of the physical torture and pain that she has been subjected to; hence, it would be a reductionist attitude to ignore the authentic spectrum of her suffering, which cannot be articulated by any linguistic system, thoroughly. It is true that as a theoretical tool, deconstruction problematizes the 'hubris' of the grand narratives; however, it is also undercut by its own ideological demarcations – that in an infinite play of signifiers, it is not possible to find meaning. Gradually stripping himself off the dogmatic inertia of such an attitude, the Magistrate realizes that an endless overflow of interpretations rooted in a "transcendental signified" (Derrida 20) does not negate the presence of ultimate meaning; rather, it celebrates the multifarious nature of 'truth' which exchanges the *either/or* dichotomy with a more welcoming stance – acknowledging that the 'key' can be *both* imprisoning/absent *and* liberating/present.

References

Ağın Dönmez, Başak. "Recent Approaches in the Posthuman Turn: Braidotti, Herbrechter, and Nayar." *Relations*, vol. 4, no. 1, June 2016, pp. 105-115. *ResearchGate*, www.reseachgate.net/publication/339956306.

Antakyalıoğlu, Zekiye. "A Deleuzean Approach to Contemporary Fiction: Some Questions." *DTCF Dergisi*, vol. 58, no. 1, Oct. 2018, pp. 257-269. *DergiPark*, https://dergipark.org.tr/tr/pub/dtcfdergisi/issue/66800/1044598.

Arendt, Hannah. *Between Past and Future*. Penguin Books, 2006.

Barad, Karen. *Meeting the Universe Halfway: Quantum Physics and the Entanglement of Matter and Meaning.* Duke UP, 2007.

Boletsi, Maria. "Barbaric Encounters: Rethinking Barbarism in C. P. Cavafy's and J. M. Coetzee's *Waiting for the Barbarians.*" *Comparative Literature Studies*, vol, 44, no. ½, 2007, pp. 67-96. *JSTOR*, www.jstor.org/stable/25659562.

Butler, Judith. "The Body Politics of Julia Kristeva." *Hypatia*, vol, 3, no. 3, Winter 1989, pp. 104-118. *JSTOR*, www.jstor.org/stable/3809790.

Cavafy, Constantine P. "Waiting for the Barbarians." *C. P. Cavafy: The Collected Poems.* Translated by Evangelos Sachperoglou, Oxford UP, 2007, pp. 14-17.

Coetzee, J. M. "Into the Dark Chamber: The Writer and the South African State (1986)." *Doubling the Point: Essays and Interviews.* Edited by David Attwell, Harvard UP, 1992, pp. 361-368.

—. *Waiting for the Barbarians.* Vintage Books, 2004.

Derrida, Jacques. *Of Grammatology.* Translated by Gayatri Chakravorty Spivak, The John Hopkins UP, 1997.

Eagleton, Terry. *Literary Theory: An Introduction.* Blackwell P, 1996.

Garrard, Greg. "Ecocriticism." *Keywords for Environmental Studies.* Edited by Joni Adamson, William A. Gleason, and David N. Pellow, New York UP, 2016, pp. 61-64.

Gallagher, Susan VanZanten. *A Story of South Africa: J. M. Coetzee's Fiction in Context.* Harvard UP, 1991.

—. "Torture and the Novel: J. M. Coetzee's *Waiting for the Barbarians.*" *Contemporary Literature*, vol. 29, no. 2, Summer 1988, pp. 277-285. *JSTOR*, www.jstor.org/stable/1208441.

Iovino, Serenella, and Serpil Oppermann. "Material Ecocriticism: Materiality, Agency, and Models of Narrativity." *Ecozon@*, vol. 3, no. 1, 2012, pp. 75-91. *ResearchGate*, www.reseachgate.net/publication/291329096.

Kossew, Sue. "Colonizer/Colonized: Paradoxes of Self and Other." *Pen and Power: A Post-Colonial Reading of J.M. Coetzee and André Brink.* Rodopi, 1996, pp. 85-107.

Kristeva, Julia. *Revolution in Poetic Language.* Translated by Margaret Waller, Colombia UP, 1984.

Memmi, Albert. *The Colonizer and the Colonized.* Translated by Howard Greenfeld, Creative Print and Design Wales, 2003.

Nashef, Hania A. M. "Becomings in J. M. Coetzee's *Waiting for the Barbarians* and José Saramago's *Blindness. Comparative Literature Studies*, vol. 47, no. 1, 2010, pp. 21-41. *PROJECT MUSE*, muse.jhu.edu/article/378199.

Newman, Judie. "Intertextuality, Power and Danger: *Waiting for the Barbarians* as a Dirty Story." *Critical Essays on J. M. Coetzee.* Edited by Sue Kossew, G. K. Hall, 1998. pp. 126-138.

Rossetti, Dante Gabriel. "The Blessed Damozel." *Victorian Poetry: Clough to Kipling.* Edited by Arthur J. Carr, Rinehart Editions, 1959, pp. 50-54.

Sartre, Jean-Paul. Introduction, translated by Lawrence Hoey. *The Colonizer and the Colonized*, by Albert Memmi, translated by Howard Greenfeld, Creative P and Design Wales, 2003, pp. 17-25.

Spivak, Gayatri Chakravorty, translator. Translator's Preface. *Of Grammatology*, by Jacques Derrida, translated by Spivak, The John Hopkins UP, 1997, pp. ix-lxxxvii.

Tillman, Rachel. "Toward a New Materialism: Matter as Dynamic." *Minding Nature*, vol. 8, no. 1, 2015, pp. 30-35.

Urquhart, Troy. "Truth, Reconciliation, and the Restoration of the State: Coetzee's *Waiting for the Barbarians*." *Twentieth Century Literature*, vol. 52, no. 1, Spring 2006, pp. 1-21. *JSTOR*, www.jstor.org/stable/20479751.

Wenzel, Jennifer. "Keys to the Labyrinth: Writing, Torture, and Coetzee's Barbarian Girl." *Tulsa Studies in Women's Literature*, vol. 15, no. 1, Spring 1996, pp. 61-71. *JSTOR*, www.jstor.org/stable/463973.

Chapter 4

Brecht's Epic Theatre: Demystifying the Dogmatic Tradition of Aristotelian Drama in the Western Theatre

Onur Ekler
Hatay Mustafa Kemal University, Türkiye

Abstract

It is no doubt that Aristotle's *Poetics* has played a vital role as a theoretical guidebook in systematically shaping Western Theatre. However, ignoring the changing dynamics of the related era by fanatically adhering to the Aristotelian tenets in the contemporary drama of the related period—treating them as dogmas— has begun to consume Western Theatre deep down inside. It was not until the modernist times that the dramatists could have some unorthodox, revolutionary views and techniques in the contemporary theatre of their time. There were a few dramatists, such as Shakespeare and Corneille, who stepped out of those dogmatically assumed standards, but their theatrical mentalities were still dependent upon the theatrical illusion of the Aristotelian drama. In modernist times, there have appeared some alternative forms of theatre that aim to un-dogmatize the Aristotelian understanding of theatre thanks to their meta-theatrical techniques. These alternative theatres hold common ground in that they try to cure the infection caused by the dogmatic presence of the Aristotelian tenets in Western Theatre. Through its revolutionary understanding, Bertolt Brecht's "Epic Theatre" is one of the newly introduced theatres that have given the harshest reactions to the illusion-making business of the Aristotelian drama. For Brecht, the Aristotelian drama is a narcotic business that emotionally drives people to ecstasy by making them unconsciously involved in the illusory world of the stage. Thanks to his innovative methods and techniques, Brecht's Epic theatre aims to disrupt the illusion of Aristotelian theatre by distancing the spectators and actors from being possessed by the performance. His purpose is to awaken the spectators as well as the actors and drive them into action to challenge the putrid dogmas deeply seated in the community. To support this argument, this study will make a detailed analysis of *The Life of Galileo*, one of his well-known plays, to show how Brecht attempts to un-dogmatize the Aristotelian dramatic theatre that has long dominated Western theatre.

Keywords: Poetics, Dogma, Theatre, Aristotle, Epic

***

Introduction

If one rephrased Whitehead's widely accepted statement[1] and applied it to the Western theatre claiming that "Western drama is but a footnote to Aristotle", few would say otherwise. Aristotle's theoretical framework, which he devised for the ideal tragedy in his *Poetics*, has become a referential guidebook for the future generations of dramatists. The tenets of Aristotelian drama have been sanctified and turned into some sort of dogmas as the Western theatre has thrived. However, these dogmas have become rotten and induced infection in the Western theatre since it has lost its capacity to keep up with the changing dynamics of the relevant time. The corrosion in the Western theatre has much been felt, particularly in the modernist times when it has kept on the canonical methods of Aristotelian drama to perpetuate illusions while people have been experiencing traumatic life events in the changing conditions of recent times. It may not be wrong to claim that spectators overwhelmed by the theatrical illusion of Aristotelian drama have become like the prisoners in Plato's cave. The illusory scenes ripping themselves from the outside reality have emotionally captivated them. This rupture between real life and theatrical illusion has further exacerbated the psychological fragmentation of people. Few dramatists have perceived it infectious and boldly moved to un-dogmatize Western theatre by introducing new theatrical notions. No doubt is that Aristotelian dramatic tenets still appear in Western theatre despite these newly emerged theatres, but as a result of the meta-theatrical aspect of the newly-introduced theatres, they are not necessarily dogmatic any longer. Bertolt Brecht's Epic Theatre is one of these theatres that challenges the dogmatic presence of Aristotelian notions in Western theatre. Epic theatre, with its revolutionary understanding, manifests itself as an alternative mode of theatre to the illusion-making industry of Aristotelian drama, which has long dominated the European stage. It forges a new path to cleanse the Western theatre festered with the worn-out dogmas of Aristotelian tenets. With its break from the dramatic theatre, performances of which have caused a narcotic effect on spectators, Brecht's Epic theatre develops an experimental stage where spectators turn to critical observers through its innovative stage design, devices, and acting. Basing on the Marxist

---

[1] "All of Western philosophy is but a footnote to Plato". (Whitehead 39)

dialectic, Epic theatre, as Harrap and Epstein note, shelters the opposing forces ceaselessly clashing in one's mind and society in a way to awaken the Western man from deep sleep (218). As Antonin Artaud aims to do with his Theatre of Cruelty, Brecht also attempts to purify the infected theatre of the Western world by seeking out new dramatic techniques; however, one difference is that Brecht's plays mainly center on how economic forces may influence the sociopolitical relations of the relevant time. Re-interpreting the historical events through the alienating effects created on the stage, Brecht aims to distance spectators from the staged performance so that they can critically filter such events as if they were on an academic platform. Thanks to various devices, spectators' constant exposure to the meta-theatricality of the events on the stage is Brecht's deliberate design in order to prevent both spectators and actors from being possessed by the performance. In this context, Brecht believes that theatre should not cast a spell over people by emotionally driving them into an ecstatic world so that they can escape from the bitter facts of life. In fact, Brecht's dream theatre is to push spectators' minds to a higher consciousness without emotionally mounting them, as it is the case with Aristotelian drama. Considering the wastelandish context in the aftermath of the bloody wars, Brecht's un-bourgeoisie attitude in keeping spectators as active agents of the de-familiarized scenes of some familiar historical events on the stage also attempts to unveil spectators' eyes and ignite them to fight against the putrid dogmas in their own minds and society. One of his most noteworthy plays, *The Life of Galileo (1937-39, 1945-47)*, can be exemplified as corroborating evidence of this aforementioned argument. Deconstructing the commonly accepted notions through the de-familiarizing techniques in the plays, Brecht not only shakes spectators' body of knowledge deeply, but he also frustrates their expectation of a dramatic plot by calling the dogmatic presence of Aristotle into question. With this idea in mind, this study will be twofold. It will first discuss how Aristotle's *Poetics* has been deified over time. Then, it will mainly focus on Brecht's Epic theatre and its aesthetic attack on the dogmatically accepted notions of Aristotle by giving examples from his notable play, *The Life of Galileo*.

On the Dogmatic Presence of Aristotelian Drama in the Western Theatre

No doubt that Aristotle's *Poetics* is the first commonly accepted treatise that systematically discusses the dramatic art form inherent in Greek tragedies. Aristotle's keen observation of the plays with a scientific eye helps him put forth a theoretical framework of an ideal dramatic form that would become a guiding book for generations of playwrights since it induces a new paradigm. As Kuhn argues, "When paradigms change, the world itself changes with them" (qtd. in Margolis and Catudal 35). Taken on this ground, one may feel at ease claiming that Aristotle started a new paradigm with this groundbreaking work. He looks at some familiar plays with scientific instruments that enable him to codify some rules so that the inner workings of the plays might be understood and followed by future playwrights. However optimistic and revolutionary the paradigmatic effect of Aristotle's Poetics might sound, it has centralized Western drama, the tenets of which have begun to be perceived as the criteria to be tracked in considering whether a play is properly conducted or not. The totalizing aspect of those codified rules, particularly on plot, character, scene, and language, has begun to have a restraining and stifling authority on the playwrights' imagination since they should care about their addressees and critics' expectations that accord with Aristotelian dramatic notions. If a play were not considered ineligible and dissonant according to the Aristotelian rules, it could be snubbed and found defective (this practice was particularly common for the plays in eighteen-century drama; e.g., see Corneille's *Le Cid*). Based on the supposition that every paradigm possibly turns into a dogma in time if not updating itself with the changing dynamics, it is not wrong to claim that the paradigm that Aristotle started with his *Poetics* in the Western theatre has been dogmatized till the 20th century when every piece of dogma is brought into question. To corroborate this supposition, we will attempt to trace how Aristotelian rules have been sanctified and dogmatized in Western drama. Thus, we will delve into Aristotle's *Poetics* to examine his guiding rules that have become indispensable for Western drama over time and then trace their dogmatic impact on Western drama till modern drama.

Aristotle's famous definition of tragedy, given in chapter six of his *Poetics*, will be our initial point since it can be seen as the microcosm that has a macrocosmic effect on Western drama. Tragedy, he says,

> "is an imitation of an action that is serious, complete, and of a certain magnitude; in language embellished with each kind of artistic ornament, the several kinds being found in separate parts of the play in the form of action, not of narrative; through pity and fear effecting the proper purgation of these emotions"[2]. (Aristotle 23)

As Lucas well notes, Aristotle has a scientific treatment of the matter (14). He first defines tragedy and then discusses the manner, that is, how it should be formed, and lastly, highlights the pragmatic purpose of tragedy for the audience. As will be detailed later, each part of this multi-layered definition has turned into an ossified principle for Western drama. One may notice that the definition opens up with Aristotle's positive attitude towards mimetic art. To Aristotle, humankind learns through imitation. Unlike Plato's attack on mimetic

---

[2] The *Poetics* of Aristotle translated by S.H. Butcher.

art, which is dangerous for a well-functioning Republic and misrepresents the truth, Aristotle exalts it since art functions as organic as nature. It does not reproduce truth. As Lucas states, it is not "mechanical imitation as waxwork or photograph"(15). Aristotle justifies it by referring to the distinction between art and history. He argues that art represents what may happen rather than what it is. It acts with the law of probability. Therefore, the truth presented to the audience through dramatic art is much nobler, better, and more attractive.

Every tragedy for Aristotle must have six elements: plot, character, thought, diction, scenery, and song (Aristotle 25). He states that the plot is the soul of tragedy (29). As Dornan notes, a tightly knit plot in representing (not re-presenting) the truth is key to Aristotelian tragedy (415). By plot, what he means is the organization of the incidents (Aristotle 25). The action of the plot, he says, must be complete, unified, and whole. In other words, it must have a proper beginning, middle, and end. To do that, it must be confined to what it would later be called three unities: the unity of time, place, and action. Tragedy must focus on a single action that usually takes place in one place and a single day. It must have a coherent organizational pattern based on cause and effect relationship. For example, the audiences of Sophocles' *Oedipus* are familiar with the myth, but they watch the play with great interest since the tragic aspect of Oedipus' life is squeezed into a unified plot that takes place in a single day. To achieve a unified plot, Aristotle highlights the significance of some elements. The perfect plot, he mentions, must have peripeteia (reversal) and anagnorisis (recognition). The reversal of the action and recognition scenes almost simultaneously occur in a perfect tragedy by taking the laws of probability and inevitability into consideration. The hero's fate suddenly turns from good to bad or the other way around with a flash of awakening. The perfect plot of tragedy should consider these points. After Aristotle meticulously defines the characteristics of a perfect plot, he gives a clear picture of a tragic character. The Aristotelian hero's attributes must be consistent with his status in life. He must be true to life. He must be a good man whose misfortune in life is caused not by "vice or depravity, but by some error or frailty (hamartia)" (45). He must not be a man who moves from prosperity to adversity or the other way around. Either way does not arouse catharsis or feelings of pity and fear in the audience. He must not be necessarily virtuous or a villain but a man "between these two extremes" (45). His words or action must abide by the rule of necessity or probability. There must be no use of Deus ex-machine or no higher beings' intervention in the affairs of tragedy as in Euripides' *The Medea* (55). Aristotle also refers to thought and diction as necessary parts of a perfect tragedy. What he means by thought is the proper speech acts, and by diction is the proper use of linguistic and literary devices. For Aristotle, they are complementary to each other. A proper speech made by the character paying attention to the language devices helps to arouse catharsis in the audience (78-79). Aristotle regards song and *scenery* as mere "embellishments" (29). He asserts that scenery has the least artistic one and almost no contribution to the art of poetry (29). To him, the spectacular effects depend more on the machinist than the poet. In chapter fourteen, he further adds that the feeling of pity and fear should naturally occur in the plot. To evoke them with the aid of spectacular effects is against the soul of tragedy (49). In chapter fourteen, Aristotle also expresses that the true intention of a perfect tragedy is the tragic pleasure that results from the arousal of feelings of pity and fear. The poet's main purpose is to actualize it through "mimeticized" work. As Galgut points out, the pragmatic purpose of Aristotelian drama is the "catharsis", or the purgation or purification of the unpleasant feelings in the audiences (15). The aforementioned elements, thought to be indispensable for a perfect tragedy by Aristotle, are bound together to create an emphatic bond between the tragic character and the audience. Feagin, an important scholar on tragedy and its elements, stresses the connection between moral judgments and tragic pleasures, claiming that the audiences' emphatic feelings towards the characters on the stage lead to the activation of the moral codes in them (101). As can be noticed, the Aristotelian notion of drama creates a lifelike illusory space that would necessitate "suspension of disbelief" in the audience in order to sustain the audience's identification with the tragic character on the stage so that catharsis can be actualized.

Hadju, in his article on "The Authority of Aristotle's *Poetics*", examines the social prestige of Aristotle's *Poetics* in European Literature. He argues that whenever it has had counter-arguments, they have been refuted by its reinterpretations (49). For example, Sir Philip Sydney echoes Aristotle's argument that art beautifies the defects of nature. Mimetic art draws us closer to truth rather than drifting us away from it. As he notes, "her world [nature] is brazen, the poets only deliver golden" (qtd. in Adams 186). Dryden, in his "An Essay on Dramatic Poesy" also echoes Aristotle's definition of tragedy. He defines tragedy as "just and lively image of human nature representing its passions and humors, and the changes of fortune to which it is subject for the delight and instruction of mankind" (253). Many others, like Sydney or Dryden, have appealed to Aristotle's *Poetics* at different times and settings. Lucas is right to ask "why it is necessary, […], to hark back to the dramatic opinions of a Greek philosopher of 4th century B.C." (Lucas 10). His response to his own question is a bold statement claiming that the history of drama is evidence of his infallibility (10).

It is no doubt that *Poetics* has a decisive influence, particularly on the rise of Western drama. However, its influence has been so immense that it has begun to monopolize Western drama. Playwrights have begun to use the Aristotelian framework. They have begun to evaluate the art, if flawed or not, with regard to the guidelines given in his work. It has long been seen as a recipe to be followed for a dramatic work of good quality. The Aristotelian notion of drama has begun to make its dogmatic presence felt. This actually started with the rediscovery of classical works in Renaissance Europe. The playwrights such as Marlow, Kyd, Marston, Jonson, even Shakespeare, and many others to count made use of the Aristotelian tenets. As it is suggested in Aristotle's guidebook, they all regard the theatre as a space of illusion in order to emotionally captivate the audience. The audiences are emotionally driven by the performance on the stage so that feelings of pity and fear can be aroused. Jaques's famous statement in Shakespeare's *As You Like It* well summarizes the perception of theatre in the Elizabethan world: "All the world's a stage, And all the men and women merely players" (60). There is no difference between life and theatre on the Elizabethan stage. Both audiences and actors are emotionally attached to the performance. Kinney's reference to Henry Jackson's letter written in 1610 in which he mentioned how he was emotionally moved by the performances of *Othello* can be seen as a clear manifestation of the theatrical illusion created in the Elizabethan plays (9). It is unfair to say that Shakespeare was a strict follower of Aristotle. He brought some novelties to the stage, violating some Aristotelian rules. To illustrate, he made the performance of on-stage bloody scenes possible. He fused tragic and comic elements on stage. He violated three unities. Despite his unique style, he still followed the theatrical illusion of Aristotelian drama, the end of which is the purgation of negative feelings in the audience. The audiences are the passive recipients in Shakespeare's stage that are emotionally carried by the performance on the stage. Moreover, the actors are deeply engrossed in the roles to make the performance more credible. As in Aristotelian drama, the emphatic bond between the characters and the audience is aimed to suspend disbelief and make the audiences feel overwhelmed by the performance.

The influence of Aristotelian dramatic rules has much more been felt, starting with the Restoration drama. The playwrights' adherence to the Aristotelian tenets has led to sameness in style and approach. This sameness, which I boldly call infection, has collared the dramatists' imagination. If a play did not comply with the Aristotelian standards, it would get little or no public attention since it would be considered a degraded work. Their obsession with the Aristotelian rules has ironically poisoned the soul of tragedy. They have prioritized shape, standard, and symmetry over the organic aspect of drama. This has eventually exacerbated the corrosion of the Aristotelian drama over time. However, the audiences seem to have no complaints since they feel opiated by the dramatic illusion fully performed with regard to the Aristotelian tenets.

One among many details that appears to be particularly obsessive for the Restoration playwrights is the distinction made by Aristotle between tragedy and comedy in chapter II of his *Poetics*. There, Aristotle says, "Comedy aims at representing men as worse, Tragedy as better than in actual life" (13). The

Restoration Comedies such as Wycherley's *The Country Wife* or Sheridan's *The School for Scandal* performed during this period bear some resemblances in style and approach. They both stage grotesque figures, the lower types such as rakes, imposters, and coozeners, to delight the audience. Although the praxis (story) of the plays changes, the muthos (plot) is quite Aristotelian. Both the playwrights and audiences seem to have become volunteer captives of the Aristotelian drama. Like Sisyphus, they appear to be stuck in repetition and sameness with no awareness that they are automatically drawn to the illusory world of Aristotelian drama, which is getting more infectious in time as it can not keep up with the changing dynamics of the related period.

As in the Restoration drama, the Aristotelian mimetic drama based on illusion and identification with the character on stage, as Annette Saddik notes, has still become a dominant factor in the nineteen-century melodrama (18). Melodrama, she argues, has an artificial style and a predictable V-shaped Aristotelian structure "with closed, decisive endings" (18). Melodrama's sentimental and emotional plot creates an illusion that casts a spell over audiences so that they can feel as if they were experiencing reality. Lichte calls it "shallow, commercial, entertainment theatre" (243). However, the illusory stage of melodrama that creates an artificial world through the mimetic representation was harshly rejected by the realist drama of the playwrights such as Ibsen and Strindberg. They offered truth on stage with a more realistic setting in contrast to the artificial world of sentimental drama. Realist playwrights such as Ibsen try to see the stage as a public forum. They bring various problems of Bourgeois society for discussion on stage. As Lichte argues, every sphere of Bourgeois life at the end of the nineteen-century is surrounded by lies (262). Ibsen and others, in their plays, attempt to give a realistic portrayal of life by destroying the illusions or lies. One problem that surfaces in the realistic drama is that the realist playwrights, as Saddik points out, also adopt an Aristotelian approach suggesting that the representation on stage is so lifelike that the audiences can develop empathy towards the characters in terms of their sufferings that result from the destruction of life-illusions. (19). Although realist theatre reflects the disturbing social issues of the time with an idealist vision of triggering a social change, the emotional attachment of the audiences to the characters on stage thwarts their critical thinking skills and leads them to be emotionally captivated by the performance, which is quite Aristotelian.

The dogmatic aspect of Aristotelian drama seems to have been an undeniable fact since it has been practiced, albeit through different methods in each period till the 1900s. Although realist theatre has made an attempt to make it questionable by bringing a new look at theatre as a political forum, its approach ironically heightens the effect of illusion. Fredrick Jameson explains the reason why it has failed with these words: "The "realistic" work of art is, therefore, one which encourages and disseminates this attitude, yet not merely in a flat or mimetic way or along the lines of imitation alone" (205). Instead, he suggests the application of "realistic and experimental" methods and techniques (205). He expresses the urgent need in theatre to reconsider the relationship between the audience and the stage. The swift, immediate changes in the twentieth century's social, political, and philosophical atmosphere uphold Jameson's insightful views on the necessity of redeeming the stage from the Aristotelian mimetic representation of truth. The expected response to the needs of the time comes with the rise of Bertolt Brecht's Epic Theatre, which has begun to influence the stage direction with its non-Aristotelian innovative understanding. The next section will shed light on the distinctive aspect of Brecht's Epic theatre as an alternative mode of theatre that demystifies the dogmatic tradition of the Aristotelian drama through the detailed discussion of the characteristics of Epic Theatre via Brecht's most notable play, *The Life of Galileo.*

Brecht's Epic Theatre: Demystifying The Dogmatic Tradition of Aristotelian Drama in The Western Theatre

As Wirth justifiably states, Brecht's calling himself "Einstein of the new dramatic form" is not an exaggerated statement (qtd. in Lehmann 33). His epoch-making theatre has led to the dissolution of the Aristotelian drama. Dickson rightly states that Brecht consistently describes his theatre as 'non-Aristotelian' since Brecht regards the Aristotelian drama as "religion" or "Opium furs Volk" (111). In his influential article on "Non-Aristotelian" Theatre, Gruber similarly features Brecht's belief of Aristotelian drama "to be a kind of sickness or addiction that requires a cure or antidote" (201). Gruber further states that Brecht's plays were somehow a response to Aristotelian drama deeply committed to his supposed precepts (200).

One question to be answered here is what drives Brecht to condemn the Aristotelian drama narcotic or hypnotic or what conditions have grounded the eligible floor for such a revolutionary theatrical form. Stephen Unwin, an important critic of Brecht, tries to explain it with the traumatic conditions of his time, such as the growing competition of colonialism, industrialism, and the aggressive foreign policies of the countries (2). As a result of these events, the First World War broke out. It was catastrophic, especially for Germany. It also led to the Russian Revolution of October 1917. The Bolshevik Revolution that promises to recover the working conditions, was especially inspired by the ideas of German thinkers, including Marx and Engels. Their revolutionary ideas were actually thought to take root in Germany (2). The German Revolution, called The Spartacus Risings in 1918-19, were brutally suppressed, and its leaders were executed (2). Moreover, The Great Economic Depression in 1929 resulted in a worldwide economic crisis and badly affected the war-inflicted Germany (3). Amidst the crisis, Hitler came to power, turning the chaos into his own advantage; he came to power in 1933. With Hitler, Fascism grew across Europe. The countries like Italy, and Spain, began to be governed by dictatorial regimes (5). Hitler's ambition to create a "Greater Germany" led to the breakout of World War II. It was an atrocious war that led to the deaths of millions of people. During the war, The Nazi brutality was no match. They committed mass massacres. They built concentration camps where they attempted to exterminate the so-called enemies of Germany, mostly including the Jews (6). The Nazi's brutal policies caused the intellectuals to emigrate to Germany. Most of them set to leave for America till the downfall of Hitler's Germany. Unwin calls this period "the dark times" in which Brecht lived (13).

'The Dark Times' did not stop Brecht from being productive. On the contrary, the traumatic events functioned like fertilizers for his intellectual soil. He wrote his first two plays, *Baal (1918)* and *Drums in the Night (1918-20)*, in the period following the end of WW1. He wrote his third play, *In the Jungle of the Cities* (1921-24). In 1924, He directed Marlow's *Edward's II* with his friend, Feuchtwanger (14). What makes this production special is that Brecht came up with the idea of Epic theatre for the first time upon having a challenge of how to cope with the vast scope of action and the appearances of soldiers (Benjamin 94). Brecht also worked at some innovative theatres of his time, such as Max Reinhardt's Deutsches Theatre and Ervin Piscator's Volksbühne. He wrote *Man Equals Man* in 1924 (Unwin 15). He was introduced to the writings of Karl Marx. In 1927, in collaboration with Kurt Weill, the composer, he wrote some operas such as *The Rise and Fall of City of Mahagony* (1927-29) and *The Threepenny Opera* (1928) (15). He wrote his only novel, *The Threepenny Novel* (1934). He also wrote three of his most notable plays, *The Good Person of Szechwan* (1938-42), *Mother Courage and Her Children* (1939), and *Life of Galileo* (1937-39, 1945-47). The impending war forced him and his family to leave Germany. They had some stops in different countries, including Denmark and Finland, before they travelled to America. In Finland, He wrote *Mr. Puntila and his Man Matti* (1940) (15). Moreover, Brecht penned some war plays, including The Resistible Rise of Arturo Ui (1941), *Schweyk in the Second World War* (1941-43), and *The Caucasian Chalk Circle* (1943-45) (16). After the end of the war, Brecht returned to Germany. He founded Berlin Ensemble, a place identified with Epic Theatre. There, he staged his most famous plays most related to the Epic theatre (16). Lastly, to mention regarding his intellectual life, it is important to note the intellectual contributors to the development of his original theatre. Unwin highlights Brecht's Marxist friend, Korsh, the intellectual philosopher Walter Benjamin, who helped him with the aesthetic aspect of his art, Georg Lukacs, who had some public arguments with Brecht, Kurt Weill, the composer, Caspar Neher, the producer of many of his plays and Piscator, his mentor (21). To

Unwin's list, Brecht's guide to English literature, Elisabeth Hauptmann, and Charles Laughton, the translator, and actor of *Galileo*, can also be added.

The swiftly changing dynamics of the time lead Brecht to introduce a new kind of theatre called Epic Theatre since Aristotelian drama is, as Saddik argues, static (20). It fails to respond to the needs of the time. Brecht views the Aristotelian mimetic process does not represent real imitation. His ideas can exactly be seen in his poem on imitation:

> He who only imitates and has nothing to say
> On what he imitates is like
> A poor chimpanzee, who imitates his trainer's smoking
> And does not smoke while doing so. For never
> Will a thoughtless imitation
> Be a real imitation. (qtd. in Barnett 176)

What Brecht has in mind is actually the imitation of a dynamic process that discloses the social and material forces that shape one's life. Williams pinpoints the main problem in Brecht's mind regarding his rejection of conventional drama. That is "the illusion of reality", which is the likeness of real life that seduces "both dramatist and audience" (278). Similar to Williams, Dickson also mentions that the purpose of Brecht's new theatre is "to inhibit empathy as a reactionary narcotic and to reveal a society which needs changing" (114). Brecht aims to destroy the theatrical illusion through an intended distance between theatre and life. Gruber defines it as "untheatrical theatre", the purpose of which, as he explains, "is not to deny emotion or enforce dogma but to insist upon the distinction between representations and the original event" (205). Robinson similarly expresses his opinion on Brecht's purpose, claiming that Brecht attempts to awaken the anesthetized audience with the techniques of depersonalization (or estrangement) (xii). Brecht, in one of his conversations, talks about the intoxicating power of conventional drama. He says, "We have got to get away from the prevailing muzziness [...] I am for the Epic Theatre! The production has got to bring out the material incidents in a perfectly sober and matter-of-fact way" (Willett, 15). His lifelong friend, Walter Benjamin speaks of Brecht's Epic theatre as the theatre of knowledge rather than entertainment (110). The ideal drama for him is to make the spectator a critical observer of the events on the stage. Unlike the overwhelmed audience of the Aristotelian drama, the spectator of his ideal drama should leave the theatre with a bag of questions that would trigger some change in one's life. Each scene in Brecht's drama is an end in itself rather than having a cause-effect relationship. As Williams notes, the scenes move with "sudden leaps" (278). Unlike the tragic hero of the Aristotelian drama, whose catastrophic end is inevitable in order to arouse catharsis in the audience, Brecht's character changes depending on the circumstances and thus producing oneself.

In his theoretical work, *A Short Organum for the Theatre*, regarded as a guidebook to his understanding of Epic theatre and also a critical response to Aristotle's *Poetics*, Brecht blames the Aristotelian drama for turning into "Bourgeoisie narcotic business" (Willett 179). Brecht compares the audience in the Aristotelian drama to a child "who climbs onto one of the horses roundabout". He claims that both are eager to be in full possession and take delight in being carried away (188). To Brecht, these are weaker pleasures of no intellectual profit. He describes the mode of theatre in his mind with these lines:

> We need a type of theatre which not only releases the feelings, insights and impulses possible within the particular historical field of human relations in which the action takes place, but employs and encourages those thoughts and feelings which help transform the field itself. (190)

To Brecht, strong pleasures appeal to reason. This can be achieved in Epic Theatre since, as Brecht argues, "the stage began to tell a story. The narrator was no longer missing, along with the fourth wall" (71). Objecting to Aristotle's claim that epic and dramatic forms belong to different aesthetic realms, Brecht features the fluidity of boundaries between the narrative and dramatic forms due to the latest technical advances, including the facilities of projection, film, and machinery through which stage design can be faster (Martin and Bial 22). Thanks to such facilities, the events are de-personalized and can stand on their own as independent elements. The background presents an alternative; sometimes counter voice that speaks itself through various means of production. This alternative voice narrates the happenings through videos, quotations, and documentaries and exposes them to a process of de-familiarization so that both actors and spectators may not lose themselves in what Brecht calls "simple empathy" (22). Brecht's keen observation of the reactions of the audience related to the play in the dramatic and epic theatres best shows how the alienation effects of the epic theatre release the strong pleasures in the audiences by keeping them constantly awake during the performance thanks to the background voice created by the modern stage props previously mentioned.

The audience in the dramatic theatre says: Yes, I have felt that too.—That's how I am.—That is only natural.—That will always be so.—This person's suffering shocks me because he has no way out.—

This is great art: everything in it is self-evident.—I weep with the weeping, I laugh with the laughing.

The audience in the epic theatre says: I wouldn't have thought that.—People shouldn't do things like that.— That's extremely odd, almost unbelievable.—This has to stop.—This person's suffering shocks me because there might be a way out for him. —This is great art: nothing in it is self-evident.—I laugh over the weeping, I weep over the laughing. (Martin and Bial 23)

Gorelik, a renowned director, points out that catharsis is deliberately prevented in epic theatre since the function of the epic theatre, he argues, is to help the playgoers feel better and enlightened. Epic theatre primarily calls for the mind to observe the events on the stage critically.

As implied above many times, central to Brecht's Epic Theatre lay 'Verfremdungseffekt' (alienation effect). They usually call it V-effect. Some critics like Eddershaw and Esslin find its English translation unfortunate since V-effect for them is beyond the emotionally distancing effect (Eddershaw 16; Esslin 132). It also shelters the arousal of different feelings that appeal to reason. Brecht explicates the term in detail in his article, "Alienation Effects in Chinese Acting". As Martin expresses, much impressed by the Chinese acting in Mei Lanfangs' Beijing opera that he watched in Moscow in 1935, Brecht is able to find answers to the challenging questions in his mind regarding acting performance in his own theatre (Martin and Bial 227). Brecht appreciates the acting techniques used to distance the actors from throwing themselves into the roles they are performing. This, for Brecht, creates a critical zone where actors can talk to the audiences about the roles they are acting. This, as Martin well puts it, facilitates the manipulation of "character" independent of the actor (227).

Emotional distance in Epic theatre is indicative. An actor should not get lost in the action. One must demonstrate the character s/he is performing so that total identification can be prevented. In "Die Straßenszene", Brecht compares the actor to an eyewitness of an accident who shows how the accident happened to a group of people (qtd. in Mclean 174). What Büdel says of the actor is "a teacher with a pointer" (75). For Esslin, the positive side of the V-effect is to enable the spectators to look at the issues in a detached and objective manner, thanks to which the de-familiarization of the things familiar provides new insight into social life (136). Like others, Dickson positively interprets the V-effect as the technique to expose the spectators to the problems in society and recuperate them (115).

In addition to the alienating forces of Epic theatre, such as the unusual use of stage props, the incidental songs, and the aid of visual techs that disrupt the illusion of Aristotelian drama, it is noteworthy to mention 'gestus' as his most innovative and original contribution in terms of acting technique. Unwin associates gestus with the English word "gesture", but he claims that it is something much deeper (61). It is the combination of gist and gesture (Willett 42). Unwin defines gestus as the physical embodiment of social relations that enables the spectators to visualize the image of a social event (61). Squiers, in his notable work on Brecht, similarly defines social gest as the eidetic substance of social relations (97). Squiers also highlights Jameson and Barthes's emphasis on gestus as "the signification of particular gestures" (28). Gestus, to their views, exposes what is present but not seen. "It makes the obscure obvious" (28). Brecht discusses the importance of gestus in his *A Short Organum for the Theatre*, claiming that the complexity of social attitudes, including physical appearance, facial expression, tone of voice as well as private attitudes such as pain, cannot be expressed with a single word. He goes on to say, "The actor must take care that in giving his image the necessary emphasis he does not lose anything, but emphasizes the entire complex" (Willett 198). Squiers interprets it in the way that the possible redemption of the spectators from the poisonous codes of Bourgeois' ideology lays in the reduction of the social relations to gestus (97). This, as he justifiably asserts, gives the opportunity to the spectators to perceive the complete image of social reality. Curran, in her article on "Brecht's Criticisms on Aristotle's Aesthetics of Tragedy", argues that gestus is a means to demonstrate the relationship between the individual and the social, which is not possible in Aristotelian drama (174). Curran makes an analogy between Brecht's social gest and Aristotle's hamartia in terms of understanding the action of the play, but she adds that Brecht's gestus reveals the social attitude while the latter focuses on individual causes (172). Glehn's point about gestus is also remarkable. He says:

> The Gestus is the action that shows the 'natural' as determined, as coming from somewhere and having its own repercussions. It has a self-referential, enquiring effect: 'When you show: this is how it is, show it in such a way that the viewer says: but is it like that?' (91)

Gestus renders the action on the stage questionable. It should give a critical impression by creating a contradictory situation. Glehn exemplifies it with *Kuhle Wampe*, 1932 film, the script of which was written by Brecht. The central point in the film is about unemployment during the crisis of the Great Depression. When it was premiered in Moscow, the audience, as Glehn stresses, begins to question "why a man who owned a watch would commit suicide" (91). As noted, the contradictory situation puts the audience in a critical position. This is what can be called the gestic action. The gest for Brecht "allows a conclusion to be drawn about the social circumstances" (Willett 105). By social gest, Brecht meant "the mimetic and gestural expression of the social relationships prevailing between people of a given period" (Willett 139). Gestus, as Martin describes, is "emblematic" of larger social practices" (227). Brecht points out that a director should have a historian's eye in order to find out the proper speech and gest since a little scene might be an emblem of a larger social event (Willett 83). To have proper conduct of acting performance, Brecht, in collaboration with his friends, wrote some experimental works called "Lehrstücke", or learning plays, in order to find out the proper gests to be acted out. These learning plays are, as Jameson describes, "master classes" (qtd. in Negri, Xii). A note on the Lehrstück performance says:

You must act like pupils. The pupil will use a particularly clear manner of speaking in order to run over a difficult passage again and again so as to get at its meaning or fix it in the memory. (Willett 33)

Lehrstücke plays remove the so-called fourth wall, and create a learning space for both actor and audience. Distancing actors from the characters they would perform by using some techniques such as reading aloud of the text or changing roles helps actors to observe the full inconsistencies in character and thus choose the proper gest that characterizes the exact social attitude related to the historical moment. As Worthen well expresses, the emphasis on the theatricality of the performance by the intentional distance between actor and character, audience and character, stage and setting unravels the emphatic bonds of the realistic production (Willett 150).

Brecht's *Life of Galileo* as Anti-Aristotelian Play

As discussed in detail above, Brecht's V-effect devices of Epic theatre render the dogmatic aspect of Aristotelian drama questionable. This assumption clearly manifests itself in his remarkable plays, such as *Life of Galileo (1937-39, 1945-47), Mother Courage and Her Children (1939), The Good Person of Szechwan (1943), and The Caucasian Chalk Circle (1944)*. In these plays, thanks to his innovative methods, Brecht presents a critical attitude toward the plays rather than creating a theatrical illusion.

The Life of Galileo, written in fifteen scenes, actually had three versions. With the actor Charles Laughton in Los Angeles, He worked on the English version of the play[3] under the threat of Atomic war. He directed the play with Joseph Leroy at Coronet Theatre in 1947. It can be regarded as one of the best examples of Epic theatre in terms of an attack on the dogmatized ideas of Aristotle in style and action. In the first scene, Galileo tells Andrea about how old, stinky, infectious assumptions of the past will be abandoned since he says, "the most sacred truths are being looked into. Things that were never held in doubt are being doubted now" (Brecht 4). The quote gives us the gist of Brecht's theatrical notion. Like Galileo, Brecht doubts the supposedly sacred truths of theatre with the experimental techniques used in this play.

The play takes a wide range of critical reception. One critic calls it a "Lehrstück" (Willett and Manheim 12). Some, like Charlie Chaplin, comment

---

[3] The translated version jointly studied by Brecht and Laughton will be our main text in this study.

on the lack of its dramatic qualities, and they did not find it theatrical (14). What they mean by 'theatrical' is the habitual form of Aristotelian drama that emotionally elevates the audience. Brecht's notion of theatre cannot be interpreted within the norms of conventional drama. As a reaction to Chaplin, Eisler stresses the meta-theatrical aspect of Brecht's play, arguing that Brecht never wants to "'mount' the things" (17). As for the negative labelling of New York Times on *The Life of Galileo* as "stuffed with hokum", Brecht's emphasis on the impossibility of evaluating the play within the norms of Bourgeois ideology is remarkable to note (18). The anti-realistic attitude of the play is a deliberate design to disrupt the illusion. The Bourgeois audience did not get used to seeing such performances appealing to their reason as a sort of intellectual entertainment.

One essential point in Brecht's theatre is to make the audience conscious of the theatricality of the performance. The audience must constantly be exposed to the notion that it is a theatre. Regarding the stage design of *The Life of Galileo*, Brecht says:

> The stage decor must not be such that the public believes itself to be in a room in medieval Italy or in the Vatican. The public must remain always clearly aware that it is in a theatre. (qtd. in Williams 148)

As well as the violation of the three unities of Aristotelian drama, the clear-cut scenes of the play with different titles also disrupt the causal relationship behind the illusory stage of Aristotelian drama. One can note a different gestic attitude of Galileo, special in each scene. The double role Brecht stresses in his *Short Organum* makes it possible. The actor and the character that one is showing must appear on the stage interchangeably. He exemplifies it by the interchangeable appearance of Laughton the actor and Galileo the character on the stage:

> Laughton is actually there, standing on the stage and showing us what he imagines Galileo to have been. Of course the audience would not forget Laughton if he attempted the full change of personality, in that they would admire him for it; but they would in that case miss his own opinions and sensations, which would have been completely swallowed up by the character. (Willett 194)

Laughton does so to reflect all the inconsistencies in Galileo, the character who changes over time from a bright scientist to a weary prisoner due to the harsh realities of the time. Brecht's Marxist readings seem to be quite influential in reflecting the gestic attitude of Galileo since he tends to show a contradicting profile swinging between Galileo the idealist and Galileo the materialist. The social gest is revealed in the clash of his sensual and idealistic attributes. In the first scene, one sees Galileo as a greedy figure enjoying his sensual appetites drinking his milk, making his body washed on the one side, and on the other side teaching idealistically to Sarti, his housemaid's boy, on the solar system with the aid of some props on the stage. Some are bothered by "the intellectual utterances from a half naked man" (Willett and Manheim 224). However, Brecht uses the co-existence of physical and intellectual activities at the same time as an alienating force in the play. It aims at blocking any sympathy or empathy towards the character (222). A similar effect is created in the scene where Mrs. Sarti questions Galileo about his weird teachings to her son. Galileo quite excitingly answers, "A new age has dawned, a great age, and it's a joy to be alive" while he is drinking his milk (Brecht 5). The colliding forces in Galileo's nature create an ironic situation that is also devised to be preventive of empathy.

Galileo's economic restraints force him to teach and sometimes even to tell lies. His demand for a pay rise is rejected. The Procurator's covert threat relevant to his wish for a pay rise can be interpreted as a deterrent factor for Galileo: The Procurator says, "The republic may not pay as much as certain princes, but don't forget, it guarantees freedom of inquiry" (8). As a response to the Procurator's offer related to the freedom to study without payment, Galileo says that free study counts nothing without having a good salary to meet the expenses of a luxurious life (Willett 199). This causes a split in the audience's perception of Galileo, the idealist, since he likes to indulge in a life of welfare rather than displaying altruistic acts. This rupture will create a sort of alienating distance between the spectator and the character on the stage. As implied in the example above, Brecht portrays Galileo as a man bound to economic relations. This clearly manifests itself in his presentation of the telescope as his invention. Upon realizing the truth, the Procurator angrily talks to him:

THE PROCURATOR: Do you realize that this invention of yours, "the fruit of seventeen years of patient labor," is for sale on every street corner in Italy for a couple of scudi? Made in Holland, I might add. At this very moment, a Dutch freighter is unloading five hundred telescopes in the harbor. (14)

Galileo's unethical behavior in making an unfair profit in this scene also frustrates the spectators' expectation of heroic codes. Upon Sagredo's questioning, Galileo tries to justify his position claiming that "How can I do my work with the bailiff at the door? [...], Besides, I like to buy books, and not only about physics, and I like to eat well. I get my best ideas over a good meal" (15). The inconsistencies in his character constantly amaze and confuse the spectators. He seems to be noble and dignified but also knavish, and Machiavellian one is applying his reason to make an easy profit whatsoever.

Caspar Neher's well-prepared stage design reflecting the atmosphere of the period eschews the acting performance in *Galileo*. Brecht, in his Organum, states:

> Neher set *Galileo* in front of projections of maps, documents and Renaissance works of art; [...] used a background of reversible flags bearing inscriptions, to mark changes in the political situation of which the persons on the stage were sometimes unaware. (Willett 224)

The stage props are quite in harmony with the color scheme used in the play. In the Preface to Laughton's *Galileo*, the use of a different color thought to be a perfect fit for the scene is mentioned (Willett, and Manheim 220). It is also stressed that Galileo's social stance is indicated by colors in the play (220). In the court scene, "the silver and pearl grey" tone is preferred to reflect the gloomy atmosphere of the court (220). Both Brecht and Laughton agree that all the stage set and props, including the color scheme, must make the spectators feel that they are at the theatre.

Apart from the contributions of the stage sketches and color scheme to the performance of *Galileo*, music and songs are also an integral part of it. Brecht states admirably of Eisler's genius in tying "the triumphant and threatening music" to the revolutionary cry of the lower classes in relation to Galileo's astronomical theories (Willett 203).

THE BALLAD SINGER: Good people, what will come to pass

>> If Galileo's teachings spread?
>>
>> The server will not serve at mass
>>
>> No servant girl will make the bed. Now that is grave, my friends, it is no
>>
>> matter small: For independent spirit spreads like foul diseases! (49)

Unlike Aristotle, who regards music and spectacle as the least important elements in tragedy, to Brecht, thanks to their distancing effects, they are highly effective in making the spectators conscious of the theatricality of the performance.

In his song at the carnival, the Ballad Singer calls Galileo as "the Bible smasher! (50)" since he is trying to un-dogmatize some assumptions deified by the Church. Implying the material interests as the driving motive for the Church members' fanatical adherence to such assumptions, Galileo, in his talk to Little Monk, questions:

> Why does he put the earth at the center of the universe? Because he wants the See of St. Peter to be in the center of the world! That's the crux of the matter. (39)

Galileo's discovery is thought to be threatening to the authority of the Church. As Sagredo warns him, it is a dangerous path that will lead Galileo to perdition (18). Galileo's unorthodox view, "Heaven Abolished" that he wrote in his diary, is thought heretical since it means destroying the hegemonic order of the

Church, which is identified with the Aristotelian view of the world that it is at the center of the universe. The Very Old Cardinal admonishes Galileo with a stout tone, saying:

> I walk with assurance on a firm earth, it stands still, it is the center of the universe, I am in the center, and the Creator's eye rests on me, on me alone. [...].everything depends on me, man, the supreme work of God, the creature in the center, the image of God, imperishable and . . . (32)

In the Masked Ball of the Cardinals, Bellarmine and Barberini, everyone but Galileo is masked. He symbolically represents the naked truth, but Barberini jeers his unshakable loyalty to the truth with these lines:

> BARBERINI (taking Galileo's other arm) Whereupon he changes back into a lamb. You too, my friend, should have come here in disguise—as a respectable doctor of scholastic philosophy. It's my mask that allows me a little freedom tonight. When I wear it, you may even hear me murmuring: If God did not exist, we should have to invent Him. Well, let's put our masks on again. Poor Galilei hasn't got one. (36)

The thought-provoking scene suggests how truth can be shaped according to one's interests. In the Marxist reading of the scene, one may notice that the Aristotelian ideology still has some use-value and sign-value for the Church authority. They find it still of service since all of their power rests on this assumption. However, one may define Galileo as "the fetish worshipper" with an insatiable appetite for the observable nature of things. In this respect, similar to Marx and Engels's point, "the crude appetite of the fetish worshipper smashes the fetish when it ceases to be of service" (22); Galileo wants to destroy the worn-off assumptions in order to create a new path in light of a new understanding based on observation and experimentation.

One of these assumptions is the deification of the Aristotelian ideology in the play. To illustrate, The Procurator says in the first scene, "Where no one cares how the pebble falls, but only what Aristotle writes about it" (Brecht 9). The Church dogmatically values Aristotle's teachings. Everyone cares about his teachings in every corner of science and religion. In scene four, Galileo has some guests, including a philosopher and a mathematician. Despite Galileo's insistence to them about looking through the telescope in order to observe his discoveries, they do not seem willing to do it, but instead, they prefer to quote from Aristotle.

> GALILEO I'm used to seeing the gentlemen of all faculties close their eyes to all facts and act as if nothing had happened. I show them my calculations, and they smile; I make my telescope available to help them see for themselves, and they quote Aristotle. (24)

The area is metaphorically infected with the dogmatic tradition. They have blinkers that block their eyes to the truth. Galileo's statement, "truth is the child of time, not authority" is an allusive implication to Bourgeois society which is dogmatically infected with tradition due to their resistance to change (24).

> GALILEO Your Highness. In these nights, telescopes are being directed at the sky all over Italy. The moons of Jupiter don't lower the price of milk. But they have never been seen before, and yet they exist. The man in the street will conclude that a good many things may exist if only he opens his eyes. And you ought to back him up. It's not the motions of some remote stars that make Italy sit up and take notice, but the news that doctrines believed to be unshakeable are beginning to totter, and we all know that of these there are far too many. Gentlemen, we oughtn't to be defending shaky doctrines! (24)

Galileo's bringing the topics of astronomy and economy into the same pot is again another stimulus for the audience to stave off any emphatic relations with the characters. Throughout the play, Brecht attacks Aristotelian tradition in action and style. It is not wrong to claim that Galileo is the mouthpiece of Brecht since one can easily trace a lot of references to Brecht's own fight against authority in developing his new mode of theatre, Epic theatre. As Grimm argues, Aristotle is both the enemy of the non-Aristotelian drama, and the ideological villain in *Galileo* (qtd. in Willett 205).

Moreover, Brecht drifts apart from Aristotle in terms of the anti-heroic characteristics of Galileo. Unlike Sophocles' Oedipus, praised much as the ideal tragic hero by Aristotle in his *Poetics*, Galileo is not a man who can act at the expense of suffering. Although both seek out some ways to cleanse society from infection, their methods differ greatly. To rouse catharsis in the audiences, peripeteia and anagnorisis are almost simultaneously given in the same scene where Oedipus is confronted with the bitter truths about his life. The driving force behind Oedipus' action is Self-discovery. The action is retrogressive. However, One may find a deliberate disruption of the catharsis in Brecht's *Galileo*, particularly in the scene where he recanted and abjured his thesis for fear of being tortured. His pupils and supporters are frustrated with his recantation. Andrea exclaims his disappointment saying, "Unhappy is the land that has no heroes (Brecht, 58)". As a response, Galileo says, "No, unhappy the land that needs a hero" (58). Galileo's anti-heroic attitude also frustrates the spectators' expectations. He is snubbed since he is thought to lack heroic altruism for the sake of a greater purpose. However, Galileo's anti-heroic attitude enables him to write The Discorsi, which changes the perception of the world, while Oedipus leads to a tragic fall despite having heroic qualities.

GALILEO: Better stained than empty. Sounds realistic. Sounds like me. A new science, a new ethics. (61)

Galileo's action is progressive in that he moves greater than he is, not because of his sacrificial acts but because of his cowardice. Oedipus' sacrificial acts as a hero are individualistic and tend to mount the audiences' hearts, however, Galileo as an anti-hero brings the spectators to open criticism.

Particularly in *The Life of Galileo*, Brecht's direct attack on the cult of the Aristotelian notion of drama is quite noticeable. His innovative and experimental techniques used in this play, such as the use of scene titles, the stage design, the incidental readings and songs, the co-appearance of the actor and the character, the use of colors, and also the character's anti-heroic qualities can be seen as a revolutionary attempt to subvert the ideology of Aristotle in action and style.

Conclusion

So far, we have traced the anti-illusionistic devices of Epic Theatre that create a deliberate fissure in the Bourgeois audiences' consciousness, having been long opiated by the narcotic business of Aristotelian drama. Also, we have realized how this fissure provides the audiences with unformulated freedom to critically observe the performance on the stage in an interactive way. The demystifying effects of the newly introduced methods of Epic Theatre help to decentralize the hegemony of Aristotelian drama by creating alternative possibilities for European theatre.

As discussed in *Galileo*, most of Brecht's plays bear the characteristics of Epic theatre that aim to estrange the spectators from the stage. *Mother Courage and Her Children* (1939) is one of them. As in *Galileo*, there is no unifying structure in the play. It includes different scenes that reflect different time span in the Thirty Years' War (1618-1648). As Curran stresses, Brecht chooses a historical war to alienate the spectators and actors from the war-struck Europe of the 1940s (172). Like Galileo, Mother Courage has an ironical and contradictory nature. She acts as a protective mother but has no hesitation to bring them closer to perdition in the war. She is a profiteer of war situations. At some points in the play, the spectators see her mother's instincts upon her curses on the war, but at other scenes, her cries on the possible end of the war at the summit of her career. Even after losing her children in the war, she still chases for some profit in war. The contradictory nature of the character as an alienating force can also be seen in Brecht's other plays, such as *The Good Person of Szechwan (1943)* and *The Caucasian Chalk Circle (1944)*. The ambivalent nature of Shen Teh in *The Good Person of Szechwan* is observable in her wish to disguise her mild, good character in a ruthless businessman like Shui Ta. She justifies her disguise in order to survive in the bloody capitalist world. Brecht calls it a "parable play" in which, he defines, "a passing historical situation (i.e., one that should be made to pass) is depicted realistically" (qtd. in Unwin 206). The split in identity shows the dependency of social relations on the economic circumstances in the play. *The Caucasian Chalk Circle* similarly has a protagonist of paradoxical nature. Grusha heroically defends Michael, the governor's son, left alone during the revolt against all the dangers on the way to which she ironically brings him closer. The paradoxical nature of the characters is Brecht's special design not only to shake the indomitable elements of the Aristotelian tragic hero but also to blur the spectators' body of knowledge so that they can stay alert during the performances.

As well as the use of the contradictory characters as an alienating force thanks to the gestic performance, the use of songs, historical events, the uniqueness of the scenes as detached episodes, and stage designs, including mechanical props, all contribute to these non-Aristotelian plays.

Brecht's Epic theatre does not stand alone in its revolutionary path to create an alternative form of theatre that aims to decentralize the Aristotelian notion of drama in the twentieth century. To make the argument of this study more comprehensible and insightful, it is worthwhile to refer to some other important theatrical initiatives that can be called as non-Aristotelian theatres. The first of them is Antonin Artaud's 'Theatre of Cruelty'. Like Brecht, Artaud sees the cure for the infected Western drama in the Far East. When he watches a Balinese performance in Paris, he is fascinated by its incarnational elements, such as vibrant sounds, costumes, music, and dance. Artaud aims to bring the theatre back to ancient rituals. The Western theatre, as he argues, lacks in the physical language that can express everything theatrical (Artaud 38). By physical language, he means that the characters' "roaring, spinning around, flaunting their instincts or their vices creates a dream-like state where "a sort of majestic fate vibrates" (Artaud ix). Although Brecht and Artaud have some different theatrical understandings, they both feature the spectacle, unlike Aristotle. Another alternative mode of theatre that subverts the Aristotelian drama is the Theatre of Absurd. This Post-War theatre disrupts the Aristotelian action and attempts to un-dramatize the traumatic experiences of war-struck people in the cyclical pattern just as they are trapped in the myth of Sisyphus or in a broken record that rewinds to the same point. Beckett's use of a repetitive structure that kills action in his masterpiece, *Waiting for Godot*, Stoppard's subversion of Shakespeare's *Hamlet* by making the minor characters the heroes of his groundbreaking play, *Rosencrantz and Guildenstern are Dead* can be regarded as outstanding examples of non-Aristotelian drama. Another non-Aristotelian play, Pirandello's *Six Characters in Search of an Author* is revolutionary in terms of the meta-theatricality that disrupts the dramatic illusion thanks to the actors' questioning of their roles and their search for the author. Pirandello's groundbreaking play seems to attain his goal since the spectators are furious at the unusual performance that prevents their identification with the characters. Jerzy Grotowski's 'Poor Theatre' is another non-Aristotelian theatre that aims to perform by mainly focusing on the acting performance and excluding what is superfluous, such as props, spectacle, costume, et al. Although all of the above-mentioned non-Aristotelian theatres differ in style and approach, they have one thing in common. All of them aim to un-dogmatize the Aristotelian drama in Western theatre.

The paradigm shift caused by Aristotle's *Poetics* unintentionally creates a dogmatic tradition in the Western theatre beyond his intention. The playwrights like Brecht find it too restrictive to meet the needs of the time. They attempt to decentralize it with their revolutionary theatrical modes (paradigm-shifting theatres?). One nibbling question is whether such alternative modes of theatre, such as Brecht's Epic theatre, can be deified over time like Aristotelian dramatic theatre. This puzzling question will hopefully bring forth new studies in the field.

Works Cited

Adams, Hazard, and Leroy Searle, eds. *Critical Theory Since Plato.* Harcourt Brace Jovanovich College Publishers, 1992.

Artaud, Antonin. The Theater and Its Double. Grove Press, 1958

Artaud, Antonin. *The Cenci.* Grove Press, Inc. First Evergreen Edition, 1970.

Barnett, David. *Brecht in Practice: Theatre, Theory and Performance.* Bloomsbury Publishing, 2015.

Benjamin, Walter (1977). "Conversations with Brecht". In Theodor W. Adorno (ed.), *Aesthetics and Politics.* Verso. pp. 86-99.

Brecht, Bertolt. *Collected Plays [of] Bertolt Brecht: The Life of Galileo, Mother Courage and Her Children.* Vol.5 of Brecht: Collected Plays, eds. John Willett, Ralph Manheim, Bloomsbury, 2014.

Butcher, Samuel Henry, ed. *The Poetics of Aristotle.* Macmillan, 1902.

Büdel, Oscar. "Contemporary Theater and Aesthetic Distance". *Brecht: A Collection of Critical Essays. Twentieth Century Views Series.* Peter Demetz, Editor. Princeton Hall, Inc, 1962.

Curran, Angela. "Brecht's Criticisms of Aristotle's Aesthetics of Tragedy." *The Journal of Aesthetics and Art Criticism* Vol. 59, no. 2 (2001): 167-184.

Dickson, Keith. "Brecht: an Aristotelian Malgré Lui." *Modern Drama* Vol. 11, no. 2 (1968): 111-121.

Dornan, Reade. "Dramatic Comedy: A History of European and American Plays" *Western Drama Through the Ages: A Student Reference Guide.* Kimble King, Editor. Greenwood Press. 2007: pp. 414-424.

Eddershaw, Margaret. *Performing Brecht.* Routledge, 2002.

Esslin, Martin. *Brecht: The Man and His Work.* Vol. 244. Doubleday, 1971.

Feagin, Susan L. "The Pleasures of Tragedy." *American Philosophical Quarterly*, Vol. 20, no. 1, 1983: pp. 95–104. *JSTOR*, http://www.jstor.org/stable/20013989. Accessed 12 Jul. 2022.

Fischer-Lichte, Erika. *History of European Drama and Theatre*. Routledge, 2002.

Galgut, Elisa. "Tragic Katharsis and Reparation: A perspective on Aristotle's Poetics." *South African Journal of Philosophy*, Vol. 28, no.1, 2009: pp.13-24.

Gruber, William E. "Non-Aristotelian Theater: Brecht's and Plato's Theories of Artistic imitation". *Comparative drama* Vol. 21, no.3, 1987: pp. 199-213.

Harrap, J., Epstein, S.R. *Acting with Style*. Eaglewood Cliffs, N.J. Prentice Hall, Inc, 1982.

Hajdu, Péter. "On the Authority of Aristotle's Poetics." *Neohelicon*, Vol. 27, no. 2, 2000: pp. 49-61.

Jameson, Fredric (1977). "Reflections in Conclusion". In Theodor W. Adorno (ed.), *Aesthetics and Politics*. Verso. pp. 196-213.

Kinney, Arthur F. *Shakespeare and Cognition: Aristotle's Legacy and Shakespearean Drama*. Routledge, 2006.

Lehmann, Hans-Thies. *Postdramatic Theatre*. Routledge, 2006.

Lucas, Frank Laurence. "Tragedy in Relation to Aristotle's." Poetics. London: Hogarth Press, 1927.

Margolis, Joseph, and Jacques Catudal. *Quarrel between Invariance and Flux: A Guide for Philosophers and Other Players*. Penn State Press, 2010.

Martin, Carol, and Henry Bial, eds. *Brecht Sourcebook*. Routledge, 2000.

Marx, Karl, and Friedrich Engels. *On Religion*. Courier Corporation, 2012.

McLean, Sammy K. "VII. The Dramatic Theory". *The Bänkelsang and the Work of Bertolt Brecht*. De Gruyter Mouton, 2019: pp. 150-202. https://doi.org/10.1515/9783111342542-008

Negri, Antonio. *Trilogy of Resistance*. Trans. by Timothy S. Murphy. Cambridge University press, 1979.

Robinson, Douglas. *Estrangement and The Somatics of Literature: Tolstoy, Shklovsky, Brecht*. Johns Hopkins University Press, 2008.

Saddik, Annette. *Contemporary American Drama*. Edinburgh University Press, 2007.

Shakespeare, William. *As You like it*. Clarendon Press, 1953.

Squiers, Anthony. *An introduction to the social and Political Philosophy of Bertolt Brecht: Revolution and Aesthetics*. Vol. 44. Rodopi, 2014.

Unwin, Stephen. *A Guide to the Plays of Bertolt Brecht*. Bloomsbury Publishing, 2015.

Whitehead, Alfred North. "Process and reality: An essay in cosmology, corrected edition, DR Griffin and DW Sherburne." 1978: 83-109.

Willett, John, ed. *Brecht on Theatre: The development of An Aesthetic*. New York: Hill and Wang, 1964.

Williams, Raymond. *Drama from Ibsen to Brecht*. Oxford University press, 1969.

—. *Drama in Performance*. C.A. Watts & Co. Ltd, 1968.

Worthen, William B. *Modern Drama and the Rhetoric of Theater.* University of California Press, 2015, pp. 205-220. https://doi.org/10.1525/9780520963047-008

Web Source

Brecht, Bertolt. *The Life of Galileo.* Trans. by Wolfgang Sauerlander and Ralph Manheim. Retrieved from http://zrperry.com/wp-content/uploads/2021/10/The-Life-of-Galileo-by-Bertolt-Brecht.pdf. Accessed on Feb, 10, 2022.

Chapter 5

Multiply Fabulous: The Sacred in the Feminine Body in Jeanette Winterson's *The Passion*

Sezgi Öztop Haner

Dumlupınar University, Türkiye

Abstract

Human beings have a need for subjective imagination as a dynamic, creative force to make sense of the world. It is within the realm of imagination that one can recreate one's own world and readapt to different notions of reality. The act of reading has effects on how we think since the words on the page force us to imagine, and actions, scenes, and bodies are evoked before us as we read. Then, we can imagine ourselves in connection with the bodies on the page. As a result of reading, readers interact with the ideologies in the texts they read in consideration of their own experiences and tell themselves and others many stories about that interaction.

Here, the role of the writer is to critique the dominant ideology of the text from which artifacts are abstracted. Then, the specific work of imaginary representation, such as novels, provides a means of shaping ideology by incorporating artifacts that already include ideological importance in a new text so as to use these artifacts to change the ideas they support into a new signification subtly. In this respect, instead of simply retelling the conventional stories that solidify ideology into a dogma that is enforced rather than criticized, Winterson recounts and subverts them in her own fashion, incorporating more variances and possibilities into a multivalent connection of the body, love, desire, sexuality, and gender as well as showing life how it could be rather than as it is.

This study will then draw attention to Winterson's representation of the body in The Passion as the site where divinity, sexuality, and gender are interrogated in order both to accomplish these subversions and to cause the critique of Western culture within the parameters of institutionalized religion. More precisely, through her depiction of Villanelle's body, the only body throughout the novel with the divine attributes of her webbed feet, Winterson can be considered to attempt to harness the dogmatic interpretations of Biblical truths and images, containing a female Christ figure, Villanelle. The Passion is essentially concerned with crises of religious faith and crises of faith in luck, love, and fetishes. Therefore, the novel extends the parameters of spiritual faith to include categories that have been eliminated by dogmatic religious institutions.

Keywords: dogma, divinity, sexuality, gender, Jeanette Winterson, The Passion

***

Introduction

Human beings have a need for subjective imagination as a dynamic, creative force to make sense of the world. In fact, the power of imagination is open-ended in the sense that its creativity derives from its potential to endlessly build upon itself, explore and reconstruct its existing methods and structures, and master its inner capacity. Then, As Campbell states in the first chapter of *Contours of Ableism*, "[i]magination is integral to human growth. To imagine is to consider desire, to dream of possibilities, to see life differently" (19). Accordingly, our spontaneous and creative imaginings as a form of consciousness reflect our different outlooks and our politics because the choices we make show the values we embrace.

These choices also extend to what kind of books we read and how we construe them, but the process of reading and interpretation will not be just a one-way interaction. We are acting upon the text to create our own reading and interpretation of the text as well as being acted upon by the text. Thus, it can be safely said that an interaction that we tend not to see occurs between the body of the reader, the body of the text as the words take form in the reader's mind, the body of the author that we can feel on the page, bodies written by the author, the body of language and the body of the book. The intersection of all bodies serves as a medium of transmission for political meaning.

At this point, in an interview with Helen Barr, Winterson explains her aims in reference to her readers: " I see my books as gateways, as opportunities: beginnings, not ends [...] for the readers to think about, to make up their own minds" (31). Then, she refers to the preceding quote in an interview with Mark Marvel with comments which elaborate on her point:

> [I]n the rewriting of stories, of history, of myths, I'm not saying, 'Look, here's the definitive version.' I'm saying, 'Here's another story about that story, so what do you think?' [...] I'm hoping all the time that it will challenge people, both into looking more closely at these things they

thought were cut and dried and also, perhaps, into inventing their own stories. (168)

Apparently, Winterson's biographical and fictional worlds depend on the power of the female imagination. It is within the realm of imagination that one can recreate one's own world and readapt to different notions of reality. Imagining one's life has come to be seen as imagining against the background of what one knows. For example, the act of reading is decidedly a physical act, but it has effects on how we think since the words on the page force us to imagine, and actions, scenes, and bodies are evoked before us as we read. Then, we can imagine ourselves in connection with the bodies on the page. As a result of reading, readers interact with the ideologies in the texts they read in consideration of their own experiences and tell themselves and others many stories about that interaction. Effectively, the reader inserts him/herself simultaneously into the ambiguity, instability, and continual transformation of language and its signifiers.

Instead of simply retelling the conventional stories that have been, until recently, the only foundation of our literary heritage, Winterson recounts and subverts them in her own fashion, incorporating more variances and possibilities into a multivalent connection of the body, love, desire, sexuality, and gender as well as showing life how it could be rather than as it is. Likewise, as Laura Doan suggests in her article "Jeanette Winterson's Sexing the Postmodern," Winterson considers fiction as a site to question, subvert, trouble, and tamper with sexuality, gender, and identity, seriously inviting readers to imagine the liberation of "natural" and "normal" from the totalizing influence of patriarchy and heterosexuality (154). In this respect, this study will draw attention to Winterson's representation of the body in *The Passion* (1987) as the site where divinity, sexuality, and gender are interrogated in order both to accomplish these subversions and to cause the critique of Western culture within the parameters of institutionalized religion.

More precisely, through her depiction of Villanelle's body, the only body throughout the novel with the divine attributes of her mysteriously webbed feet, Winterson can be considered to attempt to harness the dogmatic interpretations of Biblical truths and images, containing a female Christ figure, Villanelle. It is also important to note that since Villanelle's body possesses the divine capability of walking on water, like that of Christ, her body implicitly challenges the relationship between divinity and maleness. In this sense, Villanelle's body reveals the cultural construction of the divine as male and points out that under the imposition of Christianity, a religion of dogma, a woman has no voice.

Villanelle's ability to walk on the watery alleys of Venice thanks to her webbed feet, a Christ-like attribute customarily rumored to enable male boatmen to walk the Venetian waterways, comes to be a certain kind of preternatural power, which is suggestive of the divine. In this respect, one should notice that Winterson's *Passion* plays with the conventions of religious romance by reflecting the relationship between an individual and divine love, one being exploited by the other in the multiple blends of Winterson's eponymous passion. One of the most obvious common features of *The Passion* is then the rejection of totalisation, the celebration of exteriority, the opening of doors, and the relentless exploration of the unknown, the foreign through romance. For Winterson, romance is employed within the novel to free romance from its constraints, as is stated in the author's remark prefacing *The Passion*: "The Passion is not romance, except in so much as all our lives are marked by the men and women with whom we fell in love". It is a way to withdraw from the rhetoric of the same towards a confrontation with that which is the other, the exterior, and the foreign.

At the same time, *The Passion*'s very title implies the passion of Jesus Christ in the Garden of Gethsemane before His crucifixion when Christ's faith in and love for God the Father was put to the ultimate trial. In this sense, the novel examines passion in relation not only to religion but also to causes, love, games of chance, sex, and public idols. Then, *The Passion* is essentially concerned with crises of religious faith together with crises of faith in luck, love, and fetishes. Therefore, the novel extends the parameters of spiritual faith to include categories that have been eliminated by dogmatic religious institutions. Then, this study focuses on the marginalized subject's destabilization or distortion of longstanding religious traditions and discourses from a place both inside and outside Christianity's discursive parameters. In a critical dynamic, since the main character Villanelle within the novel is positioned inside religious stories or myths, these foundational religious scripts are subject to question. For instance, if the holy second Person of the Christian Trinity, Christ, is undermined, the longstanding religious tropes are subverted. The effect is that the marginalized as a part of foundational religious texts both exceeds and precedes the normative religious tradition and exposes that Christian narrative tradition was never singularly hetero or singular.

In addition, in connection with Villanelle's body, the female body, which is usually regarded as either sexual and depraved or pure and virginal, comes to be simultaneously holy and sexual. Winterson is well aware of the significance of bodies, specifically to women, with respect to the close relation between living in a female body and the construction of female subjectivity. In establishing the strong connection between how one imagines oneself and how one thinks of and treats one's body, Winterson attempts to invite female readers to reimagine and empower themselves in a different way, both physically and subjectively.

1. The Hybridization of History as a Totalizing Master Narrative and Fantasy in *The Passion*

What happens in a text when supernatural or miraculous elements blend with historiographic references? Jeanette Winterson's *The Passion* seems to be driven by this question. Then, Winterson employs a transgressive confrontation between the fantastic and the historically real, which is at once taboo, may still be our most important and thus sacred. Accordingly, the combination of fantasy and historical realism within the single text suggests a transgression because each is identified with a pole dependent upon the assumption of the fact-fiction continuum. Such a confrontation manifests itself as a notice to reexamine normativized discourses through which the real has been conventionally constituted and understood.

The Passion follows the adventures of Henri, a fictional first-person narrator, against the backdrop of early nineteenth-century European history. The chronicle of the Napoleonic wars in *The Passion* is stated mainly by a poor French peasant, Henri, who joins the army to be a soldier for the sake of the master narrative of Napoleon. Henri's first passion is Napoleon, a man obviously beyond the reach of Law, who attempted to conquer the world. Napoleon, Henri states, "was in love with himself, and France joined in. It was a romance. Perhaps all romance is like that; not a contract between equal parties but an explosion of dreams and desires that can find no outlet in everyday life. Only a drama will do, and while the fireworks last the sky is a different colour" (13). Witnessing Moscow burn together with Henri's recollections of his years in Napoleon's army, Henri eventually recovers from his love and his passion changes into obsessive hate and self-hatred. While Henri's experiences in Napoleonic wars are blended into the labyrinth of Venice, a fluid space of danger and transformation, the story turns out to be fantastic in its details, such as a priest with a telescopic left eye, an icicle that will not dissolve and in its junction with that of the second character, Villanelle. Her narrative is completely less conventional in the sense that Villanelle, the novel's bisexual, cross-dressed, and web-footed character, begins to experience feelings of love across the roulette wheel with a woman characterized as the Queen of Spades. Throughout Villanelle's story, love is appeared as gambling, which turns out to be unpredictable, thrilling, and compulsive. Her love is a desire which is a route beyond the principle of pleasure.

The second narrator of *The Passion*, Villanelle, also works for Napoleon's army, where she provides services for Napoleon's higher-ranking officers and serves for a while as a camp prostitute as well. Villanelle started life, however, as the fatherless, web-footed daughter of a poor Venetian boatman. Soon, she turns out to be a socially abject figure in the sense that she is a female with a peculiar genetic characteristic part of mythic and legendary status, making her gender ambiguous. Such ambiguity is reinforced by Villanelle's habit of cross-dressing in order to work in a Venetian casino, which attracts the passion of both sexes. Through Winterson's fantastic images of cross-dressing and webbed feet and, thereby, the association of sexuality and fantasy, Villanelle challenges both rational truth-seeking in relation to Winterson's denial of the equation between sex and reproduction as well as physical rules. In the novel, desire and fantasy are connected by the image of the webbed feet and the cross-dressing trope, which denaturalize the normative categories of desire and sexual identity.

Similarly, the collapse of the boundary between invention and the narrativized fact is illustrated when Villanelle asks Henri to get back her "lost heart". Villanelle loses her heart to the Queen of Spades. Henri is obliged to steal into the house and return it back to her in a jar. Putting his hand over the surface, her heart should occupy, Henri notices that Villanelle tells the truth. A similar kind of collapse between the real and metaphorical can be seen when to secure Henri's promise to get back her lost heart, and Villanelle creates a gift from a mutual friend, a gold chain in a miraculous manner enclosed in an icicle shaped by the dying man's tears. Here, Henri's approval of Villanelle's miracles enables us to notice what Brian McHale calls the "banalization" of the supernatural phenomena in postmodern fantasy (76). The final collapse in signification indicates Henri's madness, which happens at the most intense crash between realism and fantasy in the text – his rescue of Villanelle's lost heart and his violent murder of her husband.

Within the prescribed cultural scripts, Henri has performed his role. On the other hand, operating within the authorizing discourses of the dominant order, Villanelle has rejected to perform hers, accepting his heroic demonstration as an act of companionship but rejecting him as the reward of her body. This reveals what Judith Butler describes in *Gender Trouble* as the regulating fiction of heterosexual coherence, which demonstrates heterosexuality as an ideal (137). In the case of Henri, it is exposed as fiction in Henri's state of mind and explains his reluctance to accept Villanelle's rescue attempts as a form of negation. He cannot even accept the possibility of a female hero. Removed from the masculine within the heterosexual quest narrative, Henri loses his constructed self and the conception of himself as a hero.

In *The Passion*, it is Henri who carries the responsibility of scattering the seeds of disturbance against religious authority and Bonaparte's dictatorial policies. Henri's subversion of patriarchal and religious politics suggests the suppression of a set of principles that he had been raised to take for granted. His childhood memories introduce the reader to a boy who occupies and support his encompassing patriarchal world and discovers to be in close connection with its two representative Father images, God and Napoleon, especially under the influence of the priest who is in a position of control of his education.

Due to the specific education, he takes as a child, Henri's refusal of patriarchy appears to be progressive. He notices that the reality in which he moved forward unconsciously after signing for his recruitment does not agree with the descriptions of the priest. When he comes to the camp at Boulogne, he is unable to avoid juxtaposing what he has been described by the priest with what he really sees. In this regard, the portrayal Henri creates of the brothel he is urged to visit to conform to the rules of patriarchy together with Bonaparte's cook:

> I had expected red velvet the way the priest had described these seats of temporary pleasure, but there was no softness here, nothing to disguise our business. When the women came in they were older than I had imagined, not at all like the pictures in the priest's book of sinful things. Not snake-like, Eve-like with breasts like apples, but round and resigned, hair thrown into hasty bundles or draped around their shoulders. (14)

In addition, Henri had been informed that "soldiering is a fine life for a boy" (8), but his first impression is quite distressing, dependent upon the representation he makes of Bonaparte's storeroom:

> The space from the ground to the dome of the canvas was racked with rough wooden cages about a foot square with tiny corridors running in between, hardly the width of a man. In each cage there were two or three birds, beaks and claws cut off staring through the slats with dumb identical eyes. I am no coward and I've seen plenty of convenient mutilation on our farms but I was not prepared for the silence. Not even a rustle. They could have been dead, should have been dead, but for the eyes. (5-6)

Stillness, distortion, muteness, and the choking sensation of being a captive in a wooden cage are employed here to indicate the cruel state in which Napoleon preserves his chickens. Evidently, Napoleon's passion for chicken is metaphorically juxtaposed with his passion for victories and power. Like his chickens, soldiers turn out to be objects in the hands of the Emperor. More importantly, Henri ends up revealing that the image of Napoleon that the priest has served him is a construct – "I invented Bonaparte as much as he invented himself" (158) -the logical consequence of an individual longing for superiority that justifies and maintains patriarchal values. Only when Henri frees himself from his idealistic state of mind does he show the realization of his own fault: "They [the Russians] called the Czar 'the Little Father', and they worshipped him as they worshipped

God. In their simplicity, I saw a mirror of my own longing and understood for the first time my own need for a little father that had led me this far" (81). Here, Henri denies the three holding points of patriarchal ideology: the Czar, as the figure of political power; God, as the ultimate religious authority; and the Father, as the only authority in the family. It also indicates the determined turn of mind and his decision to abandon, as he admits that "I think it was that night that I started to hate him. If the love was passion, the hate will be obsession [...]. The hate is not only for the once loved, it's for yourself too; how could you ever have loved this?" (84). In fact, Henri never manages to break free from that "hate for oneself" and its following feelings of shame and guilt despite the fact that he rejects all connection with the outer world so as to attempt and leave behind his personal "nightmare of history" (84), initially, to discover a free space in which to look into his inner self, next, and, finally, to put down in writing the memoirs that adapt *The Passion*.

In addition, Henri plainly represents the beaten, not a victorious hero who, having been sent to the madhouse/ prison of San Servelo after killing Villanelle's husband, prefers to stay there in what could be explained from the psychoanalytic perspective as a return to the mother's womb: "mother is here. She looks just as always, perhaps a little younger" (135). Nevertheless, in San Servelo, Henri is spiritually reborn to a new angle of vision that overwhelms the constraints of History as a grand narrative and appreciates the power of words to build reality in favour of memory. Interestingly enough, Henri begins to write his memoirs as a way to examine his inner self when he is secluded from the outer world: "There was a time, some years ago, I think, when [Villanelle] tried to make me leave this place, though not to be with her. She was asking me to be alone again, just when I felt safe. I don't ever want to be alone again, and I don't want to see any more of the world" (152). The end of his exploration points out the beginning of his venture as a writer who struggles to understand his past experience as a means to learn more about himself.

In San Servelo, Henri feels what Linda Hutcheon (1988) calls as "the presence of the past" (131), but he does not experience a nostalgic restoration of a glorious past; rather, he initiates a critical revision of his life and memories by means of his present knowledge. Rewriting his war journal into his memoirs, Henri notices that there is no such a thing as history and chronology but a variety of stories that illuminate philosophical, individual understandings of a man and a woman, or more specifically, the human condition. Henri self-consciously recognizes his mission as an author-narrator who prescribes, chooses, and excludes whatever he regards as irrelevant when he involves in the act of rewriting his life story. Henri considers himself both the author of his memoirs and its reader when he assumes that "I go on writing so that I will always have something to read" (159). Shattering all narrative frameworks,

Henri appears to be not only the narrator and the narratee of his journal but also the reader and writer of his memoirs.

His urgency for the fact that he attempts to be true to reality paradoxically fulfills the opposite effect and reinforces the fact that writing down reality unavoidably results in changing it. Language refashions reality as it symbolizes reality, and Henri's discourse is separated from reality in a twofold manner because it has been changed twice into a linguistic construct, first as a journal and then as a memoir. At this point, Susan Rubin Suleiman (1994), the renowned scholar, expands the act of remembering further:

> When are you old enough to re-member who you "are"? The hyphen makes explicit and emphasizes what is always true about the activity of remembering: it is not a passive reception of memories fixed forever like a series of faded images in a scrapbook, but an active (re)construction, a putting together and shaping (the way an artist puts together and shapes certain materials) of a life or part of a life. Similarly the self is not a fixed entity but an evolving process, not something discovered (or passively "remembered" but something made; which does not mean that it does not exist, but that its existence is always subject to revision (re-vision). (2-3)

Of special interest to this argument here is the ironic distance from which his memories are narrated by an adult Henri. Such a critical perspective the adult narrator-author preserves concerning his own past ventures as a young character when he rewrites them is one of the means of achieving a desired end in order to subvert the monolithic, patriarchal oppression by religion, sex, militarism, and class in which Henri has been realised.

In writing his memoirs, Henri does not present a chronological account of events; rather, he employs memory as a structuring component. Similar to the most representative writers of modernism, Henri's use of memory serves as a means of obtaining temporary freedom from both the imminent and forced submission to the clock and the nightmare of history. To put it in Randall Stevenson's words, "just as modernist authors turned away from the increasing pressures of social reality to the private inner space of consciousness, so they also moved into an inner dimension of memory; into what *Orlando* calls 'time in the mind' rather than 'time on the clock'" (46). In this respect, Henri seems to imitate the modernist notion of the artist writing for himself in a conscious manner, ignorant of and indifferent to the external world, kept in a perpetual present.

On the other hand, Villanelle does not refer to such notions as memoirs, reality, or truth. She employs an interpretative verb, "recreating", which attracts the reader's attention to the fact that, for Villanelle, the act of writing is an imaginative and productive process. Then, the narrative progressively highlights Henri's disappointment with the factual and pragmatic world, as stated in the journal, and his loss of certainty when confronted by collapsing grand narratives and traditional values, as revealed by his refusal to accept his memoirs as the final text. It is at that point Henri's narrative discourse confronts Villanelle's. In fact, both Henri and Villanelle take on separate lives, and thus, their narratives turn out to be juxtaposed and independent. Their joined voices introduce the way in which the result of their narratives is much the same in spite of the different ways of representation each of them takes on.

Prior to listening to Villanelle's voice for the last time, Henri recognizes that "there are voices, and they must be heard" (142). The first apparent interpretation of this statement would associate those "voices" with Henri's madness and the fact that he appears to lose contact with reality. At the same time, there is another valid interpretation of this utterance, which embodies the ideological stance stated in *The Passion*. Henri, who has undergone the burden of patriarchy, disclaims the authorial position he has asserted so far and admits fragmentation and multiplicity of both narrative and self. Henri modifies history when he notices that he is the constituent of the structure constituted of other voices which must be heard, which must be furnished with a discourse of their own.

2. "I'm telling you stories... Trust me": Ambiguous Story-telling

The critical feminist perspective seeks to demonstrate a connection between literary texts and women's emancipation by associating the semantic dimension of the text with possible social agents and, at the same time, seeks to address women, highlighting the significance of individual change and the transformation of consciousness. From this point of view, the telling of stories can change and affect one's everyday life. As Winterson explains in her novel *Oranges are not the only fruit*: "that is the way with stories; we make them what we will. It's a way of explaining the universe while leaving the universe unexplained, it's a way of keeping it all alive, not boxing it into time" (93). Stories always do much more than they appear to do. Thus, Winterson attempts to show the interaction between real and imaginary, or between how stories help construct reality and how reality can reconstruct stories. This shift or fluidity is significant since it manifests the powerful inferences of storytelling and enables, on different levels, the author, the narrator, and the readers to be actively included in shaping the world.

For Winterson, story-telling is a political act formulated to challenge individuals to question the stories of their culture and to create their own stories. From this perspective, *The Passion* can be considered as a number of stories in which, as in the Bible, the sacred steps in the lives of individuals and miracles that cannot be proven to happen. Portraying the Bible as a sacred narrative, with a variety of other genres like history, allegory, fantasy, and myth, is essential for Winterson's experiment to secularize it and seek alternative perspectives. Instead of viewing the Bible as a divine collection of sacred narratives or God's laws, Winterson addresses her readers to see it as a way of making sense of the world as the readers imagine it to be. In *Boating for Beginners*, Winterson undermines the established or assumed reality of the Bible as a privileged historical and sacred narrative:

> Just a point of interest: the Bible is probably the most anti-linear text we possess, which is why it is such a joy. [...] The Bible writers didn't care that they were bunching together sequences some of which were historical, some preposterous, and some downright manipulative. Faithful recording was not their business; faith was. They set it out in order to create a certain effect, and did it so well that we're still arguing about it. [...] But read it; read it for its arrogance, its sleight of hand. It's very beautiful, and it's a pointer for living. The mistake is to use it as a handbook. That way madness lies (65-67).

As stated above, for Winterson, the Bible promotes merging and multiple experiences of reality rather than linear, chronological, and univocal histories of society and thereby urges the readers to break the power of manipulation in the Bible. At the same time, Winterson warns her readers against the other dangers of biblical myths. Accordingly, she equates faith with destructiveness, depicted throughout God's actions, such as immediate removal from the garden of Eden or a flood.

In her third novel, *The Passion*, specifically through her representation of Villanelle's body, Winterson attempts to exploit the institutional authority of Biblical narratives and images to address the issues of sexuality, gender, and spirituality. As Alicia Ostriker states in her book *Stealing the Language*, there is a remarkable authority that falls naturally to an author through the use of myth, particularly the Bible:

> Whenever a poet employs a figure or story previously accepted and defined by culture, the poet is using myth. [...] Historic and quasi-historic figures like Napoleon and Sappho are in this sense mythic, as are folktales, legends, and Scripture. Like the gods and goddesses of classical mythology, all such material has a double power. It exists or appears to exist objectively, outside the self. Because it is in the public domain, it confers on the writer a sort of authority unavailable to someone who writes 'merely' of the private self (212).

Reappropriating culturally accepted, deep-seated narratives, Winterson utilizes experimentation to exploit the sacred and create cultural change. Thus,

Winterson takes extra authority in her storytelling by relating to the Bible. At this point, Ostriker explains in *Feminist Revision and the Bible* (1993) that invoking mainstream myths, particularly the Bible, in a positive manner is not an easy task for women writers:

> How can we—how do we—deal with that ur-text of patriarchy, that particular set of canonized tales from which our theory and practice of canonicity derives, that paradigmatic meta-narrative in which innumerable small narratives rest like many eggs in a very large basket—the Book of Books which we call the Bible? (27)

Here, Ostriker reveals some key features of the Bible, including its patriarchal inclination and its influence over canonicity, spirituality, and cultural authority. She also suggests that ignoring the Bible is not an alternative; its cultural influence is too widespread. To be more precise, women can notice within the biblical narrative the operation of patriarchy constructing itself. If women prove that women writers react plurally and multiply to this text, we can start exploring the relation of women to the canon in a broad way, moving beyond the premise that a male text is a woman's enemy. At this point, regarding the revisionist reading of Biblical narrative, Ostriker suggests the "hermeneutics of indeterminacy" as a (re)interpretative reading model which promotes plural reading and thereby fosters a multiplicity of meanings throughout the text (17). To put it in Ostriker's words, "There is not and cannot ever be a 'correct' interpretation, there can only be another and another, and another. [...] Human civilization has a stake in plural readings" (19). In this sense, Winterson seems to agree with Ostriker's viewpoint when she states in her interview with Mark Marvel that in the rewriting of history, stories, or myths, she proposes another story about the story instead of a definitive version (168). Women, or more specifically, women writers, can interpret the Bible from many viewpoints and create various rooms and strategies for female intervention. In such a case, through her representation of Villanelle's body with divine attributes in *The Passion*, Winterson calls into question the traditional interpretations of the Bible by encompassing differences.

Villanelle, one of the primary characters in *The Passion*, is the daughter of a Venetian boatman and his wife. At birth, she comes to be the embodiment of the boatman's myth through her webbed feet. Since Villanelle is born with mysteriously webbed feet and is able to walk on water, she occurs as a misfit in her culture. The portrayal of the moment of her birth depicts Villanelle as a subversive force when she tells the reader that: "there never was a girl whose feet were webbed in the entire history of the boatmen" (51). Villanelle's having been born with webbed feet would mark her throughout her life as different from the rest of the girls in her community.

The community of boatmen is phallocratic and patriarchal, and the male hegemony and power being absolutely symbolized by the webbed feet that only boatmen acquire. A "mistake" of nature enables Villanelle, a woman inherit the male power, and any attempt to get rid of the "offending parts" is futile (57). The fact that Villanelle is biologically marked by this male trait may be interpreted as proof that she has the power to challenge heterosexuality, patriarchy, and referentiality. In conjunction with her webbed feet, Villanelle also inherits boatmen's natural inclination and desire to work on the boats. Echoing Henri's mother Georgette's desire to become a nun, Villanelle would have liked to be a "boatman" herself; however, once again, society shows a reaction negatively against any such interruption in the patriarchal order: "what I would have most liked to have done, worked the boats, was closed to me on account of my sex" (53).

Nevertheless, Villanelle does not yield since she comes to be a rebel by birth: "I did take a boat out sometimes, rowing alone for hours up and down the canals and out into the lagoon. I learned the secret way of boatmen, by watching and by instinct" (53). Apparently, both skills and jobs should be available to anyone regardless of sexual identity, which is why Villanelle regards herself as a real boatman: "Boatmen don't need to swim. No boatman would end up like this. We can't go home till we're dry, I'll be made fun of" (124). Henri also makes a remark about Villanelle's ability concerning boats, which he interprets as a power to dominate him: "When I suggested to Villanelle that she was being deliberately mysterious and taking me a way I would never recognise again, she smiled and said she was taking me down an ancient way that only a boatman could hope to remember" (113).

As a mythical being, she also acquires the miraculous traits of Christ as her feet enable her to walk on the water. In fact, only Christ, a religious figure in Western culture, shows the ability to walk on water. As is evident in the Bible, the Christian disciples "see Jesus walking on the sea, and drawing nigh unto the ship: and they were afraid" (John 6:19). Throughout the novel, Villanelle's body possesses the same divine ability to walk on water, and thus her body in an implicit manner challenges the relationship between divinity and maleness. Villanelle's body also reveals the cultural construction of the divine as man and draws attention to the argument that women have no voice within the framework of institutionalized religion. Reversing the gender of a Christ figure is a strategy for Winterson in the sense that the representation of Villanelle's body occurs as simultaneously sexual and Christ-like; on the other hand, in the Bible, Christ's body is never depicted as sexual.

In *The Passion*, the Bible becomes one of the intertexts and serves as a system of meaning and as a referential point for the framework of the chaotic reality which is experienced within the book. The title of the book, The Passion, in an overt manner refers to the biblical figure of Christ, to whom the main characters of the book are frequently related. Like Christ, Villanelle can walk on water; as Henri expresses: "I raised my head fully, my knees still drawn up, and saw Villanelle, her back towards me, a rope over her shoulder, walking on the canal and dragging our boats" (129). Accordingly, Winterson's portrayal of Villanelle's body serves as an example of the Biblical revisionism stated by Ostriker in *Feminist Revision and the Bible*. In Ostriker's view, a marked "insistence on sensual immediacy and the details belonging to the flesh as holy, an insistence that the flesh is not incompatible with the intellect" (81) are all present within the novel in relation to Villanelle's body. Departing from the conventional conceptions of the sanctified and holy, which tend to draw a sharp line between the divine and the body, Winterson urges her readers to imagine spirituality and faith as moving beyond the Bible and religious institutions into areas avoided by conventional interpretations of the Bible.

More precisely, Villanelle's unusual position, like that of Christ, is foretold before her birth. Like all the mythical Venetian boatmen, her father possesses webbed feet and can walk on water. However, having gone against the custom and shown his webbed feet to a tourist for a purse of gold, he becomes lost forever and is presumed dead. In fact, at the beginning of her story, Villanelle discards her biological father by referring to his fantastic disappearance as if it were not her former times but a distant part of a fairy tale. It seems quite apparent that Villanelle has grown up with an absent father. Accordingly, she is not used to conforming to the authority of a father figure in her home. On the other hand, it's the father's disappearance that makes the performance of the ritual unmanageable for Villanelle's mother. Then, his pregnant wife, moving to the island of the dead to utter a prayer to God for a son or a clean heart for a daughter, goes against the custom by dropping a spray of rosemary into the sea when an owl strikes her shoulder with its wing and her child Villanelle is born during an eclipse of the sun. Therefore, Villanelle starts life in the middle of a series of prophetic signs that all indicate simultaneously the divine and the monstrous. As is evident in the *Herder Dictionary of Symbols*, [i]n folk customs, rosemary was regarded as a protective agent against illnesses and evil spirits, and in this sense, it was used particularly at births, weddings, and deaths (162). Also, rosemary symbolizes "love, fidelity, fertility, and immortality" (162). Regarding the image of the owl and its call, the dictionary notes that "[i]n Christian symbolism [owl] appears negatively as the image of spiritual darkness, but positively as a symbol of religious knowledge or Christ, as the light that illuminates the darkness" (144). Finally, as stated in the dictionary of symbols, "the eclipse of the sun ... is often associated with the death of the celestial body which is thought to have been devoured by a monster" (65). Apparently, the birth of Villanelle meets the requirements or expectations of all of these threatening portents, as noted in the novel: "it was when they spread me out to dry that my mother fainted and the midwife felt forced to open another bottle of wine. My feet were webbed" (51).

It is also significant to note that Winterson provides a clue in her character's name. According to *The New Princeton Encyclopedia of Poetry and Poetics*, as an intellectual challenge, Villanelle is a poetic and musical form, originally from Italy, characterized only by a pastoral subject and a refrain as well as the lines of the "rose-coloured thread" of mortality and change (56). Therefore, her name provides Winterson's character a form and a structure, and the most dominant refrains occur within the novel as her webbed feet and games of chance, which are foregrounded by the old witch whom Villanelle calls "[m]y philosopher friend," or simply "my friend" (54, 74, 114). This old woman possesses the gift of prophecy and says to Villanelle, "You're a Venetian, but you wear your name as a disguise. Beware the dice and games of chance" (54). Throughout the novel, Villanelle appears again and again in different guises, attempting to act against the control over her life, sustained by her webbed feet and games of chance.

While her name declares her as a female in an unambiguous manner, she has a body made ambiguously sexual by means of her webbed feet, as male attributes in her culture. To be more precise, before Villanelle's birth, it is made obvious that traditionally just males in a boatman's family possess webbed feet. Accordingly, her mother consents to the midwife's attempt to cut the webs between Villanelle's toes, but her knife sprang from the skin, leaving no mark. She tried again and again between all the toes on each foot. She bent the point of the knife, but that was all. 'It's the Virgin's will,' she said at last, finishing the bottle. 'There's no knife can get through that' (52).

Crying and lamenting, Villanelle's mother is not consoled until her stepfather comes home and says that the webs will be unseen together with a pair of shoes. Villanelle's stepfather always takes on a marginal position within the family and never indicates any sign of dominance. "He's a curious man," remarks Villanelle, "a shrug of the shoulders and a wink, and that's him. He's never thought it odd that his daughter cross-dresses for a living and sells second-hand purses on the side. But then, he's never thought it odd that his daughter was born with webbed feet" (61). After all, the surgical intervention, an intense, painful feeling of repugnance and fear, and the effacement of difference experienced in the novel have been conventional historically for individuals confronted with a sexually ambiguous infant body.

Julia Epstein, in her article "Either/Or-Neither/Both: Sexual Ambiguity and the Ideology of Gender" on the ideology of gender and sexual ambiguity, suggests that the transvestite gesture signals the possibility that the social body is as fluid as the private body's drapery and that the gender definitions regulating the social order may shift and mutate. The anatomically ambiguous individual is even more threatening. Hermaphrodites [...] have historically posed epistemological challenges to definitions of natural boundaries and to the very notion of gender clarity itself. (138)

For Epstein, the anatomically ambiguous individual constitutes epistemological challenges to descriptions of established boundaries between men and women and to the notion of gender clarity itself. Epstein further maintains that hermaphrodites, called intersexuals as well, have traditionally been conformed to teratology, i.e., the scientific study of monstrosities or developmental abnormalities. Although twentieth-century technological intervention has made possible our progression from monstrosity to anatomical anomalies, the availability of medical interventions to transform intersexuals into males or females has had an ambivalent effect. Thus, in Epstein's view, "individuals with gender disorders are permitted to live, but the disorders themselves are rendered invisible, are seen as social stigmata to be excised in the operating room. The difference, again, is erased" (116). From this perspective, even though Villanelle's body is not sexually ambiguous in its genitalia, her webbed feet can be interpreted as a metaphor for male genitalia since they have been characterized as attachments peculiar to male bodies. Therefore, Villanelle's body can be viewed as hermaphroditic.

Villanelle's body as hermaphroditic becomes proper to her when her desires in relation to her occupation are considered inappropriate by her parents and society. Villanelle remarks, "what I would have most liked to have done, worked the boats, was closed to me on account of my sex" (53). Because of her webbed feet, Villanelle's constraints lead her to work in a gambling casino, conducting her to be in touch with games of chance. Villanelle's webbed feet are physically concealed at the casino; on the other hand, the hermaphroditic potential of her body, though unseen, can be considered as performed by the transvestite gesture. Possessing a body with both male and female sexual features, she chooses to perform the male gender at the casino.

Such a performative disruption of gender binaries corresponds closely with Judith Butler's theory of gender performance. In *Gender Trouble*, Butler states,

> But we are actually in the presence of three contingent dimensions of significant corporeality: the anatomical sex, gender identity, and the gender performance. If the anatomy of the performer is already distinct from the gender of the performer, and both of those are distinct from the gender of the performance, then the performance suggests a dissonance between not only sex and the performance, but also sex and gender and performance (139).

Here, Butler foregrounds the notion of dissonance among an individual's sexual anatomy, gender identity, and gender performance that *the Passion* centers upon. As in the example of Vilanelle's gender performance, such a queer act serves to expose the artificiality of cultural norms and to indicate the instability of the naturalized binary of male and female by means of the resignification process of sex and sexuality. At the same time, Villanelle's body signifies the social body as fluid in the sense that her gender performances revolve around the continuously changing body and its connotation of fluidity, and thus gender is experienced as potentially flexible and on a continuum.

3. Rethinking the Body: The Body in Political Thought

The opinions concerning what the body is, what it expresses, and what part of our identities it includes have been discussed for centuries. As Anthony Synnott states in *The Body Social*,

> The body is... primarily the self. We are all embodied. Obvious though this may be, what [body] means in practice is not always so obvious. Controversies rage about the ownership of the body, the boundaries, its meaning, its value, the criteria of life and death, and how it should be lived, and loved (1).

For Synnott, the physical manifestation of being, the body, is our very self or a reflection of the self. There is, however, another side to consider. Much of Western political thought conveys an intense ambivalence toward the body. Particularly, the subject of a woman's body and its construction and interpretation is ladened with contradiction and difficulty. At this point, it is important to note that it is not the body itself that is a dilemma for women but what the female body has come to signify in a culture that denies ambiguity of the human condition. In fact, denial of that ambiguity allows for relations of domination; on the other hand, acceptance of ambiguity leads us to release from attempts to dominate others.

The female body has been described by the patriarchal discourse in such a way that her position in the social order is biologically determined, her sexuality restrained, and her voice silenced. To be more precise, Christian, Western, and patriarchal power structures establish gender norms based on the body/spirit binary. Accordingly, in that tradition, women are connected with the body and men with the spirit/soul/mind. In her article "Woman as Body", Elizabeth V. Spelman argues that Plato emphasized the superiority of the soul at the expense of the body: For Plato, the body, "with its deceptive senses, keeps us from real knowledge" and tempts us away from a virtuous life" (111). On the other hand, it is through the mind or spirit that one may "have knowledge, be in touch with reality and lead a life of virtue" (111). Apparently, the body/spirit binary is designed to perpetuate and preserve male power and thereby leads to women's objectification and degradation.

At the same time, the body/spirit dichotomy corresponds to the Eve/Mary binary in the sense that the female body has long been defined by means of two biblical characters: the temptress Eve and the virgin-mother Mary. It is in this sense that the relation between women and the body comes to mean that women are often considered as bodies in Western philosophy, a consideration that reduces women to their reproductive and sexual functions. Furthermore, since the body is a hindrance to a virtuous life, women appear to be a threat to a virtuous life. The body's uncontrolled desires and needs come to be an unwanted prompt of a woman's fleshliness.

Likewise, as Simone de Beauvoir points out in *The Second Sex*, as a male construction, the woman in the patriarchal culture is described as man's Other. Woman as Other is identified with a lack of freedom, passivity, and immanence, while the masculine subject, free of the body and necessity, is able to perpetuate the illusion of pure transcendence implicated in mastery and control of the other as the essence of man's freedom (xxii). Further, this gendered binary draws its strength from its being established in the body. That is to say, patriarchy generates, out of a sexually separated but ambiguous body, the male body as transcendent and the female body as immanent, a sort of mythical body that naturalizes oppression (xxxiv).

One of the hallmarks of women's oppression is the way it generally leads those who are oppressed to perceive their bodies as isolated from and unfamiliar to their selves. In such a case, women appear not to be in possession of their bodies. To be more precise, women and men are embodied differently. These differences will manifest themselves in different lived conditions. However, women are embodied, like the mold itself, filled with gender norms and expectations, taboos, and patriarchal prescriptions that they internalize by means of the act of socializing. At this point, in her discussion of female embodiment, Iris Young observes in the essay "Breasted Experience": "However alienated male-dominated culture makes us from our bodies, however much it gives us instruments of self-hatred and oppression, still our bodies are ourselves. We move and act in this flesh and these sinews, and live our pleasure and pains in our bodies" (192). Here, Young invites women to reconceptualize the female body from the ground of women's lived experiences and to transform the female body from being a passive sexual object of the male gaze to being an empowered, speaking subject.

Similarly, Jeanette Winterson, in her novel *The Passion*, attempts to show women's potential to reimagine themselves subjectively and physically, proposing the representation of the female body that works against the traditional representations of the female body and femininity within Western culture. It will be the aim of this study to show how Jeanette Winterson questions, reveals and rewrites the traditional cultural meanings which have been inscribed on the female body and reconceptualizes it in a new, potentially empowering fashion.

4. Performative Disruptions of Heterosexual Dogma

Villanelle seems at ease in her continuously varying disguises in Venice, where "the laws of the real world are suspended" and "all things seem possible" (114). Despite its apparently being a single place, Venice appears to be a combination of different cities, of all the cities the mind's eye may invoke. In this sense, Venice highlights its own fictional, imaginary position as it represents the conflict between reality and appearance that pervades the book at different levels. Villanelle further illustrates that "in this inner city are thieves and Jews and children with slant eyes who come from the eastern wastelands without father or mother [...]. There are exiles too" (53). Venice is a city where the high and the low breathe the same air, and walk the same ground. It is the city of Satan, a subversive place "not even Bonaparte could rationalise" (112), "the city of chance" (55), where gamblers, the poor, the dead, prostitutes, and the mad find their place. It is "the city of uncertainty" (p.58), in which everybody is in disguise, and even gondolas serve as disguises (118). The supposed alterability of Venice in The Passion, the blurring of the boundaries between appearing and being, along with the blend of the mainstream and the marginalised, the apparent allusion to the city as an outcome of the imagination and its approval of fragmentation, multiplicity, and diversity all signify the portrayal of Venice as a postmodern city, the ideal location for Villanelle who cross-dresses as a man by means of a moustache and a man's shirt which hides her breasts, to unsettle culturally established constructions of sexuality.

Then, Villanelle depicts her native city as a place of constant transformation where individuals reimagine themselves daily by assuming fresh disguises and where directions are not possible to give since buildings and streets have a tendency to rearrange themselves through the whole night (49-50). In The *Passion*, this floating and fluid city with its shadowy waterways reveals new vistas for Villanelle in the sense that Winterson positions her in a location that tends to encourage excess and transgressive pleasure-seeking. As Villanelle states, rather than involving in the destruction that is the noticeable effect of French nationalism, Venetian have clearly "abandoned [themselves] to pleasure," and Venice has come to be "an enchanted island for the mad, the rich, the bored, the perverted" (52). Since Venice fell to Napoleon, Villanelle states, Venetians have devoted themselves to the pursuit of pleasure, as if looking for relief from their weakened historical circumstances.

At the same time, however, Villanelle's workplace, the casino, is intended to utilize these pleasure-seekers for economic advantage, as stated in the novel: "Satisfying our guests is what we do best. The price is high but the pleasure is exact" (55). In addition to taking economic advantage of these pleasure seekers, in her article "Queer Theory, Left Politics," Rosemary Hennessy points out that "[r]ecognizing that pleasure does not exceed the social but is itself constituted through the often contradictory economic, political, and ideological production of social life means that its hegemonic articulation is always precarious" (107). Originally a card dealer at the gambling table in a casino, Villanelle exemplifies this argument in the sense that she identifies herself in a masculine term, like cross-dressing in men's clothes for economic reasons through the artifice of the body as a medium. Her relationship with the pleasure she defines is intricate since the cross-identification experience of Villanelle is not just for pleasure but for a dominant seductive effect that leads to an elevated economic profit. In the casino, Villanelle cross-dresses as a boy to excite male customers pleasurably or erotically. As Villanelle explains, "I dressed as a boy because that's what the visitors liked to see. It was part of the game, trying to decide which sex was hidden behind tight breeches and extravagant face-paste" (54). Although her webbed feet should give her the right to have a career as a boatman, her sex restrains her from holding the job. To compensate, Villanelle deviates from traditional gender roles and from a corporeal ideal as a cross-dresser to work in the casino. While her cross-dressing may not be too abnormal for gender performance within the "city of disguises" (92), it comes to be a dangerous one for her to hold out. Thus, Villanelle prospers amidst her disguises as either woman or a man. In doing so, her strategic disguise to keep her bodily difference secret enables her to explore her sexuality and become aware of using it to her advantage.

In compliance with her masculine birth defect, Villanelle fails to perform some accepted standards of feminine beauty while being sexually appealing in other respects. She has small breasts with "no cleavage" and is "tall for a girl, especially a Venetian" (56). On the other hand, she has "a beauty spot… in just the right place" (56), and "[her] red hair is a great attraction" (159). Not orderly classifiable according to standards of femininity or of humanity, Villanelle exists in a peripheral space that eludes categorization. Except for her queerness, Villanelle's bodily deviance is a case of visible difference.

When Villanelle cross-dresses as a man, she, in fact, emphasizes the sexual ambiguity of her body. Her sexually ambiguous body turns out to be attractive not only for the male casino patron, however, but also for the woman Villanelle calls the "Queen of Spades". She encounters the Queen of Spades while she is working at the casino in her masculine disguise. The Queen of Spades is able to triumph at Villanelle's card game, thus earning the title by which she is identified throughout the novel. Her new relationship with the Queen of Spades urges Villanelle to question the premises of her gender and sexual identity. Only having encountered Villanelle in her masculine casino costume, she presumes that the Queen of Spades thinks she is a man. In such a case, she wonders whether to come to a dinner date in a male or female costume: "Should I go to see her as myself and joke about the mistake and leave gracefully?" (71). Confronted with this decision, Villanelle thinks about the performative aspect of gender and ponders how she should define herself: "Was this breeches and boots self any less real than my garters?" (71). Although the Queen of Spades notices that Villanelle is a woman, she does not accept having sex with Villanelle until she makes an appearance with feminine clothes. Apparently, queer desire in *The Passion* causes self-examination. This confrontation with the Queen of Spades puts Villanelle in a state of alarm and confusion. She feels her webbed feet, a sign of distinctiveness and independency, slipping away. An irresistible "upsurge of self" (74) makes Villanelle wish she could not think about her lover. However, when she fears for the condition of being deprived of the Queen of Spades, she exposes herself as a female in an attempt to continue the relationship that unites two feminine subjects.

That the Queen of Spades is a married woman causes the love affair to be doubly scandalous. Although much of *The Passion* depends on the transcendency of various social norms, compulsory heterosexuality stands as an obstacle to Villanelle's happiness. "Love is a fashion these days," ponders Villanelle, "and in this fashionable city we know how to make light of love and how to keep our hearts at bay" (105). Passion must be repressed if it does not act in accordance with the social injunction with regard to heterosexuality, and Villanelle comes to think that "There is no sense in loving someone you can never wake up to except by chance" (105). At this point, Winterson considers heterosexual marriage as a medium for financial stability for the Queen of Spades and a medium for mobility for Villanelle.

When Villanelle understands that she cannot be with her beloved, she quickly agrees to an undesirable marriage. Her opinion that "Men are violent [and that's] all there is to it" (119) enables her to justify her marriage to Napoleon's cook in spite of his having raped and beaten her. As stated in the novel, Villanelle is "pragmatic about love" and has "taken [her] pleasure with both men and women" (65). Then, heterosexual sex is only functional for her and provides Villanelle with a daughter – an individual guarantee of the continuation of her history.

Having accomplished matureness and psychological individuation, Villanelle rejects passion on behalf of the freedom to choose. What she chooses is freedom and motherhood. Then, Villanelle is introduced as the representative image of the Holy Virgin, and the reflection of the woman with a baby Henri comes across on New Year's Eve at the camp at Boulogne (43) when he is hopeless to find some reassuring signs to warm his heart. A newly-born baby always serves as a source of joy, the miracle of life. For Villanelle, their daughter "is a girl with a mass of hair like the early sun and feet like his" (150). In the religious framework of *The Passion*, Henri and Villanelle's daughter symbolizes the renewal as well as the promise of the Reunion of opposites and the individual consciousness with the universe.

Henri and Villanelle's child turns out to be an individual historical account of their lives. Their daughter possesses Henri's feet and Villanelle's "consuming hair," which impresses Villanelle as an indication that her daughter, too, "will draw her lot when the time comes and gamble her heart away" (164). On the other hand, Henri's only reflection of his daughter he has never encountered is, "I wonder what her feet are like" (167). Fearing that Villanelle has transmitted her hereditary web-footedness, Henri desires and chases the nonexistent normalcy for his child, which is, in fact, a case of visual propriety. Apparently, social systems idealize normality and force human society to conform to a single model of existence with a fear of difference. Then, physical or biological deviance is made to serve as an indicator of social nonconformity, which challenges conventional boundaries and dualisms that distinguish the normal from the abnormal. As a cross-dressing, whoring, thieving, web-footed lesbian, Villanelle serves as an emblem of a multifarious nonconformity within a culture that naturalizes and values cultural ideals of normality.

Conclusion

In the end, can the complications of Villanelle's body do anything to confirm her unique being in the composition of her own subject position? Villanelle comes to be a mythical figure with multiple fabulous bodies: part sacred, part human, part animal. In *Beyond God the Father*, Mary Daly (1973) suggests that

> [t]hose who are really living on the boundary tend to spark in others the courage to affirm their own unique being... But then Jesus or any other liberated person who has this effect functions as a model precisely in the sense of being a model-breaker, pointing beyond his or her own limitations to the potential for further liberation (75).

From this perspective, Villanelle's body can be viewed as a model-breaker since her body does not possibly conform to the form of a woman regarded as appropriate in Western culture. Therefore, she can serve as a role model to women confronting difficulties since their bodies also do not suit this culture. Whatever her physical problems and deviation, Villanelle keeps or maintains an ambiguous and boundary-crossing condition, similar to the women Henri recalls from his village: "They go on. Whatever we do or undo, they go on" (27). Accordingly, sociologist Chris Shilling asserts that for people who have stopped believing in religious authorities and dogmatic grand narratives, the body primarily comes to present a firm foundation on which to rebuild a reliable sense of self in the modern world. Due to the ambiguities existing in the late twentieth century, Shilling concludes that the modern body could also be depicted as the "uncertain body": "We now have the means to exert an unprecedented degree of control over bodies, yet we are also living in an age which has thrown into radical doubt our knowledge of what bodies are and how we should control them" (3). This uncertainty has been prominently revealed in current feminist debates concerning sexual differences in the sense that the reconsideration of the category of woman is required by the appearance of the transgender community within our culture. In light of present debates, describing a woman by genitalia turns out to be problematic. Then, it is time to consider that an individual can be regarded to live at whatever point on a gender continuum he/she considers appropriate.

In this sense, Villanelle, who positions herself at various spots on this continuum at different times, can be viewed as a figure tending to liberate. If gender were more problematical to interpret and regarded as more of a continuum, it would be much harder to be partial to one gender and subjugate the other. Such sexual fluidity can be regarded as serving as a route to the politics of extreme individualism. At the same time, it could suggest that identity politics must lead to more global politics on a sexual level.

At this point, the term "queer" turns out to be politically producing the intended result in that it conceives of possibilities for different individuals to promote social change. Then, Villanelle's multiple fabulous bodies suit well with such queer identity in the sense that there is not possibly to be another like it, and it is unquestionably queer. By means of Villanelle's body, readers notice, as Henri does, to relate queer bodies to spirituality. Moreover, what Henri realizes highlights improvements in Biblical revision: immediate intuitive awareness, aspects of the flesh as holy, and an occurrence that the flesh is not inconsistent with the intellect. Henri declares specifically:

> To love someone else enough to forget about yourself even for one moment is to be free. The mystics and the churchmen talk about throwing off this body and its desires, being no longer a slave to the flesh. They don't say that through the flesh we are set free. That our desire for another will lift us out of ourselves more cleanly than anything divine... [W]ithout love we grope the tunnels of our lives and never see the sun. When I fell in love it was as though I looked into a mirror for the first time and saw myself (154).

Accordingly, Henri discovers to feel love for Villanelle for herself, instead of a myth or a fantasy or an imaginary being of his own making such as he originated in Napoleon (157). He lives through or feels her in all of her bodily characteristics, just as his own lover who cannot provide him with her heart and thus will not join in marriage to him, but he loves her in all her puzzling complexity – a queer body subverting all potential notions of a fixed bodily identity.

After all, what does Villanelle have to express herself concerning her heart, the "rose-coloured thread" interweaved with the "plait of gold and silver" of her games of chance and webbed feet? She is still dedicated to the notion of transience and alteration suggested by her heart when she states: "I content myself with this; that where I will be will not be where I am" (150). Her story is not completed, and her last remarks depict uncontrollable passion and a continuing resolution to resist the scheme of the repeated utterance of the villanelle: "And the valuable, fabulous thing? Now that I have it back? Now that I have been given a reprieve such as only stories offer? Will I gamble it again? Yes" (151).

Works Cited

Barr, Helen. "Face to Face: A Conversation Between Jeanette Winterson and Helen Barr." *English Review* 2 (1991): 30-33.

—. (1991). "Face to face: A conversation between Helen Barr and Jeanette Winterson." *The English Review*, 2(1), 30-3.

Beauvoir, Simone de. *The Second Sex*. Translated and edited by H.M. Parshley. New York: Vintage Press, 1989.

Butler, Judith. *Gender Trouble: Feminism and the Subversion of Identity*. New York and London: Routledge, 1990.

Campbell, Fiona Kumari. Contours of Ableism: The Production of Disability and Abledness. New York: Palgrave Macmillan, 2009.

Daly, Mary. *Beyond God the Father: Toward a Philosophy of Women's Liberation*. Boston: Beacon Press, 1973.

Doan, Laura. *The Lesbian Postmodern*. New York: Columbia University Press, 1994.

Epstein, Julia. "Either/Or-Neither/Both: Sexual Ambiguity and the Ideology of Gender." *Genders* 7 (1990): 99-142.

Hennessy, Rosemary. "Queer Theory: Left Politics." *Rethinking Marxism* 7(3) (1994): 85-111.

Hutcheon, Linda. *A Poetics of Postmodernism: History, Theory, Fiction*. London: Routledge, 1988.

Marvel, Mark. "Jeanette Winterson: Trust me. I'm Telling You Stories." *Interview* 20 (1990): 164-168.

Matthews, Borris. *The Herder Dictionary of Symbols: Symbols from Art, Archaeology, Mythology, Literature and Religion*. Illinois: Chiron Publications, 1986.

McHale, Brian. *Postmodernist Fiction*. New York: Methuen, 1987.

Ostriker, A. (1991). "A Word Made Flesh: The Bible and Revisionist Women's Poetry." *Religion & Literature*, 23(3), 9–26. http://www.jstor.org/stable/40059485

—. *Feminist Revision and the Bible*. Oxford UK & Cambridge USA: Blackwell Publishers, 1993.

—. *Stealing the Language: The Emergence of Women's Poetry in America.* Boston: Beacon Press, 1986.

Schilling, Chris. *The Body and Social Theory.* London: Sage, 1993.

Spelman, Elizabeth V. "Woman as Body: Ancient and Contemporary Views." *Feminist Studies 8,* no. 1 (Spring 1982): 109–31.

Stevenson, Randall. *A Reader's Guide to the Twentieth-Century Novel in Britain.* Hemel Hempstead: Harvester Wheatsheaf, 1993.

Suleiman, Susan Rubin. *Risking Who One Is. Encounters with Contemporary Art and Literature.* Cambridge, Massachusetts, and London, England: Harvard University Press, 1994.

Synnott, Anthony. *The Body Social: Symbolism, Self, and Society.* New York: Routledge, 1993. Print.

Young, Iris. *Throwing Like a Girl and Other Essays in Feminist Philosophy and Social Theory.* Bloomington: Indiana University Press, 1991.

Winterson, Jeanette. *The Passion.* London: Penguin Books, 1988.

—. *Oranges are not the only fruit.* London: Pandora Press, 1985.

—. *Boating for Beginners.* London: Minerva, 1990.

Chapter 6

Sermons on Joint: Bob Marley, Bokonon and the Religio-lyrical Affair with State Apparatuses

Ankit Raj

Government College Gharaunda, India

Nagendra Kumar

Indian Institute of Technology Roorkee, India

Abstract

Despite sharing startling similarities (geography, history, English-based creole languages, intoxicating emergent religions and racially discriminated peoples obsessed with the electric guitar), the island nations of Jamaica and San Lorenzo (the fictitious banana republic in Kurt Vonnegut's *Cat's Cradle*) are poles apart when it comes to the religion–state equation in the two societies. This chapter is a comparative study of the emergent religion of Rastafarianism in Jamaica and the fictitious religion of Bokononism in Vonnegut's *Cat's Cradle* from a theoretical framework of Louis Althusser's Ideological State Apparatuses and Serawit Bekele Debele's modes of state control of religion: repression and cooptation. The chapter begins with historical accounts of the advent of the two religions amidst the socio-political scenarios in the two countries. The coronation of Ras Tafari Makonnen as emperor Haile Selassie I of Ethiopia in 1930 gave rise to Rastafarianism in Jamaica when reacting against the colonial British Empire, many Jamaicans saw the newly-crowned Ethiopian emperor as the second messiah and pledged allegiance to the king. Bokononism was born in San Lorenzo in the 1920s when Lionel Boyd Johnson and Earl McCabe were shipwrecked on a fictitious island with a long colonial past. Johnson and McCabe assume control of the island from a sugar company, devising an elaborate ruse to rule the island: McCabe establishes himself as a ruthless dictator while Johnson escapes to live in the jungle as the enigmatic founder of the newly formed and outlawed religion. The chapter then discusses Althusser's State Apparatuses and Debele's repression and cooptation in the light of the postcolonial state injustices against racially discriminated communities in the two nations. Next, the religious icons in the two countries—Bob Marley, the iconic Rastafarian reggae musician, and Bokonon, the founding prophet of Bokononism—are compared, assessing their differing approaches to religious response to the state. While Marley employs religion as a means to urge his fellow citizens to rise against state injustices, Bokonon appropriates religion to keep his disciples from rebelling against the state. The chapter goes on to conclude how religion and religious dogma play a decisive role when acting against or in complicity with the state, in writing the social destiny of wronged communities.

Keywords: Althusser's Ideological State Apparatuses; Rastafarianism; Reggae; Bob Marley; Jamaica; Kurt Vonnegut's *Cat's Cradle*; Bokononism

***

Nestled in the Caribbean Sea between the North and South Americas lies the island nation of Jamaica—a former British colony known the world over as the home of Rastafarianism, reggae music, and the iconic Bob Marley. Located in close vicinity of the Caribbean Basin is the exotic island of San Lorenzo, not to be found on maps but in the pages of Kurt Vonnegut's *Cat's Cradle* (1963). The fictitious island nation of San Lorenzo, with its long colonial past, continues to baffle readers with its paradoxical religion of Bokononism and the enigmatic prophet who founded it: Bokonon. Despite sharing startling resemblances—geography, history, English-based creole languages, racial discrimination, and intoxicating emergent religions—the two island nations are poles apart when it comes to the religion–state equation in their societies.

This chapter studies the emergent religions of Rastafarianism and Bokononism in the Caribbean countries of Jamaica and San Lorenzo, administers to the racially discriminated societies in the two nations a theoretical framework modelled on Louis Althusser's Ideological State Apparatuses and Serawit Bekele Debele's modes of state control of religion: repression and cooptation, and goes on to examine the religion–state affair in the two nations to conclude how religion plays a decisive role when acting against or in complicity with the state, in writing the social destiny of wronged communities.

Between Fact and Fiction: Emergent Religions in Exotic Lands

Rastafarianism in Jamaica

Rastafarianism emerged in 1930s Jamaica as a reaction against the colonial British Empire. The coronation of Ras Tafari Makonnen as emperor Haile Selassie I of Ethiopia in 1930 led some Jamaicans to believe, as per their reading of the Bible, that the newly crowned emperor was literally "the black messiah" (King 49). Leonard Howell and Marcus Garvey were among the pioneers of the emergent religion. Howell, the first Rasta preacher in Jamaica, returned from New York in 1932 and encouraged Jamaicans to shift their allegiance from the English crown to King Haile Selassie of Ethiopia, also urging them to seek repatriation to the distant African country the Rastas believe to be their spiritual motherland. Towards this end, he sold the emperor's pictures "as future 'passports' to Ethiopia" (King and Foster 5; emphasis in original). Garvey challenged the Bible's alleged sidelining of persons of colour and, influenced by the idea of Ethiopianism, preached that "God and Christ were black" (Berry and Blassingame 410).

Rastafarianism is characterised by the belief in the divinity of King Haile Selassie, marijuana smoking as a ritual, and the dynamic tension between Babylon and Zion—the former referring to the oppressive West and the latter representing the Promised Homeland that is Africa. Babylon is considered "the root cause of oppression" (Hagerman 384), while Zion is "the antithesis of [B]abylon" (Gomes 114). Rastas believe that the original Bible was written in Amharic, Ethiopia's official language. Though repatriation is a central tenet in Rastafarianism, the Rastas are divided on the means to achieve it: some seeking physical repatriation to Africa while others insist on achieving repatriation through "spiritual practice without physically traveling to the continent" (Chevannes qtd. in Aarons 381).

Though Rastafarianism is vehemently opposed to the oppressive system, their religious stance on leadership and hierarchy discourages the Rastas to wage war by political means. The Rastas believe that each member of their community is an autonomous person and is bound to answer only to their individual self. Rastafarianism is thus "antihierarchical through and through" (Kebede 185) and stresses achieving its spiritual ends, such as repatriation, by transcending formal organisation and politics. There have been, however, certain Rastafarian groups, such as the Rastafarian Movement Association (RMA), that can be considered political for their outward expressions of racial pride and their insistence that Rasta involvement in Jamaican politics is the only way to achieve control over their living conditions. Although largely apolitical in its modus operandi, the Rastafarian movement "is an agency of political protest by religious means" (176). The movement's goals can be summarised as: a rejection of drug laws, an end to police brutality, better economic conditions, and access to education and equal rights.

Rastafarianism stands apart from traditional religions owing to the lack of a designated place and rigid routines for conducting prayers and other rituals, the absence of priests and ministers, and the lack of a specific doctrine or gospel (187). This gives the Rasta's freedom to interpret the Bible as they please.

The Rastafarian tenets are hence "continually evolving and open-ended propositions" (Yawney qtd. in Breiner 37). There are no unquestionable truths or the idea of blasphemy in Rastafarianism. The only Rastafarian practice that can be considered a ritual in traditional terms is reasoning. The reasoning is a collective discussion conducted at any random place and time, wherein the codes of the community are scrutinised, and new codes are created. The members smoke ganja (the popular term for cannabis-derived from the Sanskrit word *gañjā*) as a spiritual practice, there is no single preacher, and all attendants are prophets in their own right. Reasoning differs from traditional religious congregations in that there is no specific time and place for a reasoning session, attendance is not mandatory, members are free to join and leave an ongoing session, and all members are equal.

Bokononism in San Lorenzo

The Republic of San Lorenzo is a fictitious island nation where Kurt Vonnegut's satirical work of fiction, *Cat's Cradle*, is set. The exotic Caribbean island is described in the novel as having been discovered in 1519 by the Spanish conquistador Hernán Cortés and annexed in turn over subsequent centuries by France, Denmark, the Netherlands, England, Spain, and African mutineers of a British slave ship who declared the island an independent nation with an emperor in 1786. The newly crowned maniacal emperor had fortifications and a cathedral built on the island, ruling for over a hundred years until Castle Sugar, a sugar company, took over in 1916, owning "every piece of arable land on the island" (Vonnegut 88). The form of governance during the Sugar years was part anarchy and part feudalism, with "heavily armed white men" as well as "big natives" ready to "kill or wound or torture on command" from their colonial masters (89). Though the company never made a substantial profit, it managed to sustain operations year after year by paying nothing to the plantation workers, the poor natives having nothing but "a handful of butterball priests" (89) to turn to for spiritual solace.

A significant turn in governance took place in 1922, as described in the novel, when Lionel Boyd Johnson, a wealthy and educated Episcopalian from Tobago, and Earl McCabe, a high-ranking deserter from the United States Marines, were shipwrecked on San Lorenzo on their way from Haiti to Miami in a stolen ship. As soon as they arrived and saw the island's natives afflicted with diseases they could not fathom, let alone cure, McCabe and Johnson took charge of the island, meeting no resistance from Castle Sugar. Working towards their dream of making a utopia out of the poverty- and disease-infested island, McCabe and Johnson exiled the priests and set up a form of socialism wherein the nation's total income would be distributed equally among all adult citizens. The socio-economic overhaul, though it sounded idealistic in theory, came to naught upon implementation as the individual share for each citizen amounted to a paltry sum and did nothing to benefit the poor and diseased natives of the island (95).

When the two outsiders were convinced that no economic reform was enough to retain control of the island without public resistance, Johnson turned to dynamic tension—a theory borrowed from the muscle-builder Charles Atlas which states that "muscles could be built without [equipment] by simply pitting one set of muscles against another"—and reworked it to effectively govern the island (73). Johnson believed "that good societies could be built only by pitting good against evil, and by keeping the tension between the two high at all times" (73). Towards this end, Johnson and McCabe fabricated an elaborate play wherein the former invented a new religion and went to live in the jungle as an enigmatic and elusive prophet while the latter established himself as a ruthless dictator, outlawing Johnson and his religion, announcing the death on the hook for the self-styled prophet and his disciples, and organising routine hunts involving the diseased and unemployed natives, each hunt resulting in Johnson escaping miraculously "to preach another day" (124). The name Lionel Boyd Johnson was mispronounced as Bokonon by the San Lorenzans in their native creole, and Bokonon's outlawed religion, a discreet indulgence for everyone on the island, including Earl McCabe, came to be known as Bokononism.

The precepts of Bokononism, set down in prose and calypsos, are contained in *The Books of Bokonon*, an ever-expanding collection of cynical and playful musings by the eponymous prophet. The book itself, in its physical form, is hard to come by, thanks to the religion being outlawed, and the teachings of Bokonon are propagated by word of mouth among the natives of San Lorenzo. Bokononism is based on the belief that since the truth is too heartbreaking to live with, it is better to believe in harmless lies. The book begins with the oxymoronic disclaimer: "'All of the true things I am about to tell you are shameless lies'" (4; emphasis in original). Bokonon insists that "[h]armless untruths" or "*foma*" (a coinage of his own) are what make one "brave and kind and healthy and happy" (xvii; italics in original), being the only way to lead a life of blissful ignorance. Practitioners of the religion believe that mankind is organised into teams that inadvertently serve God's will. Such teams, termed "*karass*"—in its singular form—by Bokonon, are created by God and ignore "national, institutional, occupational, familial, and class boundaries" (2; italics in original). Bokonon's "'harmless balderdash'" (Morace 155; emphasis in original) comforts his followers with the belief that "God has placed each individual within an extended family" so that "no person need be lonely ever again" (Oltean-Cîmpean 208).[1] The pivot of the *karass*, or the physical or abstract entity around which the members of the team revolve in "spiritual orbits," is termed "*wampeter*" (Vonnegut 37; italics in original). A *karass*, Bokonon warns, is not to be confused with a "*granfalloon*," the latter being "a false *karass*" or "a seeming team that [is] meaningless in terms of the ways God gets things done" (65; italics in original). According to Bokonon, human constructs like nation-states, political parties, and business companies are all *granfalloons*. Vonnegut clarified in an interview with Abádi-Nagy that the names of the two terms suggest their meanings—the word *granfalloon* derived from "'grand fallacy/lunacy/balloon'" which "is expressive of something that is false or meaningless"; while the word *karass*, which sounds like "'caress,'" signifying the comforting effect the idea has on the mind (Abádi-Nagy, 29-30; emphasis in original).

Humans are the only sacred thing for Bokononists, "[n]ot even God" taking the crown (Vonnegut 151). Naturally, the most sacred ritual in the religion has to do with humans and not God. The ritual is a "foot ceremony" (113) termed "*boko-maru*" (112; italics in original) wherein two people sit down face to face with their legs stretched outward and use their feet to caress each other's soles (very likely a pun on caressing souls)—an act considered the ultimate spiritual consummation by Bokononists. This practice, though considered more intimate than the physical act of lovemaking, is not to be kept reserved for one's partner. Bokonon insists that "it is very wrong not to love everyone exactly the same" (149) and terms a "man who wants all of somebody's love" as a "*sin-wat*," or a "very bad" person (148; italics in original).

Bokononism differs from traditional religions in that it neither "provide[s] insights through a form of logical teaching" nor preaches "an understanding of cosmological order and meaning regarding people's lives or existence" (Robinson 6). Bokonon, in fact, creates a cosmogony out of scratch for his religion and, like the rest of his teachings, calls it a "pack of *foma*" (Vonnegut 136; italics in original). He goes on to preach that there is no meaning or purpose whatsoever in human existence, and our incessant efforts to decipher life are but exercises in futility. Though based on lies, Bokonon's religion serves its intended purpose

---

[1] Loneliness, believes Vonnegut, is the major cause of sadness, discontent and the death of culture in contemporary America. The need for an extended family to combat American loneliness is an idea he has often professed in his interviews (See Augustyn; Gabel; Standish; Plimpton et al.). Vonnegut's insistence on a joint family upbringing for his fellow Americans surfaces time and again in his fiction, including the cautionary evolutionary tale *Galápagos* with its evolved breed of post-humans living in harmony and the novel *Slapstick* where artificial extended families populate a dystopian society.

of turning the San Lorenzans' gaze away from their miserable existence to a state of beatific ignorance.

Religion, State, and Society

Ideological State Apparatuses

Louis Althusser, in his celebrated essay on Ideological State Apparatuses, sets down the condition required for the state's existence in power as "the reproduction of the conditions of production" (Althusser 127). He aptly diagnoses that in order for a state to exist with all its might, it "must reproduce the conditions of its production at the same time as it produces" (128). In other words, the state must ensure the "reproduction of its [subjects'] submission to the rules of the established order" (132) to maintain its status quo in the long run.

Althusser goes on to describe the ways in which the state, incorrigibly repressive by its very nature, exerts its domination over the ruled classes by engineering an elaborate system of physical and ideological state apparatuses. The physical or Repressive State Apparatus is constituted by "the Government, the Administration, the Army, the Police, the Courts, the Prisons, etc." (142-3). Althusser defines another set of state apparatuses which, though also functioning in plain view, are equipped with a subtlety lacking in their repressive counterparts. The "Ideological State Apparatuses" are "distinct and specialized institutions" (143) that serve the state's oppressive end by ideology rather than by force. These apparatuses comprise religious bodies, educational institutions, media, academia, sports, arts, and even the family. Althusser's state apparatuses (repressive and ideological) function both by violence and ideology, the difference lying in their predominant mode of operation— repression or violence in the case of Repressive State Apparatuses and ideology in Ideological State Apparatuses. It is obvious that the Ideological State Apparatuses, like their repressive counterparts, perpetrate, to a large extent, the ideology of the ruling class, i.e., the state. It may also be stated that to exert its hegemony over institutions not directly under its jurisdiction (media, arts, academia, religious organisations, etc.), the state must exert repressive control in addition to mere ideological reins. The repressive modus operandi of the state's ideological apparatuses is too "attenuated and concealed" (145), making it almost indiscernible to an unsuspecting mind. Each of the ideological apparatuses does its job of making individuals conform to the state's ideology by the means at its disposal—the political wings "by subjecting individuals to the political state ideology," the media "by cramming every 'citizen' with daily doses of nationalism, chauvinism, liberalism, moralism, etc.," the religious bodies by preaching humans to love their neighbour unconditionally and turn "the other cheek to whoever strikes first" (154; emphasis in original), and the educational institutions by instilling in children "the 'rules' of good behaviour" (132; emphasis in original) proper to the established order so that the prescribed roles of "the exploited," "the exploiters," "the exploiters' auxiliaries" and "the high priests of the ruling ideology" (133) are fulfilled without dissent.

State Approaches to Religion: Repression and Cooptation

The question of managing religion at the hands of the state has been addressed in detail by Bryan S. Turner. Turner stresses that to ensure stability and order in public life, politics and religion can no longer be kept separate, and it falls upon the state "to re-assert its authority over civil society, especially over those religious institutions that seek to articulate an alternative vision of power and truth" (Turner, 124). Towards this shift from "benign neglect to active management of religious activities" (124), he identifies two approaches to state intervention, namely, upgrading and enclavement. Upgrading refers to modernising religious groups and their practices to align the religion with the tenets of the regime. This approach includes modern educational strategies in "the arenas of religion, morals, reproduction, and family life" (Barbalet, Possamai, and Turner 3) aimed at encouraging religious groups to shun their religious uniqueness and adjust to the ways of the nation-state. Enclavement, on the other hand, is a pre-emptive and extreme form of religious management wherein a community is segregated, contained, and controlled not by means of physical borders but through means like "enclosure, bureaucratic barriers, legal exclusions, and registration" (Turner,244) in all spheres. This approach operates on the "paradigm of suspicion" (Turner, 289), especially against immigrants who are seen by the state as potential threats.

Serawit Bekele Debele draws upon Turner's concepts to identify two more forms of managing religion. Repression, the first approach, is a form of state control of religion "which entails suspending, intimidating, delegitimising and outlawing religious institutions, figures and associations" (Debele 38) when the state feels threatened by the said religion. Repression draws from Turner's enclavement in that it enlists subversive tactics to subdue the religious community. However, it differs from enclavement in that whereas enclavement is a preventive measure aimed at blocking and isolating religious groups even before they are allowed to enter a certain space, repression is more of a cure employed by the state when "the religious group, association or figure" which has "already been acknowledged and permitted to exist" is now perceived as a threat to state power (38). Debele defines the second form, cooptation, as "an appropriation of religion in the service of the status quo" (26). This approach involves controlling and manipulating religious institutions and figures to serve the state ideology by luring them with privileges otherwise beyond their reach (38). Unlike Turner's upgrading, which seeks to educate and modernise religions out of concern for the welfare of the religious group and its peaceful coexistence in the public sphere, cooptation is employed with purely political motives where the state is less invested in assisting the religious group and keener to rope in the religious figures and institutions to promote its own ideology and denigrate its opponents (38).

Prophets Flirting with State Apparatuses

Subverting State Apparatuses with Religion: Bob Marley's Reggae Resistance

In the 1950s, Rastafarianism was seen by many in Jamaica as a cult of black supremacists who wanted to rule the white man, as is confirmed by the work of George Eaton Simpson (Simpson 134-5). The practitioners of the emergent religion, seen by the common populace as ganja-smoking drug addicts in dreadlocks, were often met with frequent and violent police action (Daily Gleaner qtd. in King 50) even though they "posed little threat to Jamaica's ruling class" owing to their largely apolitical religious tenets (50). Bob Marley, an emerging Jamaican musician, experienced the state brutality and injustices against people of his skin, was enamoured of Jamaica's Rastafari counterculture and Martin Luther King Jr.'s idea of non-violent struggle against racism in the United States (Gallardo 202), converted to Rastafarianism, and armed with reggae music, found himself singing "a cultural war against" the injustices and "wickedness in high and low places" (Miller 163).

Reggae, the genre of music associated with Rastafarianism, is the "very expression of the historical experiences of the Jamaican working-class, unemployed and peasant" (Johnson 589). Marley and other reggae musicians from Jamaica used the genre to expose the poor social, economic, and political conditions of their people, who had long been victims of poverty, unemployment, lack of education, inadequate housing and infrastructure, food shortages, social discrimination, and often police brutality. Bob Marley's lyrics, in the words of Gallardo, "offered solutions to the oppressive conditions in Jamaica—these solutions were both realistic and spiritual, intended to compel the oppressed to fight for their rights and to free them from the mental slavery that still dwelled in their minds" (Gallardo 202). Marley's songs derided state apparatuses working against the black population of Jamaica, including but not limited to—the Jamaican legislation dictating what jobs the freed slaves could hold, no suffrage for the black people, police violence, and ban on reggae music by government-owned radio stations (Hagerman 383). He used the term "Babylon system" for the state apparatuses working against black people. In the eponymous song, he likens the system to a vampire sucking the blood of its black victims using not just repressive state apparatuses but ideological ones as well, like churches and universities, to feed children the white man's version of history, thus keeping the black people deceived and enslaved. Babylon has been defined by Johnson-Hill as "any oppressive system, especially the military arsenals of the superpowers, the monetary policies of multi-national companies, and the hierarchical structures of the Catholic Church" (Johnson-Hill 29), which is strikingly similar to the description of ideological state apparatuses propounded by Althusser in that it includes schools, churches, media, military and police. Babylon as a system of oppressive state apparatuses figures in many of Bob Marley's songs, illustrating issues such as police violence in 'Burnin and Lootin' and 'Johnny Was', the crookedness of political leaders in 'Crazy Baldhead', slavery in 'Slave Driver' and 'Concrete Jungle', and poverty and hunger in 'Them Belly Full [But We Hungry]'. While voicing the trials and tribulations of his people through his lyrics, Marley also proposed solutions through his songs, "beating down Babylon" (Edmonds 42) being the common undercurrent in his lyrical sermons—'Get Up Stand Up' urges the poor in Jamaica to fight their oppressors, 'One Drop' calls for resistance against the system, 'War' (derived from a speech by King Haile Selassie I) calls for a fight against racism, 'Babylon System' stresses that "Babylon must be chanted down" (Reynolds 241) by waking Jamaica's youth from the delusion induced by the ideological state apparatuses such as schools and churches, and 'Chant Down Babylon' sends a call to arms to burn Babylon down to the ground.

The initial approach of the Jamaican establishment towards the Rastafari movement was what Debele would term repression, as the establishment saw the movement as a threat to its status quo. The state reaction towards Rastas ranged from maligning their public image to using physical violence against them. In the 1950s and early 1960s, public consensus on subscribing to Rastafarian philosophy was "mental deterioration," and those embracing the movement were seen as "an urgent matter for the psychiatrist" (Nettleford 57). The police routinely harassed the Rastafarians, cut their locks, and arrested them on the slightest pretexts (Kebede 184). State apparatuses continued to indulge in repression tactics to tame the Rastas throughout the 1960s and early 1970s as the government evaded demands for repatriation, the print media painted a vile picture of the Rastas, Rasta leaders were deported, reggae musicians were arrested, and revolutionary reggae songs like Bob Marley's 'Small Axe' were banned by the Jamaican Labour Party (JLP) (King and Foster 8). Nevertheless, Marley and other reggae musicians continued to voice anti-mainstream concerns like poverty, injustice, black nationalism, sex, and marijuana throughout the 1970s. For Marley and his fellow reggae musicians, reggae music was the only way to bring down Babylon as they perceived "themselves as the agents of Babylon's destruction and reggae music as their primary weapon" (Edmonds 51). Marley's vocal disdain for American interference in Jamaican matters (Gallardo 204) and his songs like 'Get Up Stand Up' took his message beyond the shores of the island, alarming not just the Jamaican government but the CIA and the South African authorities, resulting in South Africa censoring several tracks by the dreadlocked musician (203) and an attempt on the ganja-smoking prophet's life by a gang of assassins, one of whom confessed to being trained by the CIA (Sheridan qtd. in Gallardo 205). The assassination attempt could not intimidate Marley, for he went abroad into self-exile for two years, penning songs on international issues, including the track 'Zimbabwe' to lend support to the Zimbabwean freedom fighters in the Rhodesian civil war. Not done with combating state apparatuses, he encouraged piracy of his songs beyond Jamaican shores if it ensured subverting "the logic of the global marketplace" (Stephens 159).

The state approach towards Rastafarianism and reggae music took a gradual turn from repression towards cooptation as the People's National Party (PNP) and the Jamaican Labour Party (JLP), the two warring political parties in Jamaica, began to see Rasta, reggae, and especially Bob Marley, as a means to "reproduce the conditions of [their] production" (Althusser 128) by using Marley's popularity to gain street credibility. Regardless of the state's newfound change of heart towards the Rastas, when asked in an interview on whom he would support in the 1980 elections, Marley responded, "Well I would not support anyone. I'll support myself, a Rasta, you know what I mean? Only Rasta. No one else is what the people want" (McCann qtd. in Gallardo 203-4). Consistent with his anti-cooptation views, Marley pledged no allegiance to any political party, termed the Jamaican leaders as "follyticians" (Toynbee 169-70), and wrote the song 'Crazy Baldhead' as a satire on politicians—the term "Baldhead" being a Jamaican slang for government officials with close-trimmed hair and the "uninhibited growth of dreadlocks" by the Rastas being a symbolic "throwing away of colonial hair combs" (Sheridan qtd. in Gallardo 204). Adamant on utilising Rasta support for his political career, Jamaica's new Prime Minister Michael Manley of the People's National Party (PNP) continued to appeal to the Rastafarians by employing theatrics such as adopting the biblical name "Joshua," wielding a "magical" walking stick allegedly gifted to him by King Haile Selassie I of Ethiopia and hiring reggae musicians to play at his political rallies (King 41). Manley's promises and reforms would be far from sufficient in lifting the black Jamaicans from their petty existence, and as a result, reggae would rage on as the voice of dissent.

Assisting the State with Religion: The Paradoxical Prophet of San Lorenzo

When asked in an interview about his contribution to anthropology, Kurt Vonnegut described *Cat's Cradle* as a fictional field trip of a frustrated anthropologist[2] who could never go out himself and had to content himself with San Lorenzo—a made-up Haiti (Abádi-Nagy 30). In his biting satire, Vonnegut paints a fictitious banana republic to rival those in reality. In the novel, life before Bokonon for the San Lorenzan natives was a pitiful existence as the enslaved and impoverished natives languished in the "demoniacal squirrel cage" (Vonnegut 89) of capitalism and religion, i.e., Castle Sugar, Inc. and the Catholic church. Bokonon and McCabe arrived on the island, tried and failed to create a socialist utopia, and resorted to an elaborately imaginative play of good versus evil to keep the San Lorenzan population as wretched as they had been but now gratefully content—"And I made up lies / So that they all fit nice, / And I made this sad world / A par-a-dise" (91).

The Republic of San Lorenzo, advertised in American newspapers as a tropical paradise with exotic beauties, lavish exports, and state-of-the-art infrastructure, is a far cry from reality with its paper-thin, broken-toothed, rickety-legged, murky-eyed population, dogs who never bark and infants who dare not cry. Even the national anthem of San Lorenzo, penned by Bokonon, is a mockery of its people—"Oh, ours is a land / Where the living is grand, / ... What a rich, lucky island are we! / Our enemies quail, / For they know they will fail / Against people so reverent and free" (99). Humans, who are considered the only sacred being in Bokononism, above even God (151), regardless suffer due to the religion.

For a people reeling under such poor living standards, the government and the religious state apparatuses of San Lorenzo keep dissent in check by foiling each other to the gullible eyes of the common man, thus maintaining an ever-running drama where Bokonon remains cosy in the jungle with an ample supply of thrilled disciples and the choicest organic produce while the despotic rulers (Earl McCabe, and later his successor Papa Monzano) keep organising carnivalesque Bokonon-hunts and executing hapless Bokononists once in a while "just to keep the pot boiling" (125), both parties fully aware that they need each other to keep the game afoot—"Because without 'Papa's' badness, / Tell me, if you would, / How could wicked old Bokonon / Ever, ever look good?" (73). The religious apparatus ensures that the San Lorenzans never object to anything, have no aspirations—political or otherwise—and have no concern for the purpose of life or for the progress of any sort, except for their love of the electric guitar (167-8) which remains a pastime at best and never gets to be wielded as a socio-political weapon like in Jamaica. The precepts of Bokononism, "a parody of religion as opium" (Abádi-Nagy 46), though described by Bokonon as "*foma*" or "[h]armless untruths" (Vonnegut xvii; italics in original), are

---

[2] The University of Chicago had rejected Vonnegut's master's thesis in anthropology, only to award him the degree years later for his novel *Cat's Cradle* (See Farrell 7).

nothing but damaging lies (Oltean-Cîmpean 209) reminiscent of Billy Pilgrim's fatalistic sermons in Vonnegut's *Slaughterhouse-Five* that spoil its "adherents with a venomous ideology" (Raj and Kumar 251) of indifference to suffering and injustice. The damaging lies take their toll on the gullible population as they commit mass suicide at the behest of their beloved Bokonon, who, upon being asked by his followers in the event of a human-made catastrophe to explain what God is up to, realises how his game has gone way out of hand and orders the natives to take their lives as he is "through with them" (Vonnegut 195).

Unbeknownst to the uneducated and unaware natives of San Lorenzo, the ruling state's ideology is fully active in the religious state apparatus they turn to for comfort from their state-induced suffering. As Althusser reminds us: "*no class can hold State power over a long period without at the same time exercising its hegemony over and in the State Ideological Apparatuses*" (Althusser 146; italics in original). The Republic of San Lorenzo exerts total control on its subjects by creating and maintaining, thanks to its government, military and religious state apparatuses, the class roles that sustain the state's ideology: "the exploited" (the unpaid workers), "the agent of exploitation" (the immediate superiors to the workers), "the agent of repression" (the military and the police) and "the professional ideologist" (the designers of the state's plan and the supreme leader's close aids) (155-6). The state approach to the Bokononist people of San Lorenzo remains one of repression, never taking a turn for cooptation like the latter Jamaican approach towards Rastafarianism. Like his predecessor, Papa Monzano maintains the reproduction of the relations of his regime's production by keeping in place Bokononism as the primary and dominant ideological state apparatus, while letting the blissfully unaware San Lorenzans extract routine gratification from the most outrageous and revolutionary act they can come up with: practising their religion in secret. And his reluctant successor Jonah, who before his coronation was inclined to usher in the winds of change, ultimately decides against it, letting the reader know that he intends to keep things the way they are for the good of everyone. San Lorenzans, if they are to be truly free and self-reliant, need to acknowledge their oppression and, in turn, need to recognise their beloved religion's complicity in reducing them to their pitiable state. Either by shunning Bokononism altogether or by re-engineering the faux-forbidden religion to aid their cause can, the San Lorenzans expect to subvert the dictatorial regime and command their own place on the island that is rightfully theirs. In what could be an allusion to Rastafarianism, Bokononism forbids its adherents to breed political aspirations, and the only kind of progress the San Lorenzans are shown to care about is the electric guitar. However, unlike the Rastas, the Bokononists never resort to political dissent, and their musical affair is confined to leisure times, thus keeping a Reggaesque revolution forever off the charts on the Caribbean island of San Lorenzo.

Conclusion

We have seen thus far how religions emerge amongst people discriminated against by oppressive states and provide them with spiritual solace during hard times. The tales of the Rastas and the Bokononists, however, take different routes. During the early 1980s, the leadership in Jamaica realised that the prime condition for the state's sustenance (reproduction of the means of its production) could not be fulfilled by inviting the ire of the Rastas. The state gradually managed to see Rastafarianism and reggae music not as a threat to their status quo and co-opted the emergent religion as a symbol of their nation's cultural heritage—sponsoring the music fest "Reggae Sunsplash" and marketing the island nation as an "'island paradise'" (King and Foster 9). The Bokononist population of San Lorenzo, on the other hand, met a fatal fate at the hands of religion. While their terminally ill tyrannical ruler killed himself and let loose a catastrophic chemical invention on the island, the clueless natives turned to their prophet for divine intervention and were sermoned into suicide.

The disparate fates of the followers of the two religions are set in motion owing to the differing tenets of their prophets. While the world-renowned Bob Marley led a humble life devoid of luxuries—helping his fellow countrymen in cash and kind (Miller 163), flying economy class with his crew (Blackwell 150), scheduling free concerts for freedom fighters in Zimbabwe, and engineering truce between warring political parties in Jamaica (Miller 164); Bokonon, the self-proclaimed godman, lived comfortably in the jungle—relying on gifts from his poor devotees and keeping them trapped in "designed frustration" (May 31). While the ganja-smoking Jamaican urges his people to grow wise and rise against injustice, the "false Messiah" (Schatt 36) of San Lorenzo "sells appearances" (Raj and Kumar, "Trick or Treat" 156) and blinds his pupils with *foma* and *boko-maru*. Unlike the reggae music performed high on weed that seems to make the Rastas think clearly, Bokonon's *foma* makes apolitical sheep out of men. While Bob Marley is the one who would be seen "assisting victims and providing resources" in the event of a natural catastrophe (Miller 161), Bokonon is the one who leads his docile followers to a death sermon in the abyss. Bokonon's last sermon explains his wish to write a treatise on the history of human stupidity, only to fling it at God while grinning ear to ear and thumbing his nose at Him (Vonnegut 206). This further affirms his indifference, as he would rather mock and dissent against God than preach a much-needed revolution to his gullible adherents who languish under a dictatorial regime.

We conclude by summarising that religion (and the dogma that comes with it), when used as a weapon to subvert repressive state apparatuses, can result in uplifting the discriminated from injustice, while religion, when used as a state apparatus itself to assist the state in retaining totalitarian control can lead people to fates worse than death, for in Althusser's words: "[Priests and Despots] 'forged' the Beautiful Lies so that, in the belief that they were obeying God, men would, in fact, obey the Priests and Despots, who are usually in alliance in their imposture" (Althusser 163; emphasis in original).

Works Cited

Aarons, David. "From Babylon to Ethiopia: Continuities and Variations of Utopianism in Rastafari Reggae Music." *Popular Music and Society*, vol. 44, no. 4, 2021, pp. 378–96. *Taylor and Francis Online*, https://doi.org/10.1080/03007766.2020.1795480.

Abádi-Nagy, Zoltán. "'Serenity,' 'Courage,' 'Wisdom': A Talk with Kurt Vonnegut." *Hungarian Studies in English*, vol. 22, 1991, pp. 23–37. *JSTOR*, https://www.jstor.org/stable/41273849.

—. "'The Skilful Seducer': Of Vonnegut's Brand of Comedy." *Hungarian Studies in English*, vol. 8, 1974, pp. 45–56. *JSTOR*, https://www.jstor.org/stable/41273693.

Althusser, Louis. *Lenin and Philosophy and Other Essays*, Translated by Ben Brewster. Monthly Review Press, 1971.

Augustyn, Heather. "Kurt Vonnegut's Last Interview."*In These Times*, 9 May 2007, https://inthesetimes.com/article/kurt-vonneguts-last-interview/.

Barbalet, Jack, Adam Possamai, and Bryan S. Turner, editors. *Religion and the State: A Comparative Sociology*. Anthem Press, 2011.

Berry, Mary Frances, and John W. Blassingame. *Long Memory: The Black Experience in America*. Oxford UP, 1982.

Blackwell, Chris. "Essay: Bob Marley: 'Absolutely, Truly Natural.'" *Review: Literature and Arts of the Americas*, vol. 43, no. 2, 2010, pp. 150–54. *Taylor and Francis Online*, https://doi.org/10.1080/08905762.2010.514386.

Breiner, Laurence A. "The English Bible in Jamaican Rastafarianism." *Journal of Religious Thought*, vol. 42, no. 2, 1985/86, pp. 30–43.

Debele, Serawit Bekele. "Religion and politics in post-1991 Ethiopia: making sense of Bryan S. Turner's 'Managing Religions.'" *Religion, State and Society*, vol. 46, no. 1, 2018, pp. 26–42. *Taylor and Francis Online*, https://doi.org/10.1080/09637494.2017.1348016.

Edmonds, Ennis B. *Rastafari: From Outcasts to Culture Bearers*. Oxford UP, 2003.

Farrell, Susan. *Critical Companion to Kurt Vonnegut: A Literary Reference to His Life and Work*. Facts On File, 2008.

Gabel, J.C. "The Melancholia of Everything Completed: KURT VONNEGUT (1922-2007): Highlights from Issue 27: Ode to the Midwest." *Stop Smiling*, 12 April 2007, http://stopsmilingonline.com/story_detail.php?id=794.

Gallardo, Angelica. "Get Up, Stand Up." *Peace Review*, vol. 15, no. 2, 2003, pp. 201–208. *Taylor and Francis Online*, https://doi.org/10.1080/10402650307611.

Gomes, Shelene. "Counter-Narratives of Belonging: Rastafari in the Promised Land'." *The Global South*, vol. 12, no. 1, 2018, pp. 112–28. *JSTOR*, https://doi.org/10.2979/globalsouth.12.1.07.

Hagerman, Brent. "Everywhere Is War: Peace and Violence in the Life and Songs of Bob Marley." *The Journal of Religion and Popular Culture*, vol. 24, no. 3,

2012, pp. 380–92. *University of Toronto Press*, https://www.utpjournals.press/doi/abs/10.3138/jrpc.24.3.380.

Johnson, Linton Kwesi. "The Reggae Rebellion." *New Society*, 10 June 1976.

Johnson-Hill, Jack A. *I-Sight: The World of Rastafari: An Interpretive Sociological Account of Rastafarian Ethics*. American Theological Library Association, 1995.

Kebede, Alemseghed. "Decentered Movements: The Case of the Structural and Preceptual Versatility of the Rastafari." *Sociological Spectrum*, vol. 21, no. 2, 2001, pp. 175–205. *Taylor and Francis Online*, https://doi.org/10.1080/02732170118234.

King, Stephen A. "International reggae, democratic socialism, and the secularization of the Rastafarian movement, 1972–1980." *Popular Music and Society*, vol. 22, no. 3, 1998, pp. 39–60. *Taylor and Francis Online*, https://doi.org/10.1080/03007769808591713.

King, Stephen A., and P. Renee Foster. "'No Problem, Mon': Strategies Used to Promote Reggae Music as Jamaica's Cultural Heritage." *Journal of Nonprofit & Public Sector Marketing*, vol. 8, no. 4, 2001, pp. 3–16. *Taylor and Francis Online*, https://doi.org/10.1300/J054v08n04_02.

May, John R. "Vonnegut's Humor and the Limits of Hope." *Twentieth Century Literature*, vol. 18, no. 1, 1972, pp. 25–36. *JSTOR*, https://doi.org/10.2307/440692.

Miller, Herbie. "Essay: Bob Marley: Natty Dread, Pop Icon, or National Hero." *Review: Literature and Arts of the Americas*, vol. 43, no. 2, 2010, pp. 159–65. *Taylor and Francis Online*, https://doi.org/10.1080/08905762.2010.514388.

Morace, Robert. "Kurt Vonnegut, Jr.: Sermons on the Mount." *Critique: Studies in Contemporary Fiction*, vol. 51, no. 2, 2010, pp. 151–58. *Taylor and Francis Online*, https://doi.org/10.1080/00111610903446195.

Nettleford, Ree M. *Caribbean Cultural Identity: The Case of Jamaica*. Institute of Jamaica, 1978.

Oltean-Cîmpean, Alexandru. "Truth and Foma in Kurt Vonnegut's *Cat's Cradle*." *Studia Universitatis Babes-Bolyai – Philologia*, vol. 60, no. 3, 2015, pp. 205–16. *Central and Eastern European Online Library*, https://www.ceeol.com/search/article-detail?id=298879.

Plimpton, George, et al., "Kurt Vonnegut, The Art of Fiction No. 64." *The Paris Review*, https://www.theparisreview.org/interviews/3605/the-art-of-fiction-no-64-kurt-vonnegut.

Reynolds, Dean. "Essays: Representations of Youth and Political Consciousness in the Music of Bob Marley." *Review: Literature and Arts of the Americas*, vol. 43, no. 2, 2010, pp. 237–42. *Taylor and Francis Online*, https://doi.org/10.1080/08905762.2010.514406.

Raj, Ankit, and Nagendra Kumar. "The Hero at a Thousand Places: Kurt Vonnegut's *Slaughterhouse-Five* as Anti-Monomyth." *Critique: Studies in Contemporary Fiction*, vol. 62, no. 2, 2021, pp. 239–52. *Taylor and Francis Online*, https://doi.org/10.1080/00111619.2020.1800583.

—. "'Trick or Treat!': The Trickster Figure in Kurt Vonnegut's *God Bless You, Mr Rosewater* and *Slapstick*." *The Explicator*, vol. 79, no. 4, 2021, pp. 155–59. *Taylor and Francis Online*, https://doi.org/10.1080/00144940.2021.2005515.

Robinson, David. "Vonnegut and Apocalypse: A Consideration of Kurt Vonnegut's Representation of the End of the World." *Scrutiny2*, vol. 22, no. 2-3, 2019, pp. 42–55. *Taylor and Francis Online*, https://doi.org/10.1080/18125441.2018.15 46767.

Schatt, Stanley. "The Whale and the Cross: Vonnegut's Jonah and Christ Figures." *Southwest Review*, vol. 56, no. 1, 1971, pp. 29–42. *JSTOR*, https://www.jstor.org/stable/43468244.

Simpson, George Eaton. "Political Cultism in West Kingston, Jamaica." *Social and Economic Studies*, vol. 4, no. 2, 1955, pp. 133–49. *JSTOR*, https://www.jstor.org/stable/27851011.

Standish, David. "Kurt Vonnegut: Playboy Interview (1973)."*Scraps from the Loft*, 4 October 2016, http://www.scrapsfromtheloft.com/2016/10/04/kurt-vonnegut-playboy-interview/.

Stephens, Michelle A. "Babylon's 'Natural Mystic': The North American Music Industry, The Legend of Bob Marley, and the Incorporation of Transnationalism." *Cultural Studies*, vol. 12, no. 2, 1998, pp. 139–67. *Taylor and Francis Online*, https://doi.org/10.1080/095023898335519.

Toynbee, Jason. *Bob Marley: Herald of a Postcolonial World?*. Polity Press, 2007.

Turner, B.S. "The Enclave Society: Towards a Sociology of Immobility." *European Journal of Social Theory*, vol. 10, no. 2, 2007, pp. 287–303. *SAGE Journals*, https://doi.org/10.1177/1368431007077807.

—. "Enclosures, Enclaves and Entrapment." *Sociological Inquiry*, vol. 80, no. 2, 2010, pp. 241–60. *Wiley Online Library*, https://doi.org/10.1111/j.1475-682X.2010.00329.x.

—. "Managing Religions: State Responses to Religious Diversity." *Contemporary Islam*, vol. 1, 2007, pp. 123–37. *Springer Link*, https://doi.org/10.1007/s11562-007-0011-1.

Vonnegut, Kurt. *Cat's Cradle*. Penguin Modern Classics, 2008.

Contributors

Önder Çakırtaş is currently an Associate Professor in the Department of English Language and Literature at Bingöl University, Türkiye. His research interests centre around Political and Psychological Literature. He particularly specializes in Modern and Contemporary British Drama and Literature with a keen interest in Political Theatre, Minority Theatre, Ethnic Theatre, and Race-Oriented Theatre. In the 2018-19 academic year, he was a Post-Doctoral Research Fellow in the Department of Drama, Theatre and Performance Studies at the University of Roehampton in London. Currently writing his book *Staging Muslims in Britain: Playwriting, Performance and Representation* (contracted with Routledge, 2023), Çakırtaş has prolifically written some recent works such as 'Racializ-ed/ing identities on Stage: Muslims, Angst and Response in *Snokered* and *Does My Bomb Look Big in this?*' (*Performing Islam*, Volume 10, Numbers 1-2, December 2021, pp. 5-21); 'Islamized Class and 'the Infidel Within' the British Drama: Contemporary British Muslim Theatre Around Race, Colour and Faith' (in *Class Acts: Material Relations and Performance Aesthetics*, Ed. Elizabeth Tomlin, Methuen Bloomsbury, 2023); 'Islam, Identity and 'New Otherness': Muslim Playwrights and Islamic Performances in Early Twenty-first Century Britain' (in *Muslim Writing, Writing Muslimness in Europe: Transcultural Literary Approaches*- Eds. Carmen Zamorano Llena et al., Roıtledge, 2023). His latest book *Ten ve Kimlik: Çağdaş Siyahi İngiiliz Tiyatrosu* [Skin Colur and Identity: Contemporary Black British Theatre], was published in late 2020. His latest edited book, *Language, Power and Ideology in Political Writing*, was published by IGI Global in Pennsylvania in late 2019. His other recent publications include a play-specific exercise that demonstrates how performance illuminates close reading of Wole Soyinka's *Death and a King's Horseman* (with Miriam Chirico) (edited by Miriam Chirico, Kelly Younger, published by Bloomsbury in 2020), an analysis of Samuel Beckett's *Endgame* in relation to patriography and pathography (published by Peter Lang in Oxford), and an edited book on analysis of the link between literature and psychology published by Cambridge Scholars Publishing. He has published in numerous journals including *CLCWeb: Comparative Literature and Culture, Litera: Journal of Language, Literature and Culture Studies, Forum for World Literature Studies, Hacettepe University Journal of Faculty of Letters*. Çakırtaş is the founding editor of *Essence & Critique: Journal of Literature and Drama Studies*. He is also among the editorial members of *The Journal of British Muslim Studies*. (SOAS, University of London).

Kristen Schiedel is a Ph.D. Candidate at Dalhousie University in Halifax, Nova Scotia, Canada. Her specialization is in world literature, and her dissertation research focuses on care and burnout. Kristen is especially interested in the kind of care that individuals are called upon to provide in order to fill systemic gaps and the way this care often asks of those individuals that they go beyond what they have the capacity for in terms of time, energy, and other resources. Her work is interdisciplinary and follows an amateur and post-critical approach.

Assist. Prof. Dr. **Yeşim Sultan Akbay** is currently working in the Department of English Language and Literature at Süleyman Demirel University, Isparta—Türkiye. At present, she is conducting lectures on 19th, 20th, and Contemporary British Novels and Women's Literature. Her interest area includes psychology and philosophy of literature as well as the life-writing genre.

Assoc. Professor **Beture Memmedova**, from Azerbaijan, worked as a Visiting Instructor in the Department of English Language and Literature at Süleyman Demirel University, teaching English Literature, including 19th-century novels, Modernism, Virginia Woolf and Biofiction, from 1998 up to 2022.

Seçil Erkoç Iqbal is an Assistant Professor at the Department of Western Languages and Literatures, İnönü University, Türkiye. She received her B.A. (2010) from the Department of Western Languages and Literatures at Boğaziçi University. She had her M.A. degree (2013) in English Language and Literature at İstanbul University, where she studied Aldous Huxley's Island and John Fowles' The Magus. During her graduate studies, she worked as a Research Assistant at İstanbul University and then at Hacettepe University where she got her PhD from the English Language and Literature Department with her dissertation entitled "'Out of the Maze of Dualisms': Posthuman Space in Mario Petrucci and Alice Oswald's Poetry" in 2020. Her research interests include Contemporary Nature Poetry, English Novel, Ecological Posthumanism, Comparative Literature, Contemporary Literary Theories, and Criticism.

Onur Ekler is a lecturer in the English department at Mustafa Kemal University. He earned his Ph.D. from Erciyes University. His work focuses specifically on chaos, anarchy, and Self in modernist/postmodernist literary studies.

Ankit Raj is an assistant professor of English at Government College Gharaunda, Karnal, and has a Ph.D. from the Department of Humanities and Social Sciences, Indian Institute of Technology Roorkee, Roorkee. His current research areas include Archetypal and Myth Criticism, Comparative Literature, Postmodern Fiction, Psychoanalytic Criticism, and Posthumanism, on which he has published research articles in Routledge and Johns Hopkins University Press journals. He is an editor with Essence & Critique: Journal of Literature and Drama Studies and also edits The Hooghly Review. A former engineer and rock band vocalist,

Ankit is a poet and short fiction writer published in print, online, audio, video, and comic strip formats in over thirty magazines, journals, and anthologies across ten countries. His book reviews have appeared in Indian Literature (Sahitya Akademi) and Ink Sweat & Tears. He is the author of the poetry collection Pinpricks (Hawakal, 2022). ORCID: https://orcid.org/0000-0003-4565-7682; Twitter: @ankit_raj01

Nagendra Kumar is a Professor (HAG) and former Head of the Department of Humanities and Social Sciences, Indian Institute of Technology Roorkee, Roorkee. He has published over 120 research articles in reputed national and international journals, conference proceedings, and edited anthologies, and has delivered talks in about fifty institutions across the globe, including in India, Austria, Oman, Singapore, Canada, Switzerland, Poland, Czech Republic, Denmark, and Egypt. He has been a Fellow of the Salzburg Seminar, Austria, and is the recipient of multiple academic awards, including the Outstanding Teacher Award at IIT Roorkee for the year 2015. A professional trainer specialising in language, literature, communication, and soft skills, Nagendra has trained around 2000 professionals from academia and industry in the areas of Professional and Corporate Communication, Soft Skills, Leadership, Human Resource Management, Time Management, Stress Management, Self-management, Professional Writing, etc. ORCID: https://orcid.org/0000-0002-8292-7947; Twitter: @prof_nagendra

Sezgi Öztop Haner has been an English language instructor for over a decade at Dumlupınar University in Kütahya, Türkiye. She got her M.A. degree from Dumlupınar University, the Department of English Language and Literature. She holds a doctoral degree from English Culture and Literature, Atılım University, in 2020, with her dissertation entitled "Beyond Sexuality: Transgender Bodies in the Novels of Virginia Woolf, Angela Carter, and Jeanette Winterson." Dr. Öztop Haner has participated in many international and national conferences and published original articles in the area of her studies. Her research interests include sexuality and gender studies, transgender theory, cultural studies, critical theory, and women's writing.

www.ingramcontent.com/pod-product-compliance
Lightning Source LLC
Chambersburg PA
CBHW051102230426
43667CB00013B/2403